WOODALL'S®

RV Owner's Handbook

The Complete, Illustrated Guide to Preventive Maintenance & Repairs

About the Technical Editor

Gary Bunzer has been active in the RV Industry since 1968. Author of the popular question and answer column, RV Doctor, he has been writing technical articles, service manuals and product installation instructions since the early 1970's. The RV Doctor column is now into its twenty-fourth year of continuous monthly publication.

Involved at both the trade and consumer levels, Gary has written and produced RV instructional videotapes for professional RV technicians and conscientious RV owners. He is also one of the industry's prominent technical trainers presenting educational seminars at RV service facilities and at major RV shows across the country.

He is currently the Technical Editor of Woodall Publications as well as Camping World's President's Club magazine, RV View. Gary and his wife Deborah are home-based in Southern California.

Inquiries to Gary can be sent to:
Gary Bunzer
Bunzer Consulting
PO Box 2074
El Cajon, CA 92021
FAX: 619-440-3962

Or visit Gary on the web at:
http://www.rvdoctor.com

TABLE OF CONTENTS

Publisher: Deborah A. Spriggs
Director of Distribution Services: Cis Tossi
Technical Editor: Gary Bunzer
Editor: Micki Pflug
Illustrator: Debbie Mackall
Layout: Dave Mounce

Forward

Recreation vehicle (RV) service and maintenance—we have all had exposure to this necessity at one time or another. In the vast realm of RV options such as floorplans, color schemes, chassis types, interior furnishings and other assorted appointments, there can be no denying the eventuality of maintenance and repairs. This is especially evident today, since we tend to keep and utilize our RVs longer, and each new model that is designed becomes more challenging, from a technical standpoint. Virtually all RV manufacturers agree that in order to receive the most out of our recreational investment, adequate maintenance must be performed regularly.

For example, a typical motorhome with a generator and two roof top air conditioners requires a minimum of 16 retail hours of mandated maintenance that needs to be performed each and every year. That's correct, 16 hours worth! At an hourly retail labor rate of say $60 per hour, that is almost $1000 per year just trying to avoid a major problem. Individual product makers usually recommend periodic maintenance each season on their products as a precautionary step in order to obtain the optimum use of that product. It is noted, however, that all RVs will not automatically self-destruct if the precautionary maintenance is not performed, but one will certainly gain additional service life from these units if they are maintained and checked regularly.

Some areas requiring seasonal attention that you may choose to do yourself, but are not limited to, include;

Checking and sealing the roof, windows, storage compartments and doors.

Cleaning and servicing the LP appliances.

Changing the oil in the generator and chassis engine and checking all fluid levels.

Cleaning the filters in the roof air conditioners.

Cleaning and treating your holding tanks.

Flushing and sanitizing your fresh water system.

Performing battery maintenance.

There are basically two types of RV service: crisis repairs and preventive maintenance. The aforementioned 16 hours would be classified as time devoted to preventive maintenance—the steps performed before there is an actual need for repair. Kind of like preventive medicine. Something you do now to prevent something worse from taking place later. A little insurance, if you will. Crisis repairs, on the other hand, are not optional. The problem is already at hand and needs immediate attention!

A few examples of crisis repairs would be an abnormally worn tire or blowout, a blocked cooling unit in the refrigerator, a blown engine or a burned out roof top air conditioner compressor. Here is the important thing to remember: Preventive maintenance will minimize the frequency and the degree of crisis-type repairs. Routine tire inspection and careful study of inflation pressures, checking and cleaning the refrigerator components and checking the LP gas pressure, regular oil changes and periodic cleaning of the air conditioner filters can all prevent the above crisis repairs from happening. Realize it is a choice each owner must face—preventive maintenance, or crisis repairs. There is no third option.

Do It Yourself?

Alas, this discussion is not about the types of RV service, but about whether or not you should attempt some of the maintenance items yourself. As owners, can we control our own RV repair destiny? Is that possible or feasible, or should we simply leave all types of service up to the professionals? I, for one, have always been in favor of owner involvement in the technical arena concerning RVs. I have devoted a large chunk of my time over the last three decades educating the RV enthusiast specifically in some of these areas. Additionally, Woodall Publications has, for many years, provided the very best in consumer repair manuals for the RVer. However, unless properly prepared and equipped, I do believe most owners should simply not attempt to make repairs or perform service on any RV, product or component. This is especially true during any factory warranty period of a new RV. All repairs should be performed by authorized persons during this time. In extreme cases, warranties may even be voided or manufacturer liability lessened if unauthorized repairs are performed. (In the context of the *RV Owner's Handbook*, it is assumed your vehicle is not under a new warranty situation.)

But here is a vital concern. Some maintenance items, though mandated by the product manufacturer and/or coach maker, may not be covered by new or extended warranties. Some items are simply destined to be the sole responsibility of the RV owner. Rarely are maintenance items ever covered under any warranty, yet they too scream for attention. In such cases, and in instances of out of warranty RVs, many owners actually enjoy delving into the various technical aspects of their coaches. The key is knowing when to actively participate and when to simply make an appointment at your local service facility.

So just who among us should consider performing maintenance tasks on our rigs? Here's some demographics. An informal survey taken at one of my recent owner maintenance seminars revealed that the RV owner who actively performs routine service typically:

Is mechanically inclined or has past experiences in labor trades

Has an impressive assortment of hand tools and testers

Has a keen interest in the technology of RVs.

Travels and camps in remote areas, far from any RV service
center and has no choice but to learn to become an RV technician

Has as much or more of a technical aptitude than the average professional

Is now, or has been, a full-time RVer

If you recognize yourself in these listed characteristics or are wondering whether or not you should attempt a maintenance task, here are a few considerations for you to ponder. Keep in mind, however, this list is not all-inclusive and all items may not apply evenly across the board. These are just a few thoughts to explore.

Review your own mechanical/technical aptitude. The important thing here is to realize your limitations. As you ponder a task, ask yourself, "Can I physically perform the steps necessary to do this?" Many items in, under, on and around an RV require a certain physical dexterity. Physical limitations may prohibit some of us from performing certain maintenance items. Sort of like when the brain says "yes," but the body says "no way!" Also, realize and admit it when the subject at hand is truly over your head. There is no need to be a hero. You definitely do not want to risk converting a simple maintenance task into a costly crisis repair! Cha-ching! It may cost substantially more to undo an error than to simply make an appointment with a service center if the subject is beyond your scope. You are not expected to know absolutely everything about your RV, but you should be able to honestly recognize the point at which you do not understand something. This maxim is true even with professional service technicians as well. Foolish is the RVer who trusts his coach to a service shop that proclaims it's technicians know all there is to know about RVs.

Have a willingness to learn. If you truly want to be able to perform routine maintenance and repair functions, be willing to do a little homework. Servicing LP-related appliances and components, for instance, virtually mandates a basic understanding of the sequence of operation of that appliance. Each appliance is different, but your advantage is that you only need to learn those that pertain to your rig. And it is not that difficult to learn. Oh, it requires reading and studying the literature that came with your coach and perusing this manual time and again, but for the most part, it can be enjoyable. Especially when you consider that any knowledge gained, nurtured and then applied will ultimately save real dollars in repair costs. You wouldn't even consider jumping in the coach and taking off down a road you've never been on before without a road map or at least a general knowledge of where it leads. So it is with most technical matters on your RV. You are holding that road map in your hands right now.

Be properly equipped. Be aware that many maintenance tasks require a well-balanced selection of tools and some require specialty tools that you may not have in your tool kit. An example of a specialty tool would be the long flue brush needed for cleaning and servicing the RV refrigerator. If you commit to performing this procedure yourself, purchasing that needed specialty tool would be a wise investment. Read Chapter 3: "Recommended Tools" for the detailed list of tools you should always carry with you as you travel.

Pay close attention also, when replacement parts are required for a certain task. As an example, when performing a cleaning procedure on the RV furnace, it is recommended that all gaskets be replaced. Be sure to have those gaskets on hand prior to beginning the cleaning. You will want to avoid being part way through a task and having to stop, thereby running the risk of not finding the parts you need right away. One goal should be to keep your down time to a minimum. Always keep a small assortment of frequently replaced parts on hand. Gather all the necessary tools and parts before starting your maintenance task. Chapter 18: "The Spare Parts Kit," will provide such a guideline.

Consider the time factor. Always plan your approach to any maintenance task appropriately. Realize that all maintenance requires time. Be sure to allot yourself plenty of time to complete whatever it is you are undertaking. Do not rush. You are more likely to omit a step or make a mistake if you are under pressure to complete a task when in a hurry. Remember, the next time you perform that same task, the time element will be reduced. Familiarity and repetition will breed speed.

How to "Do It Yourself"

Okay, so you feel like you just may qualify as a true RV "do-it-yourselfer," so now what? Well, it is time for some strategic planning and implementation. The following suggestions will get you started.

Prepare a proper and clean work area. Having a clean work area for the task is vital in order to avoid confusion and also help keep the RV clean if you must traipse in and out of it several times. When servicing the appliances for example, with the exception of the furnace, it is best to perform the maintenance tasks with the appliances left in their installed positions. An exception would be the RV furnace. In some instances concerning the furnace, better results are attained if the furnace is removed and the work performed on a bench. Also, in some cases, the absorption refrigerator may need to be partially removed to gain access for cleaning. Therefore, be sure to cover and protect carpeting or finished floors. When changing the oil in the generator or on the chassis engine, have an area cleared so complete access is easily accomplished. Don't forget to have your replacement oil ready and the drain pan in place before you remove the plug!

If you will be needing electricity, have your extension cord uncoiled and strategically placed prior to starting. Likewise, if using a drill motor, have the correct size drill bit, or screwdriver tip at hand. Proper preparation will make any maintenance task easier.

Have all replacement parts ready to go. Have all replacement parts prepared and laid out for easy access. If your maintenance task involves threaded fittings, a handy tip is to pre-apply the correct sealant or Teflon tape before actually starting the work. It's much neater and easier when your hands are relatively clean. Lay the fittings aside and cover them with a shop towel or cloth until needed. If the new parts need pre-assembly, do it now, before you get engrossed in the task. If some parts in a repair kit will not be needed, separate and discard them prior to beginning. This will simplify your repair and avoid any confusion you may encounter when you realize you have a few parts left over.

Obtain the necessary support materials. As mentioned earlier, have the *RV Owner's Handbook* and all wiring diagrams, service notes, installation instructions or any other type of resource open and within easy reach before starting the job. If you feel you may need additional help or support information, postpone the maintenance until all the necessary information is in your hand. Remember, preparation is much easier for a preventive maintenance procedure as opposed to an unwanted crisis repair.

Backup vehicle. It is always advisable to have access to another available vehicle "just in case." Whether it is a neighbor's second vehicle or perhaps it's the small car you usually tow behind your rig. In any event, always plan to have a mode of transportation available just in case you forgot something or for emergencies.

Establish a relationship with a local service facility. This step is vital. Even though you may be wanting to perform the maintenance and repairs yourself, always get to know a local dealer or service center in your area. Aside from being there to order parts for you, they can also be a good source of information. They should work in concert with you and not feel threatened that you elect to perform some of your own maintenance tasks. Obviously, you will need to rely on them for those technical areas you decide not to pursue, and there will be plenty left for them to do. All major repairs and many items that require costly specialty equipment is best left to the professional shop as we have discussed. Of course, you will want to check in your local area to find the appropriate service department that best fits your needs. All service facilities are not created equal.

By carefully evaluating your technical expertise, learning and gathering a resource library of sorts for those items on your coach, acquiring the proper tools and parts and most importantly, having the right attitude, you may be just the candidate to experience the fun of maintaining your investment for your leisure enjoyment. In any case, it is hoped that major repair costs are avoided, and total contentment is realized from the experiences of working on your own RV. Keep this handbook close by and refer to it often. You will not be disappointed. And remember, RVing is more than a hobby, it's a lifestyle!

Gary Bunzer—Technical Editor—1999

Oh yes! Recreational vehicles. RVs. If you are a seasoned RVer, you already know of the joys associated with RV travel. If you happen to be fairly new to the RVing lifestyle, then you will soon become aware of its multitude of benefits. RVing knows no state or provincial boundaries and has contributed more to family togetherness, environmental awareness and the simple appreciation of natural beauty than any other hobby or pastime. Though all forms of travel have some intrinsic value, none can compare to traveling in an RV. Simply talk for a few minutes with an active RVer and you will soon be exposed to the many advantages of traveling in your own "home on wheels." Spend a weekend in one at a campsite and you will be hooked for life. Whether you favor a luxurious, ultra-modern RV resort as a destination, with every amenity imaginable including Internet access and e-mail, or you prefer to be totally isolated, far from any concrete whatsoever, beside a quiet stream, simply dry-camping (camping with no hook-ups), the RVing lifestyle offers an option for you. You may prefer to travel and camp while wrapped in the lap of luxury on your own custom bus, complete with washer, dryer, satellite mapping and every digital whatchamacallit available. Or perhaps you would be happier simply camped along a secluded beach in a pre-owned pop-up tent camper passed on to you by a distant relative. Fact is, there are literally hundreds of options available, maybe thousands, for those who adopt those two little letters as a lifestyle: RV.

It has been often mentioned that an RV is considered a recreational investment. True enough, and like other types of investments, its security and viability must rely upon a valid understanding of its intricacies and nuances. As an RV owner, having a technical understanding of the various systems associated with your rig is a must. Being able to maintain, troubleshoot and repair those systems and components independently is a bonus. A bonus that will indeed reap rewards.

You are holding Woodall's revised and updated *RV Owner's Handbook*, the complete RV repair and information manual that can literally save you real dollars. This illustrated owner's manual will guide you through all the technical aspects of RVs with a system-by-system analysis of each major RV component. Many of the maintenance procedures detailed in this manual will, in some cases, virtually eliminate the need for future repairs. Written generically, this handbook is applicable to any RV. Continuing in the finest Woodall tradition, the revised edition of the *RV Owner's Handbook* will become *the book* for used or obsolete RVs and a *must have* complement for all new RVs.

We encourage you to truly embrace this RVing lifestyle and go for it! As we welcome in a new millennium, may you have many happy and safe RVing miles in your future. Enjoy!

CHAPTER ONE

RV Types and Categories

To the uninitiated, the vast diversity of RV styles may seem complicated and frustrating as well as confusing. To simplify the way to familiarize yourself with the various types of RVs, we will follow the descriptions of each category as set forth by the Recreation Vehicle Industry Association (RVIA), the industry's self-regulating agency. These descriptions and categories have been placed at this point in the book to help you better understand the complete spectrum of RVs early in your study. When appropriate, additional clarifying text supplements the official definitions.

So what is an RV? The most basic answer is that an RV is a vehicle that combines transportation and temporary living quarters for travel, recreation and camping. They can be either motorized (motorhomes), towed behind (travel trailers, fifth-wheel trailers, folding camping trailers) or they can be carried in a pick-up, (truck camper). RVs do not include mobile homes, off-road vehicles or snowmobiles.

For a new RV, prices may range from as little as $3,500 for a folding camping trailer to hundreds of thousands of dollars for a high-end motorhome or custom coach, with many levels in between. There are over 30 million RV enthusiasts in the United States alone driving around in almost 9.5 million RVs! So remember this, there is an RV for you.

TYPES OF RVS

FOLDING CAMPING TRAILER: A recreational camping unit designed for temporary living quarters which is mounted on wheels and constructed with collapsible side-walls intended to fold compactly so the entire trailer can be towed by a motorized vehicle.

Also called folding tent trailers or pop-ups, these vehicles have come a long way in the past several years with respect to ease of set-up and interior comfort. Some are equipped with hard laminated walls instead of the more common and traditional canvas or fiberglass panel. It is not unusual to find complete kitchen and bathroom amenities, along with other self-contained features normally associated with larger RVs, in folding camping trailers. Most tent trailers are relatively lightweight and can be towed by many cars and all trucks. Many can be made fully livable within 10 to 20 minutes, often by only one person—full set-up is easy. As the name implies, these RVs fold into a low profile package which, because of the smaller frontal area, helps to improve towing vehicle gas mileage. Other benefits of the low silhouette include improved handling in high winds and the ability to store the unit in a standard size garage.

TRUCK CAMPER: A recreational camping unit designed to be loaded onto, or affixed to, the bed or chassis of a truck. Designed to provide temporary living quarters for recreational, camping or travel use.

Often referred to as a "slide-in camper," this type is one of the most popular. Since they can be loaded on and off of a pick-up truck with relative ease, this is the favored type among those who enjoy the RV lifestyle on weekends, yet still favor a truck for work or transportation during the week.

Additionally, families that already own a suitable pick-up truck have an advantage over those who do not since they can become involved in the RV lifestyle with a smaller initial investment.

Modern truck campers are extremely comfortable and sometimes luxurious thanks to continuous upgrading by the manufacturers in order to meet the demands of the buying public. Often they come equipped with a full bathroom and shower, roof-mounted air conditioning, complete kitchen, including a microwave oven, sewage holding tanks, awnings and sometimes even an on-board generator.

When considering a truck camper, one must also consider the cost of a properly equipped truck prior to the purchase. If you have a pick-up already, you still need to evaluate its capability to safely carry the camper, all your gear and you. We will delve into this a little deeper later on.

TRAVEL TRAILER (GENERAL): A trailer designed to be towed by a motorized vehicle (auto, van or truck), and is of a size and weight as not to require a special highway movement permit. It is designed to provide temporary living quarters for recreation, camping or travel use, and does not require permanent on-site hook-up. A travel trailer can be one of the following types:

Conventional Travel Trailer – Typically ranges from 12 to 35 feet in length, and is towed by means of a bumper or frame-mounted hitch attached to a towing vehicle.

In addition to all the normal conveniences expected of any modern RV, travel trailers have an advantage: You can disconnect them and leave them at the campsite while the tow vehicle is used for errands, side trips or sightseeing.

As with any towing situation, aside from the RV unit, there is a requirement for a properly equipped tow vehicle capable of handling the additional weight and stress. Whether discussing autos or trucks, the key words are "properly equipped." Nearly every pick-up can tow or haul something, but a common mistake can be made by assuming that just because you have a pick-up, you can tow *any* travel trailer. That is not necessarily the case. Properly equipping a tow vehicle requires specialized evaluation and professional advice. Likewise, not all cars can tow travel trailers either. Many, in fact, can be damaged when attempting to tow a trailer. Later chapters will address these specific concerns.

The good news is that many vehicles today can fill the above requirement. Though not a mandate, it is ideal when the tow vehicle and the travel trailer purchase are considered at the same time. An analogy would be buying a suit, shirt and tie combination at the same time as opposed to purchasing the suit one day, the shirt another day and finally trying to find the right tie to match both. It can be done, but it takes proper planning and a little homework.

Conventional travel trailers are constructed with an "A" frame hitch design. Typically, this is also where the liquid propane (LP) cylinders are mounted. The lifting jack is also attached to the "A" frame to facilitate raising and lowering the tongue of the trailer. Obviously, travel trailers must be hitched and unhitched regularly and occasionally backed into an RV space when a pull-through spot is unavailable. These tasks should not be approached with fear or reservation. Trailer handling can be fun and is quite easy once you get the hang of it. As with any learned task, practice makes perfect!

Technical chassis maintenance is minimal with all types of trailers, because they lack the steering system and mechanical drive-line of a motorhome. There is no engine, transmission, differential, etc., to maintain on a travel trailer. However, these high maintenance items do exist on your tow vehicle so you still have to plan for periodic check-ups. The less expensive chassis of the travel trailer contributes to the lower purchase price of this type of RV, plus, insurance and license fees, in most cases, are significantly lower.

Fifth-Wheel Travel Trailer – This unit can be equipped the same as the conventional travel trailer, but is constructed with a raised forward section that allows a bi-level floorplan. This style is designed to be towed by a pick-up truck equipped with a device known as a fifth-wheel hitch.

Despite being sold in smaller numbers than conventional travel trailers, fifth-wheel models are popular because of their unique split-level floor plans and their propensity for slide-out rooms. Another popular benefit is the reduced length of the overall truck and trailer combination when towing. The connecting point, the hitch, is in the bed of the pick-up as opposed to at the rear of the truck. This, in effect, shortens the overall length of the towing configuration.

The name "fifth-wheel" is derived from the round plate found on the hitch mechanism used to connect the trailer to the tow vehicle. Though smaller in design, it is similar to those found on commercial tractor trailer rigs. Also, since the majority of fifth-wheel travel trailers are built with tandem axles, this type of travel trailer actually becomes the "fifth-wheel" when the combination is in motion. Some longer, more elaborate units come equipped with triple axles. Technically, these units would be considered a "seventh-wheel" travel trailer if we follow the same logic. However, the predominant features that define this unit are the split-level design and the method of attachment to the tow vehicle.

In use, the fifth-wheel travel trailer's attaching point of "gooseneck" overlaps the tow vehicle by six feet or more. As mentioned previously, this reduces the overall combined length of the two vehicles, which results in improved traction and easier, safer handling.

Many RV veterans consider fifth-wheel hitching to be easier than a conventional hook-up because the driver can visually guide the connection without the assistance of the copilot or "spotter." One perceived negative associated with fifth-wheel trailers is the manner in which they "cheat" on turns. Because the pivot point is located several feet forward than that of a conventional hitch, the trailer tires do not follow directly in the path of the tow vehicle. Instead they cut to the inside of the tow vehicle's track significantly. This condition can lead to curb jumping, especially on right-hand turns. Additionally, increased tire wear may result. Handling at highway speeds is not a problem. Many enthusiasts contend fifth-wheel towing is superior to that of conventional travel trailers. As before, a little practice makes fifth-wheel handling second nature.

MOTORHOMES (GENERAL): A recreational camping and travel vehicle on, or as an integral part of a self-propelled motor vehicle chassis. It provides at least four of the following permanently installed living systems:

- Cooking
- Refrigeration or ice box
- Heating or air conditioning
- Self-contained toilet
- Portable water system including water tank, faucet and sink
- Separate 110-125 volt electrical system
- LP gas supply
- Sleeping facilities

Conventional Motorhome (type A) – The living unit has been entirely constructed on a bare, specially designed motor vehicle chassis.

Also called "Class As," or full size motorhomes. They are very popular among RVers. As noted in the official definition, the living quarters are built on a heavy duty motorized chassis designed specifically as an RV. Mainstream automotive chassis manufacturers, as well as many specialized makers, produce a selection of chassis and frames for the RV industry. Many utilize gasoline engines; some come equipped with diesel engines. Some are "pushers" with the power plant in the rear of the coach, while some have the engine up front.

Advanced chassis technology today has increased the buyer's options when considering Class A motorhomes. Basement models have become the most popular Class A motorhome design. Constructed with a sub-floor, the main living area is completely on one level and the lower "basement" is dedicated for storage and installation of the various system components. The proliferation of the single, double and even triple slide-out rooms have increased living space immensely as well as the floor plan options. On the inside as well, many Class As come equipped with trash compactors, garbage disposals, washer and dryer combinations, ice makers, dishwashers, satellite antennae, global positioning systems (GPS), sophisticated media and entertainment centers and more. There are plenty of options from which to choose. Understandably, these units usually occupy the higher end of the price spectrum.

Many consider motorhomes in this category to be the most comfortable RV because of the typically larger interior which allows occupants to move about freely. Another big plus comes when it is time to move to the next destination. All that is necessary is to unhook from the campground utilities, start the engine and drive away.

Maneuvering and backing is generally considered to be easier than the towables since motorhomes respond to steering adjustments similar to an automobile. Excepting the larger physical dimensions and extended stopping distance requirements, learning to drive a Class A motorhome comes extremely easy to most owners.

Most Class A's range in length from 28 to 35 feet. Once they are parked and set up, most owners hesitate to disconnect the coach for a quick sightseeing trip or to run an errand. This has led to the common practice of towing a small vehicle behind the motorhome for those quick, yet necessary side trips. The subject of "dinghy towing" will also be addressed later in the *RV Owner's Handbook*.

Van Camper (type B) – A panel-type truck to which the RV manufacturer adds any two of the following conveniences:
- Sleeping area
- Kitchen facilities
- Toilet facilities
- 120-volt hook-up
- Fresh water storage
- City water hook-up
- Extended top for more head room

Van campers are popular for weekend trips and short outings. The primary advantage of these units is that they retain the versatility of a large family car or van as well as provide the amenities mentioned above for recreational camping. Van campers are capable of the same duty the ever-popular mini-van might offer during the week, but can also be used for enjoying the RV lifestyle. Another advantage of this type of RV is its relative ease of driving in traffic. In fact, the popularity of the mini-van has resulted in many being converted to this type of RV.

Chopped Van (mini or type C) – This unit is built on an automotive van frame with an attached cab section. The RV manufacturer completes the body section containing the living area and attaches it to the cab section.

Commonly called "mini-motorhomes" or "Class C" motorhomes, this variety is also very popular. Ease of handling is one of the strong selling points to this type of coach. Less intimidating than the larger Class A's, Class C units are built on a standard van chassis. The driver's section is identical to that of a production model van. The chassis is often lengthened or "stretched" to accommodate the RV portion. Lengths typically run from 18 to 29 feet. The average length is about 24 feet.

Most minis sport some form of enclosed cabover structure above the driver's compartment. Quite often this space is used for sleeping, though on occasion, it is dedicated solely to storage or for mounting a multimedia entertainment center. Many models come equipped with bunk beds or a convertible dinette that pulls double duty as a sleeping area when not in use as a table. The amenities found in Class Cs rival those found in the larger Class A motorhomes. Many are downright luxurious.

Primarily because they are shorter, other major advantages credited to Class C's include the aforementioned ease of handling or maneuverability and livability. Many floorplan options are available to satisfy just about every kind of RVer. Even those who prefer the very popular slide-out room. The most often heard disadvantage is the necessity on most units to crawl up and into the cabover section to go to bed. Also, there exists a false sense of size since the unit is built on a standard van chassis and looks just like a van from the driver's view. Gas stations, drive-up automated teller machines (ATMs) and fast food outlets take on a whole new perspective when in a Class C. It takes a little concentration to realize you are much taller, longer and wider than a typical van.

Conversion Vehicles – Vans, pick-up trucks and sport utility vehicles (SUVs), manufactured by an automaker then modified for transportation and recreational use by a company specializing in customized vehicles. These changes may include windows, carpeting, paneling, seats, sofas, and accessories.

Technically termed RVs, these vehicles are primarily intended for luxurious point-to-point travel rather than extended RVing. Some do have small sinks, an ice box, a television and/or convertible sofas, but for the most part, the typical RV systems are absent. Most owners agree that these units are suitable only for occasional overnight camping.

RV OWNERSHIP BREAKDOWN

To give you an idea of the breakdown for the most recent numbers of deliveries of RVs, the following chart displays the categories and their total deliveries in 1998. The totals are not the actual retail sales of RVs, but the number of new units delivered to the RV dealers. Many more additional RVs were sold that are not reflected in the total. Pre-owned coaches and units sold between private parties translate into many, many more families now engaged in one of America's favorite pastimes. According to RVIA, 1998 was the best year since 1978, so if you are still not an active RVer, now is the time for you to become involved!

Category	Number of RVs
Travel Trailers—Conventional	98,600
Travel Trailers—Fifth-Wheel	56,500
Truck Campers	10,800
Folding Camping Trailers	63,300
Class A Motorhomes	42,900
Class B Motorhomes	3,600
Class C Motorhomes	17,000

CHAPTER TWO

Basic Interior and Exterior Care

Undetected rainwater seeps through an inadvertent tear in the ethylene proplene diene monomer (EPDM) roofing membrane caused by a low-hanging tree branch allowing water to permeate the substrate decking below. It continues to seek its own level, as leaking water will, propelled by gravity, until it soaks the ceiling and is absorbed into the wall panels. What could be the result if left unabated? Probably a loosened rubber membrane, stained ceilings, damaged side walls and possible loss of structural integrity in the RV. The translation—a big bucks repair bill!

A finely made window dressing is removed from its position above the dinette and tossed into the washing machine after a slight spill created a small stain. It comes out clean, but now it only hangs half way down the window. These accidental damages rarely happen in conventional homes, but in RVs, they can be commonplace if owners are unaware or inattentive.

The best prevention is to be thoroughly acquainted with the various interior materials and their proper care, and to actively and assertively inspect every square inch of the exterior of your RV periodically. Although it is virtually impossible to list all of the different materials and fabrics used by manufacturers today, this chapter is designed as a general guide to basic interior and exterior care.

INTERIOR RV CARE

Interior RV walls, floors, ceilings, countertops, cabinets, appliances, fixtures and furnishings are all made from a variety of materials. A short list would include: linoleum, tile, vinyl, Formica, stainless steel, chrome, glass, plastics, painted or stained wood and various laminates. "Soft goods" such as upholstery, drapes, curtains, dividers, leather chairs, couches and bed coverings, may demand peculiar cleaning techniques common only to that product. Unfortunately, there is no across-the-board aftermarket product that will effectively clean and treat every type material or composite found on a typical RV. But here are few general tips for interior RV care.

• Read all labels and literature that is available for that particular component. Look for cleaning or washing precautions. Keep this information handy. Perhaps include it with the remainder of your RV literature. If you have Internet access, try a search for that type of material or composite.

• Use cleaning products that you have had success with in other applications, such as at home. Try them out in areas that will have minimum impact if they do not prove effective. For instance, try out a carpet cleaner under a bed or in a closet before attempting to clean the entire carpet. Or give that new spray-on wall brightener a test inside a closet first.

• Look for a manufacturer name or brand on tags or labels. If cleaning or care instructions are not readily available on the product, contact the maker directly. Most are more than willing to provide written instructions for the upkeep of their products.

• Remember that what may work well with one certain fabric or component may not work well with another. Realize that all finishes, fabrics and materials differ. Ask other RVers what works for them. Be willing to share and pass on care secrets you uncover.

WALLS: Interior walls are usually plywood or wood-grained hardboard panels with a thin veneer or wood finish on the exposed side. Wallcoverings such as wallpaper or a vinyl layer are common as well. Scratches are the most common problem. Wood scratches can be stained to match or a colored putty stick can be used to fill in the deeper grooves.

For stained wood paneling, apply a home-type furniture polish or treatment at least once a year or more often if necessary. One product that works well is "Restor-A-Finish," also available at most hardware stores and home supply depots. It can also be found in some of the popular mail order catalogs. If the wood is painted, wash it down periodically with a mild detergent and water.

Bathroom walls may be made of enamel or vinyl coated hardboard. Some may be covered with a durable wall paper. These should be wiped dry after use to prevent mildew.

FLOORS: RV floors are usually either covered with linoleum, tile or carpet. Dirt not cleaned from linoleum can become ground in and ruin the tile. Use a name brand household cleaner and wax the floor to lengthen the time between cleanings.

Frequent vacuuming before dirt has a chance to get ground in is the best procedure. Central vacuum systems make this a simple task. If you don't have a central vacuum, there are a number of reliable 12-volt auto vacuums that are inexpensive and take up little storage space. Of course, the carpet can simply be vacuumed at home before and after a trip, but an on-board vacuum is a good idea if carpeting is in high-traffic areas. Also, once a year clean the carpet with a commercial cleaner.

CEILINGS: Ceilings are usually either wood fiber panels, plywood or acoustic paneling. There is little need to clean this area often since it is seldom touched, but fingerprints and other soiling can be removed with a damp cloth. In some instances, the ceiling may be covered with a fabric. Consult your owner's manual or contact the manufacturer if you are unsure what exact type of ceiling is in your RV.

FABRICS: The list of fabrics is growing everyday. Obviously no single cleaning agent or method suits all of them, but a few general recommendations can be made. Most upholstery fabrics used in RVs are not washable, and many are not dry cleanable. Soiling is controlled by spot cleaning performed with one of the many upholstery cleaners marketed for home furniture. Use a commercial vinyl cleaner for vinyl upholstery. Curtains and drapes are usually dry cleanable, but check the tag to be sure.

WINDOWS: The usual home window cleaners will work fine on glass. On plastics though, avoid abrasives. A small amount of ammonia and a mild detergent with water is safe for both.

KITCHEN APPLIANCES AND GALLEY AREA: Appliance manufacturers routinely provide literature on care and maintenance. (If you have long since lost the literature or are a second owner of an RV contact each appliance manufacturer individually or our technical editor for specific instructions).

REFRIGERATOR: Cleaning of the RV refrigerator is similar to its home counterpart with one difference. RV refrigerators are more vulnerable to high heat. This means that attempting to speed up a defrost cycle with the aid of a hair dryer will result in damage that could necessitate a new refrigerator.

Make sure the controls are turned off and clean the interior with two tablespoons of baking soda dissolved in a quart of warm water. Rinse and dry. Wash the crisper pan and other removable parts with warm, sudsy water. Wipe the exterior with a cloth dampened in a mild detergent water, rinse and wipe dry with a soft cloth.

On older refrigerators, metal racks that seem immovable because of plastic stops can often be jockeyed out by using a screwdriver to lift up the clip so that the shelf will slide out. Be careful that you do not damage the inner liner.

Appliances

Keep RV appliances clean. To unclog range burner ports, insert a wooden toothpick. Don't use a metal object here—it would damage the port.

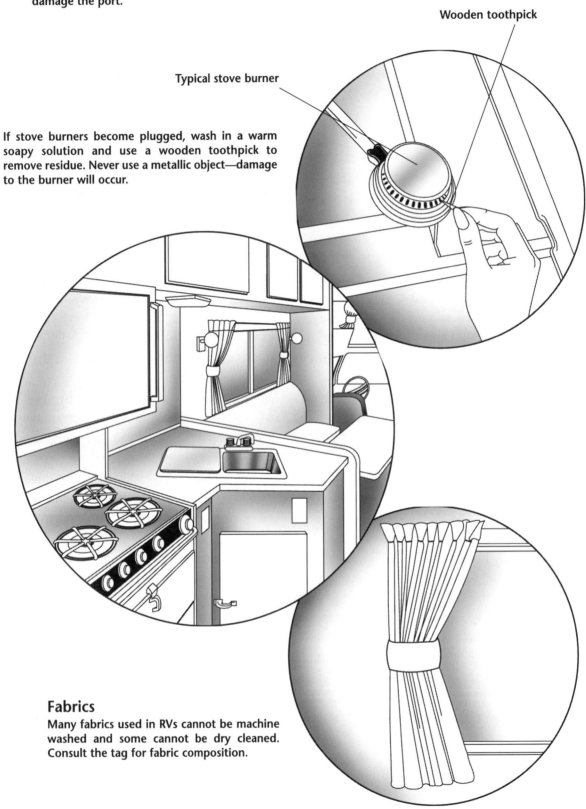

Wooden toothpick

Typical stove burner

If stove burners become plugged, wash in a warm soapy solution and use a wooden toothpick to remove residue. Never use a metallic object—damage to the burner will occur.

Fabrics

Many fabrics used in RVs cannot be machine washed and some cannot be dry cleaned. Consult the tag for fabric composition.

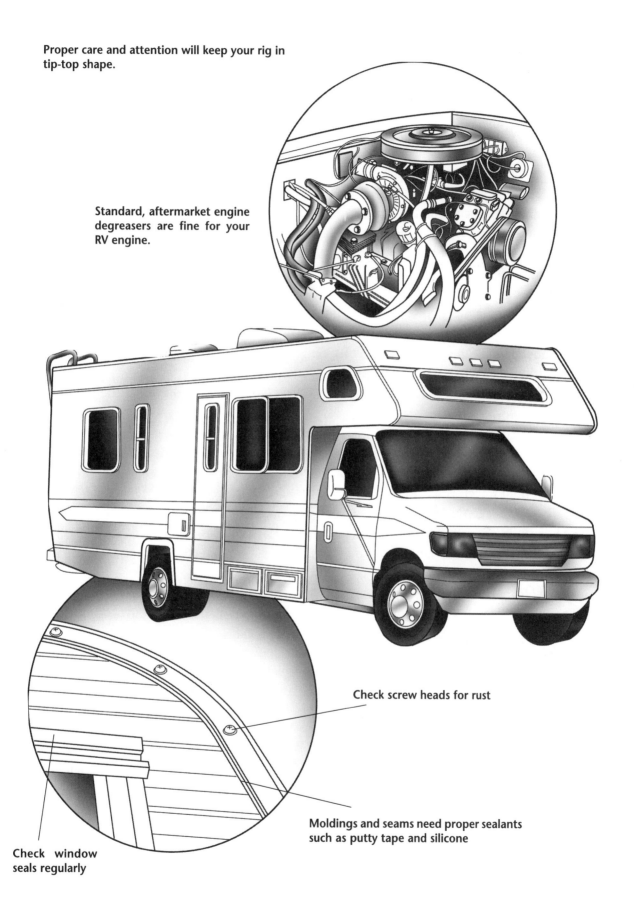

Proper care and attention will keep your rig in tip-top shape.

Standard, aftermarket engine degreasers are fine for your RV engine.

Check screw heads for rust

Moldings and seams need proper sealants such as putty tape and silicone

Check window seals regularly

OVEN: Most RV oven interiors have a porcelain enamel finish. This is easily identifiable by its smooth shiny surface. Use a mild detergent with water to remove soil before it has a chance to cook on. Wipe burned-on spots with ammonia to soften them, then clean with detergent and water. Remove plated oven racks and use a soap-filled scouring pad to clean. Rinse and dry. A solution of mild detergent and water is also good for cleaning microwave oven interiors.

A few RV ovens have a "continuous cleaning" finish on the oven's interior. It is recognized by its rough, dull surface. These ovens have porous ceramic coating that allows soil to disperse over a large surface area and the coating, with the help of baking temperatures, acts as a catalyst to "evaporate" it.

STOVE TOP: Clean the stove top often to prevent spills from becoming baked on and to keep the burner ports unclogged. Before cleaning, be sure the stove is cool and all burners are turned off. The outside metal should be cleaned with a sudsy cloth using mild liquid dishwashing detergent and water. Rinse with a cloth dampened with clean water and dry the surface with a soft cloth.

Make sure the burner ports are open by poking each with a wooden toothpick. Do not use a metal object or probe since it would damage the port. Stay away from steel wool, abrasive cleaners, cleaners containing ammonia, acids or commercial oven cleaners on any exterior portions of the range.

The underside of the stove top in may RV ranges is prone to rust. Keep this area dry and treat it monthly with a chrome cleaner to prevent corrosion.

RANGE HOOD AND VENT: Clean the stainless steel portions as you would the sink (see "metallic surfaces" below). At least twice a year, clean the filter element with warm water and detergent, or simply replace it.

STAINLESS STEEL SINKS: Ordinary detergent is good for this type of receptacle. Rinse and wipe dry with a clean cloth. If there is a problem with fingerprints, apply a cleaner that leaves a thin film of wax, then fingerprints wipe up easily.

COUNTER TOPS AND TABLE TOPS: These are usually covered with a durable plastic or acrylic laminate, Formica or a derivative. Use a plastics or glass cleaner. A word of caution about those seemingly indestructible surfaces: hot objects may injure the laminate, causing it to pull away from the bonded wood base.

METALLIC SURFACES: Metal decorative trims are easily cleaned with a glass or appliance cleaner. There are many chrome and metal cleaners, so choose a named brand product for best results.

BATHROOM FIXTURES: The lavatory, shower stall, tub and toilet are typically formed of ABS plastic. These fixtures can be damaged by the use of abrasive cleaners. Use only products recommended by the manufacturer or a mild, low-acid household detergent. Named brand plastic cleaners are acceptable.

EXTERIOR RV CARE

The most basic exterior care is simply to keep the rig clean. The cleaner the RV, the easier it is to recognize problem areas that may be masked or hidden behind a layer of dirt or caked-on mud. Realize, also, that the exterior includes the undercarriage of your RV. Do not overlook the importance of keeping the entire coach as clean as feasibly possible.

ROOF AREA: Careful inspection and cleaning go hand in hand. Check the roof in the spring and in the fall. If you have driven through an area with low hanging branches, check it again as a precaution.

By far the most popular roofing material today is the ethylene propylene diene monomer (EPDM) rubber membrane. Chapter 11, covers the complete spectrum of EPDM care and repair, which differs significantly from RV roofs covered with aluminum or fiberglass. For roofing other than EPDM, check the seams, vents and roof edges carefully. In some climates, it may be necessary to reseal the roof on an annual basis. There are a number of reliable RV roof sealants. A common sealant is an asphalt-based mix with aluminum powder that reflects sunlight. More reflective white plastic sealants are also available. In hot, dry areas, aluminum is the better choice. In rainy regions where insulation is valued, pick the white sealant.

Follow the instructions on the label and stir the sealant well, then apply liberal amounts with a trowel or brush to the edges of the roof, vent mountings and the seams. If the old sealant appears brittle and shows signs of cracking, do not apply new sealant over the old. Remove the old sealant and clean the roof area first.

CAULK OR SILICONE SEALANT: Examine the sealant around windows, storage compartments and vents for aging. The oil-based caulk used to seal joints and windows will repel other caulking compounds so scrape it off before applying fresh caulk of a different type.

SIDES: RVs with aluminum siding thankfully are not prey to the body rust that plagues auto bodies, but the baked enamel finish can become streaked from roof and window sealant residue or from oxidizing EPDM rubber membrane. Exposed aluminum also oxidizes and can develop a mottled, pitted appearance. Care includes a thorough cleaning to remove grime, bugs and stains, and a wax or protective coating to prolong the scrubbed state and restore luster to faded colors.

There are many excellent brand name cleaners, waxes and black streak removers available today. Test a few to see what works best for your application. Studies have shown that the surface type, the amount of oxidation or corrosion and the climate are the three main determining factors as to which products work best. Waxes developed for auto application are fine for luster and protection, but most require frequent application—about once every three months. Longer lasting RV products are available at a slightly higher cost. Check your local RV accessory stores for these products.

Fiberglass is the predominant material used for RV siding today. There are a myriad of cleaners and polishes made for fiberglass too. Fiberglass is quite prone to oxidation, and when ignored for long periods, substantial oxidation can permanently damage the finish beyond a simple cleaning and polishing job. However, with severe oxidation, the only true remedy is a new paint job. Most damaging to fiberglass are the ultra-violet (UV) rays from the sun. For long storage periods, especially in hot, dry climates, a total coach cover will prolong the luster of gel-coat and fiberglass components.

Proper care concerning the interior and exterior will add many miles to your RVing enjoyment level.

CHAPTER THREE

Recommended Tools and Safety

TOOLS AND THEIR USES

Since the beginning of time, humans have designed, used and improved upon a myriad of tools. Today there are thousands of different kinds and types of tools—the book you are now holding is, in itself, a type of tool. Throughout the ages it has been decidedly proven that people simply cannot survive without tools. Likewise, today's RV enthusiast cannot get by without tools.

Whether you are a tinkerer, a backyard mechanic or a seasoned technician, if you own an RV, there will be times when an adjustment may be necessary—a screw may need tightening, or a component may need replacing. You *will* have an opportunity to dig for that screwdriver or find that test light at some point in time. Consider it an RV "fact of life." Particularly if you find yourself "out in the boondocks" and miles from the nearest service facility. Full-timers especially, should be "well tooled" while living aboard an RV. Additionally, there is a justified feeling of satisfaction knowing that you repaired that water pump or found that short. Plus, having the right tool to perform a task will make the job safer and easier.

Throughout this handbook, many detailed instructions will be provided that may or may not

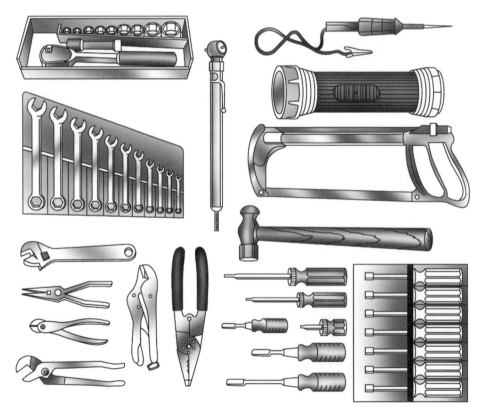

Typical Tools Found in a Basic Kit

depict all of the possible scenarios you will encounter. It is important when you follow these instructions and procedures that you satisfy yourself thoroughly that neither personal nor product safety will be compromised or jeopardized. If you are in doubt about a procedure and do not feel comfortable, do not continue. Simply call your local service facility and make an appointment with them. Safety, remember, is the No. 1 priority.

It is assumed that you now possess a basic knowledge of hand tools and at least some cognizance of mechanical aptitude. If you are not sure, try anyway. Experience is the best teacher. Even the most non-technical RVers are usually successful at tracking down squeaks, rattles and leaks. You need not feel helpless if you own an RV and are not mechanically inclined. The procedures here will give you the road map to follow. Just remember never to compromise the safety factor.

The balance of this chapter will display lists of tools that are recommended for general and specific tasks associated with an RV. They are categorized into three sections:

- Basic Tool Kit
- Advanced Tool Kit
- RV Specialty Tools

BASIC TOOK KIT: The Basic Kit is comprised of those tools that should be found in your coach even if you do not plan to get heavily involved in troubleshooting and repair. These are the common hand tools that will simply come in handy when needed.

Socket set (three-eighths-inch drive)—Typically you will only use a few different size sockets. It is also advisable an assortment of extensions of different lengths and a universal joint. You will also need a spark plug-sized socket for the spark plugs in your generator if you have one.

Combination wrench set (one-quarter-inch to one-inch)—This is the type that has a box-end on one end and an open-end wrench on the other.

Crescent wrenches (6-inch and 12-inch)—These adjustable wrenches are handy for many chores.

Pliers assortment—Needle-nose, 8" groove joint (water pump), standard slip joint pliers.

Locking pliers—One small and one large.

Tire gauge—Be sure the PSI range is applicable for your tires.

12-volt test light

Flashlight

Hacksaw

Ball Peen Hammer

Screwdrivers—(flat blade, Phillips, clutch-head, Robertson (square-head). Different sizes of varying lengths, including flat blade and Phillips "stubby," thin pocket screwdriver and one magnetic multi-tip screwdriver. You can never have too many screwdrivers.

Nut drivers—Most hex-head screws used on RVs use a quarter-inch socket. If you only choose to buy one nut driver, choose a quarter-inch.

Polarity tester—Some even come with a built in voltmeter as well.

Wire brush

Eye goggles

Rubber gloves

Pry bar/nail puller

Battery terminal post cleaner

Owner's manuals—That is right. Service literature is probably your best tool. Try to assemble literature containing parts listings and service information for all of your LP appliances and any other major component or device found on and in your RV.

ADVANCED TOOL KIT: The Advanced Kit adds a few more tools to the basic kit. The inclusion of these tools will enable you to perform some troubleshooting and minor repairs on most major systems of an RV.

In addition to the basic kit:

Caulking gun

Diagonal wire cutters

Spark plug gap tool

Portable battery charger (six amps minimum)—To be used as a small battery charger and as a 12-volt source of power when troubleshooting or "bench testing."

Volt, Ohm, multi-meter (VOM)—Preferably digital. It need not be the most expensive model, yet it should be somewhat rugged in design and accurate to within + 5 percent of full scale.

Cordless, reversible, drill—Invaluable if you need to remove more than a couple screws, drill a bunch of holes, or install accessories. A three-eights-inch chuck is recommended in order to accommodate a twist drill of that size. A fast charging, heavy duty drill is well worth the extra dollars.

Battery hydrometer (preferably temperature compensated)—An absolute must when troubleshooting your battery systems.

Crimpers for solderless terminals—Invest in a good quality pair. The cheaper, inexpensive combination stripper, crimper, cutter, etc., is not fully reliable for solderless terminals. A good crimper will deeply penetrate the terminal resulting in a lasting connection that will not pull loose.

Volt-Ohm-Mullti-Meter

Crescent wrenches (four-inch and eight-inch)—These two sizes are complimentary to the six-inch and ten-inch in the basic set. When working with LP fittings, always use a backup wrench to tighten and loosen fittings. The small four-inch size will come in handy when working on appliances.

RV SPECIALTY TOOL KIT: The RV Specialty Kit include those items that are specific to the world of RVs. The addition of these tools, coupled with the knowledge in this handbook, will enable you to attack almost every troubleshooting task and maintenance procedure encountered. However, it does not include the large major pieces of equipment that are normally found only in service shops. With one possible exception, each of the tools listed in all of the sets can be purchased for well below $125.

In addition to the advanced set:

Manometer (preferably water column type)—Available in spring gauge type or the more cumbersome water column type. Why the water column type? It is 100 percent accurate every single time. This device will allow you to set your LP regulator and test your entire coach for LP leaks.

Water Column Manometer

This type manometer is 100% accurate.

Mercury oven thermometer

Refrigerator thermometers—Two are needed: one for the freezer compartment and one for the main food section.

Brake adjusting tool

Inductive-type ammeter—This device can be slipped over a brake magnet wire to measure the current draw of each magnet without having to cut the wire or otherwise tap into the circuit. A must for testing your brake magnets the easy way. (part #810, Hayes-Lemmerz)

Circuit breaker test leads—For checking electrical shorts. Easily made by attaching alligator test leads to each post of a standard 12-volt, 20-amp circuit breaker. It is placed in a circuit while troubleshooting a fuse that keeps blowing.

Alligator test leads (attached to a 470-ohm resistor)—For testing the LED circuits of monitor panels and tank probes.

Inspection mirror—Allows inspection of components in those hard-to-see places.

Refrigerator flue brush—A soft bristle brush the same diameter as the flue. For cleaning out the flue once or twice a year.

Thermocouple tester—Available through your RV service facility or at

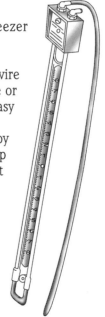

Granger's stores. This device can bench test your thermocouple while it is out of the appliance. (This tester is not needed if all your appliances are direct spark ignited.)

Thermocoupler Tester
Will effectively test all thermocouplers in pilot flame appliances

TOOL SAFETY

Now that you know the different sets of tools needed, it is imperative that you understand the issue of safety when it comes to tools. The No. 1 rule is to use the right tool for the right job. Never pry with a long screwdriver, never hammer with an end wrench, etc. Tool safety is directly proportional to your safety and the safety of your equipment. For example, when working around lead/acid batteries, always wear eye protection and rubber gloves. Inexpensive goggles can save your eyesight while working with battery electrolyte.

QUALITY OF TOOLS

It is nice to have that shiny new Cadillac, but that 20-year-old Volkswagen can still get you down the road. Use common sense when purchasing tools. If a cheaper tool will perform the same as a similar top dollar tool, fine. If a cheaper tool appears fallible or prone to breaking, thereby compromising the safety factor, buy the more expensive version. Obviously, the quality-made tools will last longer, yet may cost you more initially.

Look for a good warranty. Any tool that has free replacement value or an extended warranty is much better than one that is limited. Let your budget be your guide. You can always upgrade later. If a certain tool or brand of tool will make your task easier, faster or safer, then it could be considered a justified purchase. Take care of your tools. Do not allow them to rust, corrode or become lost.

When purchasing tools to carry with you as you travel, it is important to keep in mind space limitations. The tools listed in this chapter are simply suggestions. You may choose to add some tools of your own or delete some tools from these lists. Choose tools that you know are applicable to you and your RV. If you perform your own engine tune-ups for instance, there are additional automotive tools that you would probably need as well. Tools should be purchased for a specific purpose, and it is doubtful you could ever have too many.

CHAPTER FOUR

Electrical Systems

By far one of the most confusing yet least understood entities within the RV realm is electricity. The electrical systems found in RVs today have become far-reaching and technically advanced. Unlike years past when one could simply bypass certain functions and manually light the refrigerator, for instance, today, it is virtually impossible to use most appliances without a healthy 12-volt battery system. Electricity is vital to an RV, especially when it comes to being totally "self-contained." It is certainly one of the commodities RVers must learn to conserve.

This chapter will present a brief overview of the different systems found in the typical RV as well as more detailed looks into batteries, generators, converters, inverters and solar power. For now, here are some basic, yet necessary, fundamentals.

SYSTEM TYPES

There are two basic types of electrical systems found in an RV. Alternating current (AC) and direct current (DC). The AC system is considered the high voltage system while the DC circuits are considered low voltage. Both systems should be treated with respect. It is not the voltage in a system that is harmful, it is the current that kills.

Before we look at each system separately, there are a few shared attributes that are applicable to both. In an RV, each type (AC and DC), has these items:

- Conductors (AC utilizes solid wires, DC uses stranded wires)
- Protective device (fuses and circuit breakers)
- Resistive units (components and items that use the electricity)
- Means of switching (switches or relays)

Combined and appropriately situated, these four items form an electrical *circuit*. The AC and DC circuits must be kept separate. High and low voltages are not compatible.

DEFINITIONS

In order to better understand electricity in an RV, here are some definitions to help bring things into perspective.

VOLTAGE: The force that causes free electrons to move on a conductor as an electric current. It can also be called electromotive force (EMF), or the difference in potential.

In the world today, there are six basic methods of producing voltage. Interestingly, five out of the six are viable to RV's in one form or another. The methods are:

Friction—An example would be static electricity

Pressure—The principle found in piezo ignitors on some pilot model appliances

Heat—Also called thermoelectricity, exemplified in thermocouples used in flame failure safety systems for RV appliances

Light—Photoelectricity is used with today's solar panels

Chemical action—Our common flooded, lead acid RV storage battery

Magnetism—Used in auxiliary RV generators and automotive alternators

CURRENT: The amount of electron flow in any given circuit. It is a quantity of energy commonly called a "draw" or "drain." For instance, one might hear, "How much of a current draw does that fan motor use?" Or, "The battery has a 650 milli-amp drain on it."

RESISTANCE: That which is a form of friction to the current that impedes the flow of electrons. All resistive loads, those items that use the electricity, have a set value of resistance that is measured in a units of measurement called ohms.

POWER: The amount of electrical work used by any of the resistive loads, or the time rate of doing electrical work. Within the RV realm, this term is used quite liberally and mostly in error. "There is not enough *power* in the battery to start the engine." This statement actually refers to current.

Power in an electrical circuit is measured in watts. Watts, as a unit of measurement, equals the voltage of a circuit multiplied by the current of that same circuit.

ELECTRICAL RELATIONSHIPS

As inches are to feet and feet to yards, so also are volts to voltage, amps to current and ohms to resistance. The following chart may be helpful to separate and understand the differences between the physical property, unit of measurement and form of the electrical terms discussed so far.

Physical Property	Form	Unit of Measurement	Symbol
Pressure	Voltage	Volts	(E)
Flow	Current	Amps	(I)
Restriction	Resistance	Ohms	(R)
Stored Heat	Power	Watts	(P)

The symbol in parentheses that follows each unit of measurement is simply a universal, single letter designator used to represent each of the electrical forms, an abbreviation, if you will.

OHM'S LAW: Ohm's Law is defined as the way to express the relationship between voltage, current and resistance in any given circuit. They are mathematically relative to one another in the same unique way in each type of circuit. If any two of the three values are known in a circuit, the third can be determined by applying Ohm's Law.

There are three ways in which to express Ohm's Law. In text format, Ohm's Law states that the current equals the voltage divided by the resistance. Also, the voltage equals the current multiplied by the resistance. Or that the resistance equals the voltage divided by the current. The following diagram further illustrates the law.

Ohm's Law Diagram

By simply covering the value that is unknown *(but that you wish to determine)* with your finger on the above diagram, the remaining properties will be presented in mathematical formation.

For instance, you want to find the current in a certain circuit. Using the chart, cover the "I" *(for current)* with your finger. What remains is the "E" over the "R". As you would with a fraction, divide the known value of the resistance into the known voltage. The result will be the previously "unknown" current value.

The magnitude of the electrical current, or amperage, depends on the resistance of the circuit and the voltage applied to the circuit. Ohm's Law indicates how much current flows. Also, the resistance does not depend on either current or voltage. The characteristic of the conductors and the load itself determines the resistance. Resistance cannot be changed by simply changing the current or the voltage. Ohm's Law indicates how much resistance is contained in any given circuit.

The voltage in a circuit does not depend on either current or resistance. The voltage in the circuit is determined entirely by the health and condition of the battery in that circuit, or how much is being delivered by the generator or shoreline power source. Ohm's Law will, however, indicate how much voltage is required for a given current through a given resistive unit.

It is evident that all three of these properties are clearly related to each other in a unique way and that each pertains to simple electricity within the circuits found in your RV.

POWER LAW: Power, as mentioned earlier, is a property usually associated with alternating current circuits and components. Like Ohm's Law, the Power Law is easy to calculate as long as you know any two of the three properties. Here's the diagram for the Power Law.

Power or watts within the RV arena is exemplified when determining, for instance, the size of a generator that is needed for a particular application. On-board power plants are rated in watts or a variation of watts called *kilowatts* (watts divided by 1,000). As an example after calculating each alternating current load in an RV (most appliances and components have the amperage or current rating on the nameplate or the information can be found in the owner's manual), it is determined that a generator is needed that can produce 50 amps. Since power equals the current times the

Power Law Diagram

voltage, it can now be determined that 50 amps multiplied by the standard 120 volts equates to a need of a generator that can produce at least 6,000 watts, or 6.0 kilowatts.

Understanding the unique relationship among the above-mentioned electrical properties will greatly enhance your ability to troubleshoot them with minimal effort and downtime. But before we can successfully troubleshoot our electrical systems, let's explore more about the major systems involved.

12-VOLT DC SYSTEM

The DC systems associated with RVs are sometimes referred to as simply the battery systems. In every RV there are at least two distinct battery systems. One is the automotive system which typically starts the engine (in the motorhome or tow vehicle), powers the dash, horn and all running lights and electric brakes (on the travel trailer), among other things. The other is the house, or RV system, sometimes referred to as the auxiliary battery system. This system provides the current for everything in the house portion of the RV: the water pump, furnace blower, exhaust vents, low voltage lighting and a myriad of different 12-volt products available today.

Voltage for the 12-volt DC systems is produced by:
- Battery banks
- Power converter
- Automotive alternator
- Solar panels

Though we will take an in-depth look at each of the above, at the center of the 12-volt DC systems lies the battery. Everything 12-volt revolves around this chemical wonder, so a well-rooted understanding of batteries should be the goal of the conscientious RVer.

Batteries: If one takes into account all of the modern bells and whistles and gadgets and widgets available on an RV today, one would have to imagine the amount of battery power needed to run all those amenities.

Considering the components of even the simplest of circuits, it has been determined that the single-most confusing entity that lies within the very heart of virtually all RVs is the 12-volt battery. Not only do we have to contend with just one battery, it is not uncommon to see a minimum of three, and sometimes four or more of these current-storing wonders aboard an RV. And what is more, there are different types of batteries we must learn to understand.

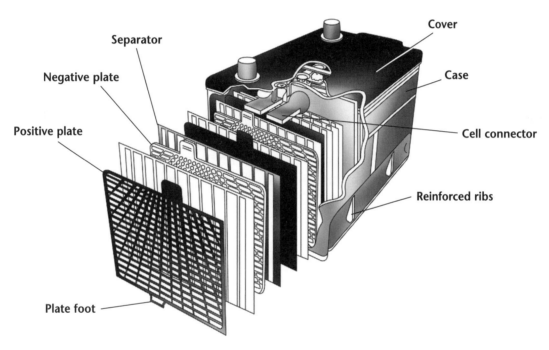

Typical 12-Volt Lead Acid Deep Cycle Storage Battery

The lead acid battery utilized today is defined as a power source or an electrical power accumulator—an energy bank, if you will. The current or amperage is the energy we are storing. The key is to be able to store more (have more on hand at any given time), than you, the system or any circumstance can utilize, waste or let slip away. In many situations, this is usually a break-even scenario at best.

Capacity and Efficiency Two overworked and seemingly nebulous terms talked about today are efficiency and capacity. A novice RVer might ask, "How much power does that thing have?" (a question of capacity) or "How come it's dead already, I just drove 50 miles getting here?" (a question of efficiency).

An important factor concerning the capacity of batteries is to remember that they will deliver the maximum amount of their available capacity if they are discharged within 20 hours or more. If the normal use or discharge on any given battery is spread out over a 20-hour period or more, that available current will be delivered at 100 percent. Notice that it was termed available capacity, as there will be a vast difference concerning exactly how much capacity any given battery might have at any given time.

To be a little more specific, the capacity of any battery is dependent upon:
- The area of the plates that is in direct contact with the electrolyte
- The actual specific gravity of the electrolyte
- The type and thickness of the internal separators and plates
- The general condition of the plates (how much sulfation has taken place)
- The limiting voltage (the limit beyond which there is very little useful amperage or energy available)

Battery capacity is directly proportional to the efficiency of a battery. How efficient a battery may be is determined primarily by the following three factors:
- The mechanical and physical condition (concerning the internal and external components)
- The state of charge of the battery
- How temperature affects it

Battery Ratings – Traditionally, batteries are rated in ampere hours (AH). This is the most common method for rating RV batteries. The AH rating is based on a 20-hour time span, which is an industry figure that is accepted for all batteries. An example would be that if a battery could deliver a constant five amps for the accepted time frame (20 hours), then it would be considered a 100-AH battery. Theoretically, as well as mathematically, a battery could deliver 10 amps for 10 hours and still be a 100-AH battery, but remember, the accepted rule is based on the 20-hour figure. If a battery manufacturer does not list the AH rating, it can be approximated if the Reserve Capacity (RC) is known. By multiplying the RC by a factor of 0.65, the result would be the nominal AH rating.

The RC rating is a figure representing the actual number of minutes during which a charged battery can supply 25 amps while maintaining a voltage of not less than 1.75 volts per cell. This is the amount of time (in minutes) the battery will last if the alternator belt flies off and the current use is 25 amps at the time, or your charging converter quits functioning while you are using 25 amps worth of current. RC can be approximated by dividing the AH by 0.65.

Another method of rating batteries is by Cold Cranking Amperage or CCA. CCA can be technically defined as the amount of current (amps) that a battery can supply for engine cranking under low temperature conditions. Usually the current rating is listed for the temperature of zero degrees Fahrenheit. If a start battery has a CCA rating of 380, for instance, that indicates the amount of amps that can be delivered for 30 seconds at zero degrees Fahrenheit, while maintaining a voltage of 1.2 volts per cell. This method of rating is pertinent for automotive start batteries.

A relatively new method of comparing batteries is by looking at life cycles. This is especially common with the newer sealed, lead acid batteries. This method of rating takes into account the depth of discharge (how low a battery is drained), in relationship to how many times that battery can be discharged to that degree. When considering an upgrade to the more costly, advanced batteries currently available, use life cycles as a factor of comparison.

Collectively these methods of rating batteries are set forth by the battery industry and are simply a way to distinguish the differences between all batteries. Using these methods any battery can be sized accordingly to the task it is being asked to perform.

Types of Batteries – There can be no discussion of batteries within the world of RVs without differentiating between what is commonly called a deep cycle battery and the standard automotive start battery. Today we can add the terms Absorbed Glass Mat (AGM), gel-filled, oil-filled and "spiral cell" design to the lingo. Limiting the immediate discussion to simply a standard automotive start battery and a deep cycle RV battery for now, here are the substantial differences that must be understood prior to continuing.

At the root level the differences are basic. Simply stated, the standard automotive start battery is constructed in such a manner that will allow for a very high rate of discharge or amp draw, with the stipulation that the duration of such current usage will be for a short time span—high amps delivered over a very short period of time. For instance, such an occurrence happens when the engine is started. The starter motor draws or uses a considerable amount of current, but only for the time it takes to start the engine. This point is proven when some unforeseen situation prohibits the vehicle from starting and a seemingly well start battery becomes very dead in a short period of time. The fact is it was designed to deliver that high amount of current for no more than just a few seconds.

The capacity of a standard auto start battery is lessened considerably each time it becomes discharged and recharged after the abuse endured in the above situation. The positive plates actually become weakened and sulfation occurs faster. Sulfation and other internal battery happenings will be discussed in detail a little later.

On the other side of the ledger, a deep cycle battery is constructed with thicker, denser plates alloyed with antimony or calcium to make them harder. Additionally, they have specially developed glass mat separators. This design allows for the consumption of current to be relatively low in amps, nominally speaking, but to be delivered over a longer period of time. Typically, this is the type usage found during dry camping while still utilizing the low voltage equipment. This also results in the battery capacity lasting almost four times longer than that of a similar size automotive type battery even though it will be discharged and recharged many times over. In many cases, when utilizing flooded batteries, two six-volt golf cart batteries wired in series is yet a better configuration since six-volt golf cart batteries are true deep cycle batteries.

In recent years, a new element of battery design has become commonplace within the realm of RVs—the SLA or sealed lead acid battery, sometimes referred to as VRSLA batteries (valve regulated, sealed lead acid). These include the flooded cell battery, the gelled acid battery and the AGM or absorbed glass mat battery. Each of which has models available for starting applications and for deep cycle, RV applications.

SLAs, typically have a higher specific gravity, but come with an increased initial cost. The initial cost, however, should not deter a RVer from upgrading to one of the SLA types. Higher efficiency, extremely low internal resistance and the ability to be charged quicker are just of few of the benefits of this newer technology. Plus they typically have longer life cycles.

One type of SLA battery available today is the gel-filled battery. In contrast to the flooded lead acid battery which uses a liquid electrolyte, the gel battery has its electrolyte suspended permanently in a thixotropic gel that contains a phosphoric acid additive. This results in the gel battery enjoying many benefits not currently found in flooded, lead acid batteries.

Developed by the German company, Sonnenschein, over three decades ago, the predominant feature of gel batteries is their fairly low self-discharge rate. They can realistically last between five to seven years, and since they contain no liquids, they can be installed in virtually any position, even sideways or upside down! Like all SLAs, they internally recombine the hydrogen and oxygen gases produced by charging and rapid discharging. They are, however, highly susceptible to heat and have a history of being sensitive to high current charging.

One nice thing about gel batteries though, is that they have equal voltages across each cell. The battery is less likely to short internally. However, because gel batteries use a mixture of silica gel and acid, voids or gaps in the gelled material inherently develop to allow the gases to pass to the vents. These voids can dry out and eventually reduce the capacity of each cell. Also, because of the high current sensitivity for RV deep cycling applications, it is often times recommended that an automatic voltage regulator and a sophisticated three- or four-step charger be employed as well.

Another newcomer to the forefront of RV deep cycle batteries is the AGM battery. AGM batteries are not gel batteries even though both types are considered SLAs. They were developed in 1985 primarily for military projects, such as the stealth bomber and one of the greatest off-road RVs of all time, the military HumVee. In such applications, safety, efficiency and reliability played a key role. Eventual adaptations to RVs was only logical. Additionally, AGM batteries are highly resistant to vibration and shock, another plus for RV applications.

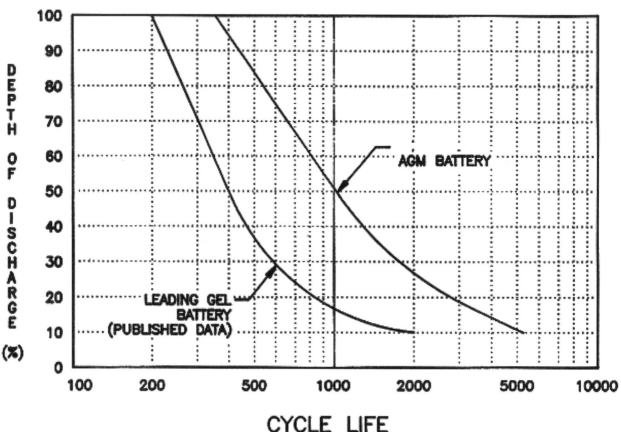

LIFE CYCLE
PERFORMANCE COMPARISON

GEL VS. AGM

Highly touted, the AGM battery has many intriguing features. Its recombinant gases are effective to about 99 percent. The hydrogen and oxygen are recombined inside the battery within each separator, unlike the gel type where the recombining occurs between the plates and the battery top. This keeps dangerous hydrogen gas levels to a minimum. Most AGM batteries vent hydrogen vapors at less than 2 percent, where 4.1 percent is needed to support flammability in air.

The inherently low internal resistance is a welcomed benefit to RVers who store their RVs much of the year. According to one maker, during storage, the self-discharge rate of an AGM battery is 3 to 10 times better than a gel battery and 5 to 50 times better than a typical flooded lead acid battery.

Because the electrolyte is not liquefied, but rather absorbed into a fiber floss glass matting with an exceptional wicking ability, faster migration of the acid in the electrolyte permits AGM batteries to deliver current and be recharged much faster and at higher charge rates. AGM batteries can be charged ten times faster than a same rated gel battery and five times as fast as a like-sized flooded lead acid battery.

As mentioned earlier, a viable method of comparing sealed lead acid batteries can be accomplished by looking at their respective life cycles. Here is where the AGM battery really excels. At the chart on the previous page, notice that an AGM battery reduced to 50 percent depth of discharge is rated for about 1,000 cycles compared to about 400 life cycles for a gel battery.

Because AGM battery technology permits more positive plate material to be saturated by the absorbed mats in each cell, there is an automatic increase in the battery's capacity in virtually every area. More life cycles, reduced internal resistances, higher amp hour rating, more reserve capacity and deeper depth of discharge cycles are some of the improvements over other types of SLAs.

Another interesting, albeit radical, design for an AGM RV battery has been developed by Optima Batteries. Their unconventional "spiral design" uses only two plates per cell: one positive and one negative. The plates are wound into a tight spiral, separated by an absorbed glass matting. The close proximity of the thin lead plates in each cell enhances the flow of current and lowers the internal resistance yet further. The spiral cells are pressure-inserted into individual cylinders in the battery case. After being inserted into their own cylinder, the cells are then injected with an electrolyte which absorbs into the mat, effectively sealing each cell. According to the manufacturer, this design prevents the active material on each plate from drying out.

Not as new, but considered by some to be equally unorthodox, is the ThermOil battery developed by Thermo-Tech. Primarily a flooded lead acid battery, the ThermOil battery contains a mixture of seven different oils that sit on top of the sulfuric acid in the electrolyte. This mixture is the reason for the high degree of success for the recombinant gases produced by the acid. Almost 98 percent of the gases are safely retained below the level of the protective oil layer on top.

Just recently the company produced an aftermarket oil additive that is applicable to most commercial lead acid battery applications. The oil additive is said to improve the performance of a flooded lead acid battery. Up to 40 percent longer life, no accumulation of corrosion, reduced maintenance, elimination of toxic fumes (by 98 percent), and a higher resistance to extreme cold or heat are but a few of the benefits extolled by the company.

For today's RVer, the options are many. One thought is important though, have on hand the best 12-volt battery configuration the coach can carry and the wallet can endure. Contact some of the current battery manufacturers and seek additional information from fellow RVers and other battery experts in order to make an informed decision as to which type deep cycle battery is best suited for your needs.

Battery Sizes – There are several sizes of deep cycle batteries available for RV use. Most are still rated in amp hours. Physical size will vary with manufacturer, yet when upgrading, overall dimensions may well be a factor when considering space limitations. The following chart lists the most common sizes of deep cycle batteries rated in amp hours. The golf cart battery listed is a six-volt battery, therefore, two batteries must be wired in series in order to produce the 12-volt DC needed for the system.

Battery	Amp Hour Rating
Group 24	85 amps
Group 27	110 amps
4 D	180 amps
8 D	250 amps
Golf cart	250 amps at 6 volts

Inside the Battery – Still the most popular as deduced by the sheer numbers of them, the flooded, wet cell battery is assertively being challenged by the AGM technology for the top spot. The accompanying diagram will illustrate, however, the physical layout of a typical flooded, lead acid battery. Keep in mind that it is not necessary to label this battery a start battery or a deep cycle battery, but only that the differences between the two be understood.

A typical battery has a case made usually of polypropylene plastic and more often than not is of a one piece construction that also includes a one piece cover. There are also indentations and ribs that impart strength to the case, however, care must always be taken never to drop a battery. Always use a proper battery strap or clamp for carrying. It is further recommended that eye protection and rubber gloves be worn whenever handling lead acid batteries.

The typical 12-volt storage battery has six individual compartments known as cells. These compartments house the positive and negative plates. The positive plates and the negative plates make up the bulk of what is inside the battery. They must be insulated and separated from each other while immersed in the electrolyte.

In between each plate is positioned the separator. This separator is usually constructed of a mat-type glass material, as it must be resistant to the acid in the electrolyte as well as heat, because charging and discharging a battery always produces a temperature rise. All of the plates in each of the cells are connected by the use of a welded strap or cell connector. They are interconnected in series. That is, the positive plates in one cell are strapped or connected to the negative plates in the next cell. With each cell producing approximately two volts each, being connected in series results in the six cells being able to produce the 12 volts required. When a battery is said to have a bad cell, this usually means that a cell has one or more of the plates that could be partially shorting out, or is sulfated. The characteristics of sulfation will be discussed a little later.

One positive plate and one negative plate ultimately end up on either end of the battery protruding through the top of the battery—the terminal posts. Some construction modifications have allowed for the emergence of side post batteries for certain situations based on design intent.

There is a portion of each plate called the plate foot which allows for each plate within each cell to be elevated above the very bottom of the battery case so that internal contamination can be kept to a minimum. This plate foot rests on the ribbed bottom of the case. Any contaminates in the sulfuric acid/water mixture that sink to the bottom along with the shedding of the active materials from each plate lie within the ribbed portion on the very bottom. The sediment can internally short circuit the cells if the level of the contaminates rises above the height of the ribbed bottom and the plate foot. This is why battery manufacturers recommend only purified or distilled water be added to the battery. They will contain less contaminates than normal tap water. Mineral water is not to be used at all.

There are certain chemicals found in all flooded lead acid batteries that play a big role in understanding what happens during the discharging and recharging of a typical wet cell battery. The electrolyte liquid in the battery is made up of sulfuric acid and water. The sulfuric acid portion of the electrolyte is a combination of hydrogen and sulfate. Water, as we all know, is made up of a combination of hydrogen and oxygen. Although these elements can be combined during the charging cycle, they can be separated, as well, during discharge.

All positive plates in the battery contain an active material called lead oxide. This is a combination of lead oxygen. Again, keep in mind that although they form a single compound, they can be separated. The negative plates contain sponge lead as its active material.

Battery Discharge – During periods of battery discharge, different reactions are happening to the positive plates, negative plates and the electrolyte, all at the same time.

The lead portion of the lead oxide on the positive plates starts to mix with the sulfate found in the sulfuric acid. This forms lead sulfate on the positive plates. At the same time, lead of the negative plates combines with the sulfate from the sulfuric acid to form lead sulfate on the negative plates. The oxygen portion of the active material on the positive plates combines with the hydrogen of the sulfuric acid to form water. This water drastically reduces the strength of the electrolyte. The battery is said to be in a sulfated condition. Both the negative plates and the positive plates now contain heavy concentrations of lead sulfate and which are immersed in a solution of mostly water. The battery is basically dead at this time.

Battery Charge Cycle – During recharging of the battery, the above chemical reactions are reversed. The individual chemicals split from their new compounds and again reform to their original state. The lead sulfate is split into elements of lead and sulfate. The water is split into hydrogen and oxygen. The sulfate combines again with the hydrogen to form sulfuric acid. The oxygen forms chemically with the lead to form the lead oxide on the positive plate, while the excess lead forms on the negative plate. The sulfuric acid that is formed replaces the water, which will increase the specific gravity and the battery becomes charged.

Testing the Battery – There are four test procedures that can be performed on any battery within an RV, be it a deep cycle or a standard start battery. Of the four tests, one employs common sense, two are tests you can use regularly and one test, though extremely helpful, requires an expensive piece of equipment. That test should be performed by a competent service facility if the other tests fail to make a determination.

Visual Test—This visual test is very basic in its intent. If the battery has cracks, bulges, loose posts or gaping holes, then it should be replaced. Some batteries that have experienced extremely low temperatures while in a sulfated condition may become freeze damaged. All such batteries should be recycled accordingly.

Specific Gravity Test—An important, yet often under-emphasized battery test is the hydrometer test, also called the specific gravity test. It can provide a viable method of determining if a battery is charged and to what extent. Why is this test so critical? When troubleshooting a battery-related problem, one of the first steps is to try to eliminate the battery as the culprit. In order to effectively do this, we must first determine that the battery in question is indeed fully charged.

The term "fully charged" is often misused. Taken literally, it means that any given battery is storing the maximum amount of current it can possibly hold while considering the chemical properties of the contents and the extent to which the battery is sulfated. That sounds like a mouthful, but this merely explains that a fully charged battery has as much stored current as it can possibly store at that time, regardless of age or condition.

One guaranteed way to determine if a typical flooded lead acid battery is fully charged is to carefully monitor the specific gravity while the battery is being charged. When the specific gravity does not continue to rise, but stays constant for a period of two to three hours, then that battery is considered to be fully charged. Any additional charging will be just wasting energy and exposing the battery to unnecessary heat and to possible gassing or boiling of the electrolyte, both of which will lessen its capacity to store current after any further discharge and recharge cycles.

Voltage readings, though important, should not be the prime factor for determining if a battery is fully charged. The exception to this rule is when testing all SLAs. Some batteries are equipped with an internal hydrometer of sorts that monitors the effectiveness of the electrolyte. With no means to apply the aforementioned hydrometer test, voltage measurements will, on these batteries, indicate the state of charge when using an accurate digital voltmeter.

Backtracking to specific gravity again, just what is it and why it is important? Specific gravity is a number that is used to compare the weight of the electrolyte to the same amount of pure water. It is a number that has no unit of measurement tagged with it. It is a stand-alone ratio to be used for comparison.

Pure water has been given a value of 1.000. A charged battery may have a specific gravity of 1.260. This means that the electrolyte in the battery is 1.260 times heavier than the same amount of pure water if the temperature is 80 degrees Fahrenheit. It is actually the sulfuric acid in the electrolyte that enables it to weigh more than water. It could be stated that the specific gravity of a battery will determine the sulfuric acid content of the electrolyte.

Earlier we learned that when a battery is in a sulfated condition (discharged battery), the hydrogen portion of the sulfuric acid combines with the oxygen portion of the lead oxide of the positive plates producing water. In other words, a sulfated battery has more water content than sulfuric acid, resulting in a lower specific gravity reading.

State of Charge	Cold Climates	Warm Climates
100% Charged	1.265	1.225
75% Charged	1.225	1.185
50% Charged	1.19	1.15
25% Charged	1.155	1.115
Discharged	1.120 & Below	1.080 & Below

When monitoring the specific gravity during or after charging, it is important to remember that the temperature of the electrolyte also has an impact on the readings taken. The standard for the above chart is always 80 degrees Fahrenheit. If the temperature of the electrolyte varies above or below that 80 degree mark, there must be some compensation for the difference. The industry accepted rule is that for every 10 degrees above 80 degrees, add .004 to your reading. Likewise, for every 10 degrees below 80 degrees, subtract .004 points. Typically, this is of no great importance in the more temperate regions of the country, however, the correction is indeed important in very cold or very hot temperature areas as the value can be substantial.

Key Points to Remember

> Do not take a hydrometer reading immediately after adding water to the cells.
> Replace any battery that has a 0.050 point difference between any two cells.
> Always use a temperature corrected hydrometer.

Open Circuit Voltage Test—This test is measured at the battery posts with the negative terminal disconnected. Since voltage is what is used to push the current through the circuitry and is not a viable indicator of the capacity of what is actually stored in the battery, this test should be used in conjunction with the specific gravity test. Remember, the amount of current (measured in amps) is what is actually being stored, and that voltage is only the force behind the moving of that current. Although voltage is relative, it should not be construed as the true condition of a battery, except in instances of gel or AGM batteries as mentioned earlier.

Open Circuit Voltage	Percent Charged
12.7 or more	100%
12.4 to 12.6	75 to 99%
12.2 to 12.3	50 to 74%
12.0 to 12.1	25 to 49%
11.7 to 11.9	0 to 24%
11.6 or less	Dead Battery

Notice the big jumps in the percentage charged compared to the small increments in voltage changes. This drastic difference is why the open circuit voltage test is not viable as a stand-alone method of battery testing. It also validates the rationale of using a digital meter to measure the voltage. It further resolves the misunderstanding that if a 12-volt battery measures 12 volts, it must be charged or healthy. Actually, if a battery measures 12.0 volts, it is possible that it is only 25 percent charged.

A variation of the open circuit test is to measure the voltage from cell to cell. The open circuit voltage from cell to cell should measure approximately 2.05 to 2.1 volts. If the voltage varies 0.5 volts or greater between any two cells the battery should be replaced.

Load Test—A most effective method of testing the battery on an RV is the load test. This test, however, requires specific and expensive equipment usually found only in well-equipped service facilities. Involving the use of a carbon pile tester, this test draws a massive load on the battery that truly determines the interior condition.

It is a high-current tester that can apply a variable amount of current that can be dialed in to the specific test rate needed depending on the size of the battery to be tested. There are many less expensive, coil-type testers on the market that claim to be battery load testers, however, in actuality they will not effectively load and test the battery as completely as the carbon pile tester. If you are unable to determine if a battery is good by performing the other tests, find a facility in your area that has the capability of performing the carbon pile load test.

Dual Battery Separation (Dual Battery Charging System) – RVs today must keep separate the two distinct battery systems explained earlier. It is important as an owner to know which type of dual battery charging system an RV has. It is equally important that it be electrically correct and sized properly in order for you to enjoy your RV to the fullest. The main types are:

- Isolator
- Solenoid
- "Smart" Isolator/Solenoid

Typical Isolator-Type Dual Battery Charging System

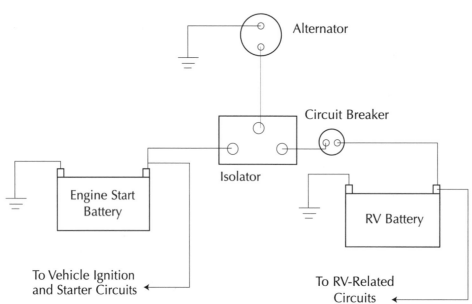

Isolater—The isolator type system employs a multi-battery isolator, a solid state, electronic device comprised of diodes that distribute the output current from the alternator to each of the battery systems independently of one another. It completely separates and isolates the two systems from each other at all times.

You have an isolator type system if you can locate an extruded, finned device usually with three or four individual terminals. Some are painted a bright blue or red, while others are simply aluminum in color. They are usually located either under the hood, in the general vicinity of the battery compartment, or on the firewall of the motorhome. It is vital that the rated capacity of this isolator exceed the rated output capacity of the automotive alternator.

Solenoid—The solenoid type dual battery charging system uses a heavy duty electro-mechanical switch that connects the two 12-volt systems together in parallel during the time the engine is running, or during the time that the solenoid is in the "closed" or energized position. It keeps the

Dual Battery Isolator

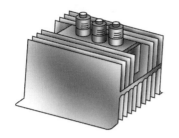

The rated capacity of the resistor should always exceed the output potential of the alternator.

two systems truly separated only when de-energized, when the ignition is off.

If you find a round, cylindrical device, silver in color, with two large battery cables attached to two large terminal posts, and either one or two other smaller terminals, you are equipped with the solenoid type. Usually not available in numerically rated capacities, it must be heavy duty and rated for continuous duty. Starter solenoids, though similar in design and mechanical movement, are not electrically capable of the high currents commonly found in charging systems. Starter solenoids are designed for momentary duty only and will quickly burn out if used as a dual battery charging solenoid.

"Smart" Isolator/Solenoid—The third type of battery separation is accomplished by the use of "smart" devices such as Hehr Power Systems Model 10-97 Smart Isolator and Sure Power Industries Models 1315 and 1314 Smart Solenoids. These devices incorporate a high capacity, electronically controlled solenoid switch within a well monitored charging system. The Sure Power Smart Solenoid comes in two varieties; one begins charging the auxiliary system only after the engine battery has reached a minimum 13.2 volts. The other couples the two systems together in parallel when either battery has reached this pivotal voltage. The Hehr Power System Smart Isolator has the added benefit of user-adjusted voltage parameters.

Hehr Isolator

TROUBLESHOOTING THE 12-VOLT DC SYSTEM: When problems arise within the 12-volt DC systems, it is usually at the most inopportune times. Since a large percentage of the amenities found aboard RVs is controlled and powered by the 12-volt DC systems, it stands to reason that there will indeed be a few instances of 12-volt irregularities during the course of your travels. However, there is no need to be intimidated by this. A great majority are common-sense related, and many more are regular maintenance items. Having the right tools and applying a few troubleshooting techniques will usually be all that is necessary to find and repair the discrepancy.

One of the most important tools is usually given when the RV is purchased—it is the owner's manual. Granted, not all RVs are delivered with a detailed owner's manual (that is why the book you are holding is so valuable), but most manufacturers will probably have, at the very least, a wiring diagram for the 12-volt DC circuits somewhere in their files. It is a necessary item for them just to construct the coach. It is also a valuable tool, a "road map" that allows you to follow the electrical path of the voltage and current. Contact your manufacturer and request a copy of the RV's wiring diagram. Be very specific about brand, model number, vehicle identification number (VIN) and other identifying data when you make your request. With wiring diagram in hand, here's how to effectively troubleshoot your 12-volt DC system.

When troubleshooting either of the 12-volt DC systems, keep in mind the following tips. Consider:

- The system in general
- The circuit in specifics
- The component in the circuit

Analyze first, to which system is the problem pertaining? The automotive system or the RV portion? Next, determine which circuit in that system is affected. And finally, pin point the component in that circuit that may be the cause. Use the process of elimination. Work from big to little, general to specific. Here is an example:

Your auxiliary battery keeps going dead. Right away you know it is in the RV portion since it is the auxiliary battery in question. By setting your VOM to the ten-amp scale, you can easily check for a drain on the battery by unplugging the shoreline if it is plugged in, and removing the negative cable from the battery. You now have an open DC circuit. Connect the red test lead from your VOM to the cable you just disconnected and the black test lead to the negative terminal on the battery. You now have a complete circuit with the meter inserted in series in the negative cable. Right away you will see a draw on the battery measured in amps or milli-amps (mA).

Next, insure all 12-volt appliances, lamps, etc., are turned off. If the drain persists, go to the fuse panel and remove and then immediately reinstall each fuse, one fuse at a time. If the drain disappears when a fuse is removed, the meter will go to zero. When that happens, that fuse is the one that is protecting the circuit that contains the problem. You notice that it is labeled "Right Side" indicating that circuit is situated on the right side of the RV. Now we have at least eliminated the left side and narrowed our search to just those 12-volt items on the right side of the coach. One by one, seek out every 12-volt item. Work from one end to the other in a systematic way. Lo and behold, you finally realize that the booster for the TV antenna was left in the "on" position creating a small draw that eventually drained the battery. Turning it off, the measured drain on the meter falls to within the acceptable standard of less than 100 mA, or one-tenth of one amp. There are a few parasitic drains on both battery systems that are normal, but if the current loss is greater than 100 mA, begin the troubleshooting.

This systematic approach can be applied to any of the 12-volt DC electrical systems. By not becoming overwhelmed at the thought of having to search for a cause, and by using your tools correctly, it can actually be fun and challenging to troubleshoot 12-volt electrical problems.

For a detailed view of RV batteries and a visual explanation to performing the various tests and troubleshooting steps discussed in this chapter, consider ordering the video tape, "Testing the Battery Systems—The Basics," by contacting the technical editor.

Battery Charging Options – In most every RV application, there has been a time or two when electrical woes have led to frustrating downtime during a RV excursion. Although not as common as in earlier years, poorly designed electrical systems, especially within the low voltage, 12-volt DC

Typical Travel Trailer 12-Volt DC Electrical Diagram

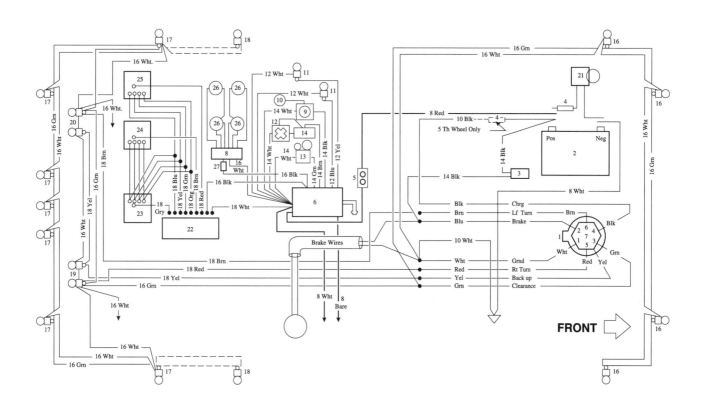

No.	Description	No.	Description
1	Car Connector	15	Refer Light
2	Battery	16	Amber Clearance Lt.
3	Break-A-Way Switch	17	Red Clearance Lt.
4	In-Line Fuse - 30 Amp	18	Amber Clerance Lt.
5	Circuit Breaker - 40 Amp		(Models over 30')
6	40 Amp Converter	19	Right Tail Light
7	Brakes	20	Left Tail Light
8	Stereo	21	Power Jack
9	Furnace	22	Monitor Panel
10	Thermostat	23	Grey Waste Tank
11	Interior Lighting	24	Solid Waste Tank
12	Power Roof Vent	25	Water Tank
13	Water Pump	26	Speakers
14	Range Hood	27	Filter

—— Wire Code ——
Number Designates Gauge

Blk - Black	Red - Red
Blu - Blue	Whit - White
Brn - Brown	Gry - Grey
Org - Orange	Yel - Yellow
Grn - Green	

systems, are still a concern for the active RVer today. Full-time RVers can relate to this fact. Even the casual weekend user has experienced his or her share of dead batteries or appliances that did not function correctly.

Ruined batteries, burned out alternators, flickering lights, converter charging problems and erratic appliance operation are just a few examples of the frustrations some have experienced in the past. In order to keep the 12-volt DC systems charged up, today's RVer has a few options available. Although not all of the alternatives can be used simultaneously, each has a viable statement to be made and a place within the realm of RV battery charging options.

These options are available to the RVer for battery charging:
- Power converter
- Power inverter
- On-board generator
- Portable battery charger
- Automotive alternator
- Photovoltaics (solar panels)

Power Converter—A power converter adds an additional voltage source for the 12-volt auxiliary system. Its job is to convert the incoming 120 volts AC to 12 volts DC, nominally speaking. Whenever possible, it is wise to plug the shoreline cord into a source of 120-volts AC. When the converter is activated, it saves the current in the auxiliary battery. Although not all converter/chargers are created equal, most today will keep some charge going into your batteries while providing the DC current to your appliances and lights, etc. The RV converter is not simply a 12-volt power supply. In actuality, some may produce a somewhat unclean form of DC electricity. The battery, wired in parallel with the converter, acts as a filter to smooth out the ragged output of the converter. In fact, some converters will not even function at the right voltage unless the battery is in the system.

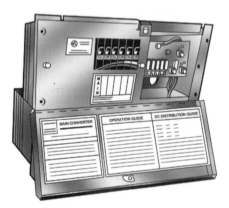

Linear Power Converter
This model houses the 120-volt AC circuit breakers on the left side of the unit, and the 12-volt DC fuses on the right.

Converters today are fully automatic. That is, all that is necessary is to simply plug in to shoreline power (or start the generator), and the converter becomes energized automatically. Converters may be configured differently and use different technologies, yet their function remains the same. It is important that you know the location of the converter in your rig. If they are not directly located within the converter, you also need to know where all the DC fuses are situated. Be sure to carry spares with you as you travel.

Some converters are built into a distribution panel that features 120-volt AC circuit breakers on one side, and the low voltage, 12-volt fuses on the other side. It can be thought of as sort of an electrical control center. A full section on power converters and converter/chargers follows later in this chapter.

The power converter, with a well-designed charging feature, is a very good method of keeping the RV portion of the 12-volt DC charged, especially if your unit is equipped with a sophisticated, three- or four-step converter/charger. The drawback to the AC to DC power converter is that 120 volts AC must be present before the converter can be put to work. That means you must either plug in the shoreline cord or run the generator if so equipped.

Power Inverter—There is a charging option on some sophisticated DC to AC inverters that will transpose the inverter into a charger once another form of 120-volt AC is employed. This means the inverter becomes a high-output charger when, for instance, the shoreline is plugged in. A more in-depth look at the inverter follows later in this chapter.

On-Board Generator—As a stand-alone 12-volt battery charger, the generator is a very poor choice. Although some, indeed, may have an inherent trickle charge of sorts, most can rarely charge above 3 amps at best. If a 100-amp batter is 50 percent discharged, replenishing it at an average 2.5 amps per hour would take at least 25 hours. With the generator consuming an average of a gallon or more of fuel per hour, this option does not seem to make much sense.

However, the value of having access to a power plant in the first place is to be able to produce 120-volt AC. To maximize generator efficiency, use the resultant 120-volt AC voltage to power the charging converter, the charging inverter or the next option, the portable battery charger.

Portable Battery Charger—The advantage of having a small portable charger is that it can be connected to either of the 12-volt battery systems. Sure, the sophisticated charging converter may be able to pump 50 amps or more into the system, however, most are only configured to the RV battery system. The automotive battery system sits dormant when parked overnight in a campground or when dry camping in the boondocks. Nothing could be finer than to be able to charge the automotive start battery while connected to shore power. Having a 10- or 15-amp portable charger on board will enable you to keep both systems charging whenever connected to shoreline, running the generator or using the quiet form of 120 volts AC, the inverter.

Automotive Alternator—By design, the one element common to both battery systems found on the typical RV is the automotive alternator and its associated charging system. The alternator in the motorhome or tow vehicle is located at the heart of one of the types of dual battery charging systems found in RVs today. But is not uncommon to discover that the stock automotive alternator supplied by the chassis maker is drastically undersized for the demanding loads attached to the modern RV.

This is probably another good place to mention that you, may occasionally spot references sporadically placed throughout this handbook extolling the benefits of the RV aftermarket products. Aftermarket products do offer the RVer various options that include upgrading and improving many

Hehr Alternator

aspects of RV life. One of those upgrade areas includes high performance alternators. Hehr Power Systems line of Powerline alternators offers models to an output of 250 amps. Certainly an upgrade to a high performance, a high-output alternator is a wise consideration. Many times these high performance units are a simple bolt-for-bolt replacement using common hand tools.

Photovoltaic—One of the newest forms of technology to come upon the RV scene within recent years, and certainly one that will become more prevalent as time goes on, is the science of photovoltaics or solar energy. Free electricity from the sun is becoming more integrated into the RV industry each year. In recent years, a valid interest has developed at the manufacturing level as well as at the aftermarket level.

Many manufacturers of RVs are implementing pre-wired packages similar to the air conditioner or generator pre-wired packages of recent years. Others simply are installing solar panels and complete systems at the factory.

Photovoltaics – Solar Power from the Sun The terms "solar power" and "RV" have indeed been mentioned sporadically in the same paragraph since the 1970s, however, not many in the industry gave it much credence. Except by a relatively small group of believers, its value has not been truly embraced by all. Recently though, technology has finally legitimized the viability of adding solar power configurations to the 12-volt DC system found in RVs. Today, more and more RVers, especially full-timers and those who like to travel off the beaten path and dry camp often, are learning how to capture and utilize that free energy from the sun.

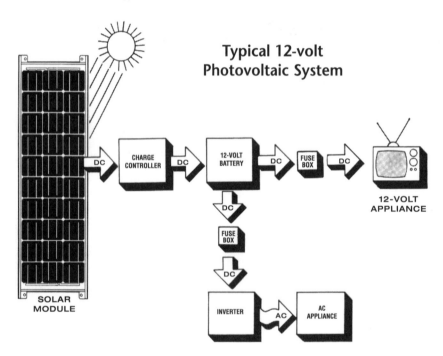

The science behind photovoltaics and the refinement of solar cell technology is quite interesting and warrants additional study should you feel so inclined. For our purposes here, though, the instruction will be kept relatively brief. The following diagram illustrates the process of converting light into electrical energy.

Major RV solar equipment manufacturers, such as Siemens Solar Inc., maximize their discipline by using single crystalline silicon technology as opposed to thin film, or amorphous processes. This allows better efficiency overall for RV applications as well as other applications.

Components of the Typical Solar System
(Drawing from Siemens Solar Industries)

Sunlight
Energy in the form of light.

Solar Module
Converts sunlight into DC electricity.

Charge Regulator
Prevents overcharging and excessive battery discharge

Battery
Electricity generated by the solar modules is stored in batteries.

Inverter
Used when AC electricity is needed. DC electricity into AC.

Load
Systems can be designed to meet virtually any electrical requirement, large or small.

The making of solar panels begins with the process of melting purified crystalline silicon and inducing the growth of silicon ingots in a cylindrical mold of sorts. (For an analogy, this is similar to early grade-school experiments of making simple rock candy to grasp a close analogy.) The ingots are then sliced longitudinally into a squared-off shape and sawed into thin wafers that are given their electrical characteristics through a diffusion process of phosphorus-doping the previously boron-doped wafers. These wafers are cut as thin as 200 microns. Silver paste is then applied to each side of the cell, and electrical circuit contacts are formed by the subsequent screen printing process. The cells are electrically connected together, laminated in an embedding medium, sandwiched in glass, secured and framed.

Major Components of an RV Solar System

Solar Modules and Panels—Mounted on the roof, these collect the sunlight and convert that light energy into DC electrical current. Connecting the panels in parallel alignment will increase the current capacity. Your specific need will dictate how many solar panels will be necessary in the array. In order to produce enough voltage to properly push the current through the system, you will need panels with at least 33 cells each.

Building a Solar Panel

Polycrystalline silicon is melted, doped with boron, and then drawn into a single crystalline ingot, which is usually round. The ingot is then squared and sawed into wafers. The surface of each wafer is grooved and etched into a microscopic pyramid shape to create more surface area and improve light absorption. The boron-doped wafers are then doped with phosphorous.

An anti-reflective oxide coating is applied to each wafer, and silver paste is screen-printed onto the front and back of each cell to form electrical circuit contacts. The wafers undergo a firing process to provide maximum electrical conductivity.

After testing, 30, 33, or 36 solar cells are electrically connected into strings. The strings are arranged in an embedding medium and placed between a special front glass and a multi-layer back sheet. The components are laminated at a high temperature to form a protected encapsulation, and the module is then fitted into a torsion-resistant anodized aluminum frame. Depending on the model, diodes and junction boxes may then be installed.

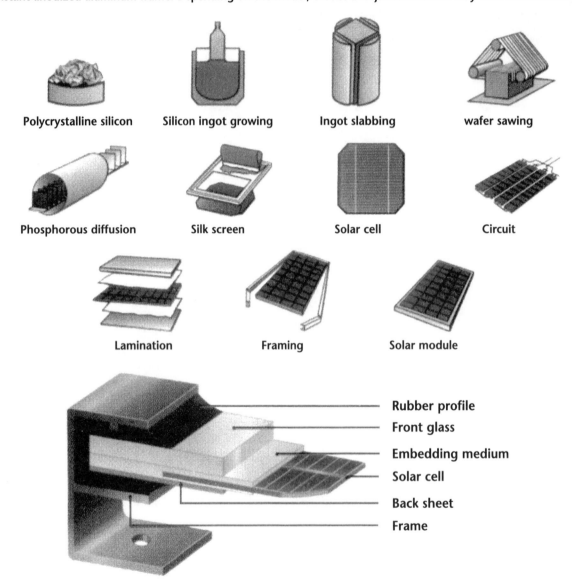

Polycrystalline silicon   Silicon ingot growing   Ingot slabbing   wafer sawing

Phosphorous diffusion   Silk screen   Solar cell   Circuit

Lamination   Framing   Solar module

Rubber profile
Front glass
Embedding medium
Solar cell
Back sheet
Frame

Storage Batteries—Although most solar panel installations are typically wired directly into the existing auxiliary 12-volt battery system, it is important to note that not all batteries are compatible with photovoltaics. Until recently, one of the most neglected aspects of RV photovoltaics was the lack of capacity to adequately store that free current extracted from the sun. It may be necessary to upgrade your auxiliary 12-volt DC system to be able to properly store the current your particular array will provide. As mentioned previously, the advances in battery technology have now made solar possibilities more viable than ever. Today, many battery makers produce very compatible batteries for solar applications.

Charge Controller—In some inexpensive pre-packaged systems, this item may be listed as an optional voltage regulator. In reality, it is a must in order to protect the battery bank from overcharging. If photovoltaics is to be a consideration to augment your dry camping potential, insist on a voltage regulator. Only the very smallest of solar "trickle" chargers should be installed without one. A good rule of thumb is if the peak charging current of the solar panel is greater than 1.5 percent of the total battery amp-hour capacity, insist on a quality charge controller.

Voltage Regulation – The voltage regulator or charge controller is the device that monitors the voltage and current being passed to the battery. It is an important component in the conscientiously planned photovoltaic system. Without it, current from the solar panels will flow uncontrolled into the battery system. It is obvious what the result would be. Overcharging is one of the most detrimental forms of 12-volt abuse administered to the battery.

Overcharging causes a heat rise in the battery that not only shortens its potential to store current, it also creates a fire hazard resulting from the manufacture of hydrogen gas at the battery. In most every case, voltage regulation is mandatory.

Four types of photovoltaic voltage regulators/charge controllers used in RV applications are:
- Shunt type
- Single Stage
- Dual stage
- Multi-stage, pulse width modulated

The shunt type represents the most basic of types and is considered simply an on/off switch at best. This least expensive type simply allows the current generated from the solar module to charge the battery at whatever voltage is available. The regulator monitors the voltage and switches the charging current from the battery through a low resistance transistor to ground when the battery voltage has reached a predetermined value.

Allowing the charging current to be dissipated and wasted through such a regulator creates an inordinate amount of heat that requires heavy heat sinks to dispel. There also are strict limitations on how much current this type of regulator can handle. Typically, not much more than two to three amps can be routed through a shunt type regulator.

The single stage controller, also an on/off device, eliminates the need for heavy, cumbersome heat sinks commonly found on the shunt type. With this type, the current is simply shut down when a predetermined value of percent charged is attained. This is by far an improvement over the shunt type of regulation, but not nearly recommendable.

The dual stage charge controller is more useful, as it eliminates the need to have any solar energy wasted as heat. This type monitors the battery voltage and applies direct charging capability from the solar array to the battery. However, when the full charge limit has been reached (approximately 95 percent), the regulator switches its circuitry to a trickle mode which slowly tops off the battery and minimizes an overcharging probability. Though energy is seldom wasted, efficiency and battery optimizing are still lacking.

The multi-stage, pulse width modulated charge controller is by far the most sophisticated and most highly recommended. Pulse width modulation (PWM), is a complex method of battery charging that will maintain the battery bank at its highest state of charge at all times. PWM charge controllers pulse on and off literally thousands of times per second. The "off" pulse gets a little longer as the battery voltage rises.

The technology for this type controller employs the use of highly efficient MOSFET transistors in the circuitry. Power MOSFET technology also prohibits night-time reverse flow battery discharges commonly associated with less sophisticated, inexpensive controllers. Other features of these state of the art controllers include reverse polarity protection, over-temperature protection and an LCD digital readout display for battery voltage, output charging current and an optional current tracking of what is being consumed by the RV systems.

Heliotrope General, a leader in these series type four-stage charge controllers for RVs incorporates full-time 30-amp charging capability including temperature compensation (extremely important) and automatic battery equalization. The equalization charge is basically a very slight overcharge at regular intervals, (30 minutes every 24 hours), to help prevent battery plate sulfation and to allow all cells in the battery to reach the proverbial "full charge." Advanced charge controllers such as the Heliotrope General line employ user-defined parameters for battery voltage, size and type. Their model RV-30S controller is designed for single battery bank applications, such as on travel trailers. The model RV-30D also has a circuit to connect a motorhome's starting battery to the solar array. Although each unit is rated for 30 amps continuous, individual components carry a hefty 50-amp rating—a wide safety margin by anybody's standard.

Typically, the four charging stages found in these top of the line controllers are: bulk charge, taper charge, float charge and the previously mentioned, equalization charge.

Heliotrope General Charge Controller

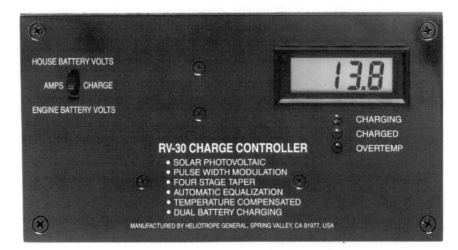

Another manufacturer of advanced charge controllers is RV Power Products. Their Solar Boost 2000 actually increases the available charge current from a solar array as much as 30 percent, though, at present, the maximum charge capability is limited to 20 amps. Continuously recalculating the module's peak power voltage as the charging characteristics change allows the Solar Boost to recapture wasted wattage, which increases the charging current proportionally.

Solar Modules—Much like a dual battery isolator that must be sized to the current output of the alternator, or the generator that must be sized to its electrical demands, the same thing must happen with photovoltaics on RVs. Avoid the common mistake of simply buying the panel that happens to be on sale or the one in stock that the salesperson is pushing. Forethought is required when designing a solar array for your RV.

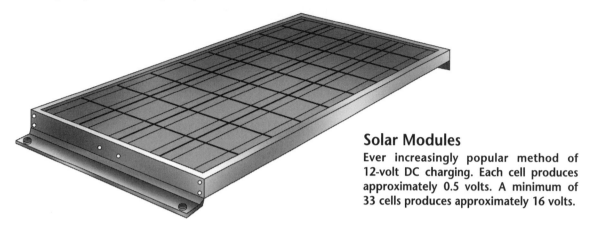

Solar Modules
Ever increasingly popular method of 12-volt DC charging. Each cell produces approximately 0.5 volts. A minimum of 33 cells produces approximately 16 volts.

Remember that each solar panel is an arrangement of individual solar cells. Each cell produces approximately 0.5 volt DC. Therefore, a 33-cell panel will have a voltage output of approximately 16 volts DC. A 36-cell module will have nearly 18 volts. Although solar panels today are routinely rated in watts, they are easily converted to amps by applying the Power Law which states that power (watts) equals the current (amps) times the voltage (volts).

Each cell in a panel is connected in series. In systems where more than one panel is needed (an array), the panels are connected in parallel. The variables concerning the output of solar panels are determined by the number of cells in the panel, the degree of light intensity absorbed by the panel, the cleanliness of the panel and the ambient temperature. Also, panel shading has a reducing effect on a modules ability to produce its rated output. The time of year you predominantly travel also plays an important role in properly sizing a system for your RV. Dry camping in winter, for example, will produce less overall current than the same scenario played out in the summer months while in warmer climates. More on sizing appears a little later in this section.

Also, just as charge controllers are not created equal, so it is with solar modules. Varying technologies exist with some manufacturers gaining the edge over others. Siemens Solar Inc., a longtime leader of RV solar configurations, has formulated RV kits complete with the module, wiring harness, charge controller, mounting hardware and easy to follow instructions. Sized for specific tasks (for instance the RV Power Kit 100 can furnish 22 to 26 amp-hours per day), the line offers something for just about every RVing scenario.

Another leader in solar module design is BP Solar. Their highly efficient laser-grooved, buried-grid technology leads the field in the peak power voltage ratings race. By cutting grooves in the individual cells with a laser and filling them with electro-plated material for the circuitry, efficiency can be increased to 17 percent compared to an average of 12 to 15 percent for the remainder. The deeply buried grid reduces the occurrences of shadows on the cells resulting in a higher peak power voltage. This is important because of the inherent voltage drop associated with heat. Panel output voltage decreases as the cell temperature increases. In some cases, temperatures nearing 150 degrees Farehnheit would cause a voltage loss of nearly two volts! Power and charging current would suffer as a result.

A typical module with 33 cells has a PPV rating of 16.0 volts at 77 degrees Farenheit. A larger module with 36 individual cells will produce 17.0 PPV at the same temperature. But the LGBG design of the BP Solar module will produce 18.5 PPV with those same 36 cells.

Sizing a Solar System—When "sizing" a system it is important to remember two things: First, the solar components must be "sized" to your particular RVing requirements and second, the battery bank must be adequately "sized" to accommodate the current produced by the solar array. To be avoided is the situation where the RVer adds an undersized, small solar panel without consideration of the battery size and ends up with too much storage capacity and wonders why the batteries never seem to fully charge, or worse yet, a woefully undersized battery is ruined by too much charging current produced by the solar array. In all cases, the sizing must be closely coordinated. Both the solar array and the battery capacity will be determined by the actual consumption of electricity as predicated by your habits, RVing lifestyle and the equipment found on your RV.

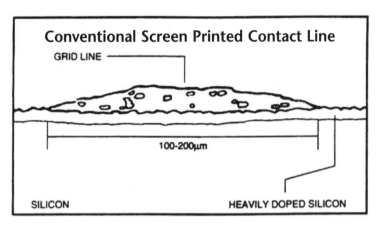

Conventional screen printed cells have large shading losses.

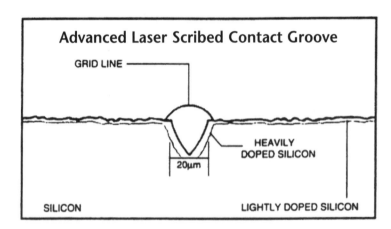

Laser-grooved buried-grid cells have low shading losses enhancing the short circuit current.

Another factor to remember is that some RV electrical current ratings are listed in amps, while others are rated in watts. To accurately determine the solar requirements, all consumption demands must be made using the same common denominator. There are many charts and graphs available listing many of the common current ratings for devices found in most RVs, so there is no need to replicate them here. All solar brochures will list the common requirements, but in truth, it will ultimately be necessary to go through your RV and calculate exactly what your individual requirements truly are.

Calculate all the DC loads and determine exactly hour many hours each day you will use those loads. Additionally, calculate your AC loads, again determining how many hours each day those loads will be activated. List only those AC loads that will be powered by an inverter. The loads covered by the AC on-board generator need not be factored here.

It is also prudent to add another 30 percent to the average daily DC requirements and to add an additional 40 percent to the AC requirements to accommodate system losses, normal parasitic drains and other deration factors such as inverter losses, local weather patterns and seasonal changes. Finally, add your total usage requirements together to come up with a figure that represents all your loads per day. Keep in mind that every RV will be different. There is no stock answer.

How Many Modules? Solar modules are available based on their output rating. Some may be rated in watt-hours, so again, either convert your daily requirements to watts or convert the module output to amp-hours so all formulas have the same common denominator. By dividing your daily requirement by the output values of the modules you are considering, the number of panels in the array can be determined.

How Many Batteries? Once the electrical loads and the number of panels have been determined, the next step is to figure out exactly how many batteries will be needed to store the necessary current for the system. Battery autonomy or "reserve factor" should also be included in the formula. The reserve factor is the number of days you will need current from your batteries without the benefit of having solar charging capability when dry camping. Usually a factor of two days is average, but take into consideration where you travel, time of year, localized weather conditions, etc. In addition to the reserve factor, an additional 30 percent of the capacity is recommended as a safety factor.

By taking the daily power or amperage requirement and multiplying it by the reserve factor, plus adding the 30 percent safety factor, the total battery bank capacity can be calculated. The next step is to consider the type of batteries for the solar array. Remember, not all batteries are adaptable to photovoltaics, especially automotive start batteries. Deep cycle, marine batteries will suffice, however, if you are seriously considering delving into harnessing the free energy from the sun, consider the gel type battery or the highly rated AGM battery discussed earlier.

Keep in mind that even though some automatic charge controllers allow the user to choose between either a flooded lead-acid battery or a sealed lead-acid battery, the newer AGM battery, although sealed, is not a gel battery. When using AGM batteries in a solar application, the controller must be set to the same setting as a standard flooded battery. To be sure, check with the manufacturer of the charge controller. Also, keep in mind that AGM batteries do not require as many equalization charges as standard flooded batteries.

Properly calculated, the DC and AC loads on a typical RV can now be adequately covered by applying the newest technology found in the sophisticated advancements of the modern photovoltaic community. Startup costs can be quickly dissipated, especially for the full-time RVer. The age of harnessing the free energy from the sun is upon us.

POWER CONVERTERS: The tireless role of the RV power converter is relatively simple: convert 120-volt AC shoreline or generator power into regulated 12-volt DC to energize all the 12-volt devices found in the RV. Though doing this every single time a unit is plugged in is quite a monumental task.

The power converter is located at the busy intersection of the 12-volt DC system and the 120-volt AC system. Although previous RV power converters were basically simple in design and intent, recent advances in technology has brought new terminology such as "MOSFET," "high frequency switching," and "smart chargers" to the RV enthusiast. Still, by and large, the RV converter is blamed for more electrical problems than which it is actually accountable. Surveys have approximated that as many as 90 to 95 percent of all converters returned as defective were in actuality, fault free. It appears that the real causes for some electrical problems are apparently being overlooked and the finger is often arbitrarily pointed at the converter as the culprit; even though many converter/chargers face unrealistic expectations by RV owners.

Where some converters do fall short, is in the area of effective battery charging. Only rarely and under close monitoring does a battery bank ever approach the 65 to 70 percent charged level. A true, fully charged system is even rarer. Optimizing the 12-volt battery systems has become one of the most important challenges RVers face. We fear overcharging the batteries yet are confused when the battery bank is rarely charged properly or fast enough to suit our needs.

In recent years, commonplace RV charging converters have been designed in a manner that achieves, at best, a compromised balance between the overcharge/undercharge extremes. The result is that many auxiliary battery banks never attain full capacity during the charging cycles, nor are they ever 100 percent fully protected from being overcharged. Each result minimizes the useful life of the battery bank and in some cases drastically shortens battery life. There are solutions, but let us first take a look at the basic converter components.

Although considered old technology by today's standards, the design of the most common RV converter is relatively simple. There are three main components to a basic converter:

- Transformer
- Rectifier section
- Method of switching

The *transformer* is the first step in the conversion process. It steps down the incoming 120 volts AC to 12 volts AC. It is lower voltage, but still alternating current.

The *rectifier section* then converts or *rectifies* the 12 volts AC to 12 volts DC. This is done via blocking diodes, silicon controlled rectifier diodes (SCRs), and other related electronic components. Because the voltage that is allowed to pass through the blocking diodes becomes pulsed or erratic in nature during this process, capacitors are sometimes needed to smooth out the deliver of the current.

Since the converter has a 12-volt DC output as does the battery, and they are directly connected, a *method of switching* must be employed to be able to differentiate between the two. Most converters use automatic relays to accomplish this. In years past and in some special applications today, a manual switch was activated to do this. Although today, most all are fully automatic.

Newer "smart converters" employ much the same paradigm, yet utilize different technology. Power supplies and electronic switching devices adapted from the computer industry have varied the voltage transformation process somewhat. In modern, refined converter/chargers, the incoming 120 volts AC is first rectified to 120 volts DC, and then reduced through a much smaller and lighter high frequency transformer to the lower voltage. The pulsed output of the high frequency transformer is further rectified to produce an extremely clean and smooth current flow into the batteries.

Types of Converters – Typically there are four types of converter/chargers found in RVs today:

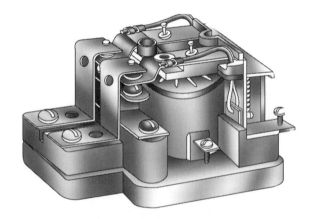

Automatic Switching Relay Found in Power Converters

An audible click can be heard when the relay is energized, thereby switching from battery power to converter power.

- Dual Output
- Single Output Ferroresonant
- Single Output Switching
- Single Output, Multi-stage

The dual output, or split system converter, employs two distinct DC output formats: one for the various DC circuits found in the coach, and a single, separate output for the battery connection. Largely for economic reasons, this type of converter has been extremely popular among RV manufacturers for many years. Many models incorporate the 120-volt AC breakers within the same cabinet structure as the converter, so all 120-volt AC breakers are located in the same location as the 12-volt DC fuses. Some of the common characteristics of dual output converters include:

- Less expensive to replace individual components
- Utilize common parts that are readily obtainable
- Because of heat, are more prone to component failure
- A limited charging capability: five to eight amps maximum
- For large battery banks, charge times may be quite long

The single output ferroresonant design allows for all of its rated output current to be utilized as battery charging current when needed and if the conditions are right. If the branch circuits (lights, water pumps, fans, etc.), are not being used on a 50-amp ferroresonant converter, for instance, then all 50 amps will be available for battery charging purposes. Another advantage is that the ferroresonant type will compensate for variances in the AC line voltages.

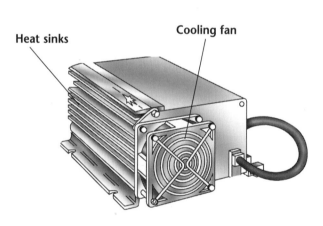

Heat sinks

Cooling fan

Ferroresonant Power Converter

Models like this one can deliver 50 amps for battery charging if conditions are right.

The disadvantages include poor output voltage regulation. Substantial changes in the output voltage can occur with changes in the output current. In other words, as the RV appliances are used, the output voltage drops significantly resulting in an inappropriate voltage for effective battery charging. And like the dual output converter, charging times can become exasperatingly long.

Because of the heat factor, many ferroresonant converters are equipped with a cooling fan to dissipate the heat generated by the conversion voltage. However, all converters are susceptible to heat and, therefore, camping gear and supplies should not be stored in, on or around them. A separate 12-volt DC fuse box or distribution panel is needed in conjunction with the ferroresonant converter.

Characteristics of the ferroresonant converter include:

- Able to charge the RV battery at full-rated output capacity
- Contains no SCRs, diodes or PC boards
- Are more costly for component replacement
- Higher potential for battery overcharge

Additionally, ferroresonant converters can utilize the battery as an augmentation if any load so requires. For instance, if when powering a 12-volt electric tongue jack on a travel trailer, the load becomes more than the rated capacity of the converter, the current stored in the battery can be utilized and added to the current supplied by the converter. A dual output converter in the same situation would overheat and either trip a breaker or burn wires or other components.

The single output, switching type converter/charger provides a single circuit connected in parallel with the coach battery and the branch circuits. Again, the rated output current can be split between the charging duties and for powering the coach.

Similar to a stand-alone 12-volt power supply, these types of converters/chargers are able to power the coach even without a battery in place. Another advantage of this type is that the output voltage regulation is quite good and some models offer a user-defined fixed output level. This results in a shorter charging time when compared to the dual output type or the ferroresonant type, but mandates strict monitoring of the battery charging procedure in order to avoid overcharging the battery. A little of the "automatic" will be compromised with this type.

The single output, multi-stage converter/charger is by far the most advantageous. Most all sophisticated, multi-stage charging converters include, or offer as an option, a highly developed monitor panel for measuring battery voltage and current flow to and from the battery bank. This is a must for the active RVer or full-timer. They employ state of the art charging criteria developed specifically for deep cycle batteries while optimizing the charging parameters by taking into account the battery temperature, the total amp-hour capacity of the battery bank and the type of electrolyte used.

Multi-stage charging converters such as RV Power Products Model #6210 offer three distinct charging cycles, while Statpower Technologies Corporation produces a line of converter/chargers with the added benefit of a fourth stage, an equalization charge. Much like the photovoltaic charge controller discussed earlier, this new breed of charging converter employs the use of microprocessor controlled power MOSFET technology along with PWM for optimum efficiency and performance.

Four Charging Stages – The typical multi-stage charge sequence involves a bulk charge which basically pours all of the converter's available output into the depleted battery bank until the voltage approaches the gassing point (around 14.2 to 14.4 volts). This *bulk* stage will bring the battery up to about 75 to 80 percent capacity in the shortest amount of time. Though the charging current is slowly reduced as the voltage increases, this stage is considered a constant current stage.

Next is the *absorption* stage, sometimes referred to as the acceptance charge. In this stage, the battery is charged at a constant voltage as the current flow to the battery bank slowly decreases to about one amp/100 AH capacity of the total bank. Statpower's Truecharge 40+ will charge at 14.4 volts until the current decreases to about five amps. At this point the battery bank is considered fully charged.

Statpower Smart Charger

After the current has been reduced during the absorption stage, it enters a maintenance type of charge sequence called the *float* stage. This float charge is commonly referred to as a "trickle charge." A constant voltage of about 13.3 to 13.5 volts is applied at a low current of about one to three amps (some chargers deliver a float current of 1/500 to 1/1,000 of the total battery capacity). This is the point at which many typical converter/chargers begin to boil the electrolyte when left connected to shore power for extended periods since their voltage may remain higher than the gassing voltage limit. Because of their design, the True*charge* 40+ and the Model #6210 eliminate this fear, and most all RVs can be left plugged in indefinitely when equipped with this newer type of charger. The exception is when the battery bank consists of true deep cycle batteries such as two Trojan T-105, six-volt golf cart batteries. Most true deep cycle batteries are best utilized when charged and discharged deeply between charge cycles. They are not designed for prolonged periods of float charge. The Truecharge 40+ considers this and allows the RVer to choose a charging cycle sequence that only includes two steps: the bulk charge and absorption charge. A third, constant output voltage mode can also be selected if necessary.

A fourth stage, the *equalization* stage, is also available on the Statpower True*charge* 20+ and 40+ models. This equalization mode is simply a controlled overcharge designed to minimize or prevent sulfation from occurring in flooded batteries. During normal charge cycles, especially in the hotter climates, higher temperatures and impurities in the electrolyte may prevent some cells from attaining a full charge while allowing a higher degree of sulfation on the plates. Typically, this is not a problem for most gel batteries as mentioned earlier in the battery section. Since not all batteries require a regular equalization charge (most sealed, lead acid batteries in fact, do not), this feature is user-induced rather than automatic. Close monitoring of the specific gravity is recommended during any equalization charging mode.

Other advantages of the CSA- and UL-approved True*charge* 20+ and 40+ models include the ability to choose between gel, flooded or AGM battery types, a 21-day automatic battery top-up cycle which prevents against battery self discharge, and three separate outputs for charging the engine start battery of a motorhome, the auxiliary battery bank and perhaps a separate generator starting battery if so equipped. Over-temperature protection, overload protection and reverse polarity protection are additional benefits.

In most every case, an upgrade to one of these highly efficient, "smart" power converter/chargers is a wise investment and may very well eliminate or at least minimize the 12-volt battery charging woes so prevalent today.

Troubleshooting the Converter – When troubleshooting the power converter, here are five basic preliminary steps:

(1) **Verify the proper incoming AC voltage**—Be sure the incoming voltage falls between 103 volts AC and 130 volts AC. High and low voltage can have a damaging effect, not only on the converter, but other AC components as well.

(2) **Verify the correct polarity**—Reversed polarity or an open hot or neutral wire somewhere in the 120-volt supply system can indeed be harmful to the converter. Always check the polarity and test the GFCI each time you enter a new campground. If it is not correct, move to a new site or simply do not plug in the shoreline. Likewise, check the polarity of the DC conductors from the battery. Some components may be damaged if the battery is mis-wired.

(3) **Eliminate the battery as the culprit**—Because of the close association, many times the converter is blamed for battery or other DC system-caused problems.

(4) **Make sure all electrical connections are clean, dry and tight**—Many electrical problems are associated with loose wires and connections. It is a common occurrence because of the jostling most RVs endure during their lifetimes.

(5) **Analyze the symptoms closely and carefully**—Take notes as you go through the process of checking. Follow a systematic approach by first considering the DC system in general. Next, look at the problem area in specifics. Third, consider the components in the sequence. And finally, accurately measure and record the following voltages:

- The incoming AC line voltage
- The battery voltage in an open circuit test
- The output voltage with the converter without the battery in the system
- The output voltage with the battery connected

Should you need to call a service facility or seek advice, having the above voltage information handy will provide a starting point to begin troubleshooting.

Internal Repairs – Due to the level of sophistication in today's power converters, if a problem proves to be interior to the converter, it is recommended that the converter be shipped off for repair. Some well-trained RV service facilities may offer internal converter repairs as a service, but most are probably not fully equipped to handle all possible scenarios. Many components are not field repairable, yet they can be repaired or replaced relatively inexpensively. (Some do have module boards that are easily replaced if necessary.)

All converter manufacturers have a service and repair facility in-house or one that they can recommend to perform internal converter repairs. Contact your converter manufacturer for the details of their service policy. If your converter has out-lived its manufacturer (it does happen), contact Master Tech at 800-848-0558. This company is positioned to troubleshoot and repair virtually any RV converter.

Common Complaints – Although not always at fault, many times converters are blamed for a particular ill. The below listed complaints are general complaints followed by possible causes. The possible causes are listed in the following priority order:

- Easy to check and most likely the problem
- Easy to check but least likely the problem
- Difficult to check but most likely the problem
- Difficult to check and least likely the problem

1. Converter overcharges the battery:
   - Faulty battery
   - Loose or corroded connections
   - Faulty PC board
   - Excessive AC volts
   - Shorted SCR
   - Faulty transformer or rectifier section

2. Converter does not charge the battery (not likely with ferroresonant):
   - Blown fuse
   - Faulty connections
   - No AC input
   - Faulty PC board
   - Faulty LED (if equipped)
   - Faulty SCR
   - Faulty transformer

- Open thermal breaker
- Open limiting resistor
- Open diode

3. Converter automatic relay chatters:

- Low AC volts
- Reversed AC polarity
- Very low frequency (should be 60 Hertz)
- Faulty relay
- Loose internal connections

4. 12-Volt bulbs blow when on converter power, but are fine on battery:

- High AC volts
- Reversed AC polarity
- Improper capacitor used
- Faulty transformer

5. Radio/Television interference with converter on:

- Radio not wired properly
- Battery charge line too close to speaker wires
- Too small radio ground wire
- Speaker wires in same harness as 120-volt AC Romex
- Faulty filter or no filter in system

6. Converter drains battery:

- Branch circuit drain
- Weak or faulty battery
- Faulty PC board
- Bleeding diode
- Faulty SCR
- Faulty transformer
- All batteries have a normal internal drain and all converters have a normal resistance that does cause some current loss. Anything under 20 mA is considered normal.

7. No converter DC output:

- No incoming AC voltage
- Tripped breaker
- Blown fuse
- Faulty connections
- Faulty relay
- Faulty diode or transformer

Additional Thoughts – The National Electrical Code for RVs mandates that power converters be UL-listed for use in an RV. It is not permissible to permanently install a battery charger instead of a converter, for instance. Thermal overload (high temperature cut-off) protection is required on all power converters, not so for simple battery chargers.

The NEC states that power converter cases must be bonded to the chassis of the RV by means of a stranded or solid eight-gauge copper wire. If your converter is a combination converter and 120-volt AC panelboard, however, then this is not a requirement.

Many times when troubleshooting 12-volt DC systems or converters, the return path, or ground wire is often overlooked as a possible cause. In direct current applications, the negative side of the circuit is just as important as the positive side. An open can exist on either side of the resistive unit. Many 12-volt misfortunes are caused by an undersized or inadequate ground wire. As a general rule, make sure the ground wire in any 12-volt circuit is at least the same diameter, preferably one size larger, than the positive wire. This pertains to converters as well. It's always wise to have a large ground wire from the converter firmly attached to the frame of the RV or even directly to the auxiliary battery bank. The ground wire should not be confused with the bonding conductor. The ground wire is a return path for the electron flow, the bonding wire protects and bonds the metal case of the converter to the chassis.

All in all, the power converter of today is an electrical workhorse. To keep it in shape takes very minimal effort. There is not an abundance of preventive maintenance to perform. Just remember that with any electrical component or connection, it must be clean, dry and tight. Periodically check the terminals and connections. Some may work loose over a period of time. Also, make certain the immediate area around the converter is kept clean. Converters do produce heat, so air flow can be crucial with some high performance, high output units. And finally, be aware that having a healthy battery will contribute to a healthy power converter. They must work together.

120-Volt Alternating Current (AC) System

The system most familiar to you is probably the 120-volt AC system. It is very similar to what you are accustomed to in a typical house. In the RV, the 120-volt AC can be produced three ways:
- Shoreline hook-up
- On-board generator
- Inverter

The major components typically found in the alternating current electrical system include the shoreline cord, a distribution panel (breaker box), circuit breakers and resistive units. If the RV is equipped with an on-board power plant or generator, then a means of switching from shoreline to generator would also be included in the list of components. That means of switching can range simply from manually plugging the shoreline cord into a generator output receptacle, to the more common application of utilizing a sophisticated, voltage sensitive, automatic relay.

Modern RVs are usually comprised of automatic switching devices to keep these high voltage components in order. All are constructed with safeguards against over-loading and accidental activation of two or more sources of electricity at the same time. In years past, most switching was done manually and required the user to remember the specific when and how.

How and when to use these various sources is usually dictated by the camping environment you find yourself in at any given time. The priority order should be if shoreline power is available, such as in the campground or at a permanent campsite, then by all means, plug in. If you are in an area that requires quiet and there is no shoreline connection, then power up the inverter for whatever 120-volt needs you may have. If noise is not a problem, and you have a full fuel tank, fire up the generator.

Regardless of which source you utilize, conservation of energy should always be your foremost thought. Even when on shoreline. Get into the habit of good, energy efficient RVing.

The resistive units mentioned above are the common AC loads found in the coach. They may include, but certainly are not limited to:

• Roof air conditioners	• Ice maker
• RV refrigerator	• Blender
• Power converter	• Televisions
• Microwave oven	• VCRs
• Computers	• Hair dryer

...or any other device you wish to simply plug into any receptacle.

Assorted duplex receptacles are located throughout the RV making it very convenient to plug in virtually any electrical accouterment such as a stereo, drill motors, coffee makers, vacuum cleaners, electric fry pan, etc. The list, seemingly, is endless.

Another device found in the 120-volt AC system is the Ground Fault Circuit Interrupter (GFCI). This device is manifested as either a receptacle (usually located in the bathroom), or as a circuit breaker (located at the breaker box). It is mandated by the electrical code for RVs and protects all receptacles located near sinks and those that are located on the exterior of the RV.

It is a common misconception that the GFCI is a circuit breaker or an over-current protector. Such is not the case. While breakers and some fuses do obviously protect against over-current, they cannot sense or protect against the potentially lethal low level ground faults. Additionally, GFCIs will not sense a direct short to ground. The exception, of course, would be the breaker type GFCI, which does both.

The benefit of the GFCI is evident in the fact that it will indeed sense the low level current leakage that might occur in an alternating current system, lethal current that the circuit breaker would naturally overlook. The GFCI used in RVs will sense and monitor current leakage up to 5 mA (.005 of one amp), and then it will interrupt the circuit. Here is how it works:

Current from either the shoreline cord, generator or inverter flows through one wire (the hot wire), to a device and back to the power source through the neutral wire. All RVs have a separated and isolated ground wire that is ultimately bonded to the chassis. Unlike conventional household wiring, a common connection between the neutral wire and the ground wire should not occur within the RV system.

In most cases this current to the device and from the device is always equal. The current alternates between the hot and neutral wires in a given circuit. If the current to and from the device is equal. It is said to be balanced. The GFCI constantly monitors this balance between the hot and neutral wire. If the GFCI senses an imbalance between the two currents, and that current differential approaches four to six mA, the GFCI will trip, interrupting the current at that point. Depending on the type of GFCI used and how the GFCI is wired into the circuit, the circuit will be opened and current flow will be stopped to all protected receptacles downstream as well as the GFCI.

How the GFCI senses and opens the circuit determines the speed at which it will open the circuit. One method invokes the use of a mechanical relay, such is commonly found in a circuit breaker. Another more common method of sensing is by the use of an electromagnetic, electronic

Receptacle-Type GFCI

Push the test button while connected to 120-volt AC power. The reset button should pop out slightly, indicating proper operation. Push the reset button after it pops out to reset.

Circuit Breaker-Type GFCI

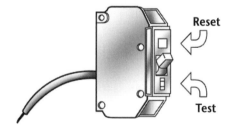

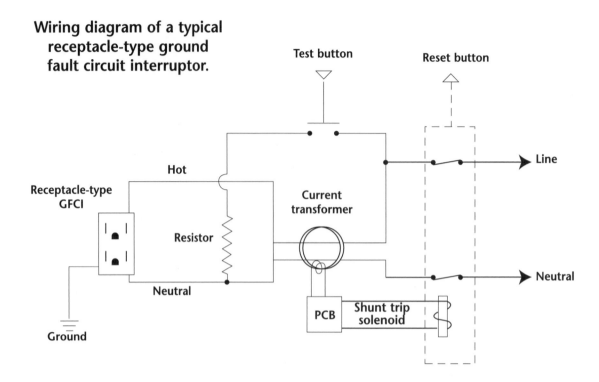

Wiring diagram of a typical receptacle-type ground fault circuit interruptor.

shunt trip solenoid (see the accompanying wiring diagram). In most cases, both methods will react fast enough that if a shock current is felt at all, the time duration will not be enough to injure.

All GFCIs usually contain a bypass or test function that is user invoked. This test function allows testing of the internal electronic components of the GFCI. It also verifies the integrity of all receptacles on that same branch circuit. The GFCI should be tested regularly.

DC TO AC POWER INVERTERS: Like recent advances in photovoltaics and in AC to DC power converter technology, so has the DC to AC power inverter made great technical strides. The power inverter can now be considered a truly viable alternative for producing 120 volts alternating current. As many RVers are aware, campgrounds often restrict the use of efficient yet noisy power generators after certain hours, yet power is still needed for the online RVer equipped with the latest in computer equipment. And whose RV family does not require AC power periodically for clothes ironing, watching television or drying heads of hair? Because of the improved ability to store lots of DC current with the new advances in battery design, inverters are quickly becoming one of the most reliable forms of maintaining true "self-containment."

The power inverter is the electrical opposite of the power converter. That is, DC power from the auxiliary battery system is inverted to 120 volts AC power output. Electronically processed, this inversion is totally silent. There are no moving parts aside from an occasional cooling fan application.

The sophisticated models even have battery charging capabilities so whenever you plug into shore power at a campground, for instance, the inverter senses another form of 120-volt AC, switches modes, and becomes a high output, three step battery charger. Other safeguards typically built into the modern inverter include:

- Overcharge protection
- Automatic switching
- Ease of installation

- Simple two-wire hook-up
- Overload protection
- Simmer or idle circuit
- Low battery protection

Best installed near the batteries to minimize voltage drop, many inverters can be mounted horizontally or vertically making aftermarket installations a relatively easy task. If you are considering adding an inverter to your present RV, realize that certain upgrades are prerequisite to adding the inverter. It is recommended that the following items be employed with inverter systems.

- High quality, properly sized 12-volt battery bank
- High output automotive alternator (motorhomes)
- Upgraded battery cables and wiring harnesses
- Isolator battery separation
- Accurate battery monitor (voltmeter and ammeter)
- Solar panels to aid in charging
- Advanced AC to DC converter

Inverters designed for RV applications are available in two basic output waveform technologies: quasi-sine wave (sometimes referred to as modified sine wave), produced by low frequency transformers, and pure sine wave, a produced by microprocessor-controlled, high frequency circuits and components.

Although low frequency inverters are less expensive and considered efficient devices, they are, however, prone to voltage fluctuations which can cause disturbances in some DC circuits in the RV. Pure sine wave inverters, on the other hand, are extremely sophisticated and can produce AC power at or above the quality levels of shoreline power grids.

Comparisons can be effectuated by looking at the total harmonic distortion (THD), produced by each type. The harmonic difference between the low frequency RV inverter wave form and true sinusoidal wave shape is a percentage figure that affects the operation of induction type loads such as motors, compressors, or other capacitor-started devices. The higher the percentage, the higher the heat factor. The higher the heat factor, the more damaging to the device. THD (purity of waveform), produced by low frequency inverters can exceed 40 percent with some units purported to approach 47 percent.

The PROsine inverter technology developed by Statpower Technologies Corporation produces a true sine wave with less than 3 percent THD. Additionally, voltage stability is far superior with high frequency inverters. Voltage stability is crucial in many RV applications such as microwave ovens, battery chargers and some televisions. Unpredictable cooking times, buzzing in stereo equipment and video distortion on televisions and computer monitors can be virtually eliminated by installing a high frequency inverter. If you are one of the many RVers with computer equipment on-board, a high frequency inverter is a must for laser printers.

Battery charging in the PROsine line of inverters employ the much touted three-step charging methods discussed in the power converter section earlier in this chapter with the advantage of a higher power factor. A higher power factor rating means that the battery charge circuit draws approximately 30 percent less AC current to deliver the same DC charging current. This is another area to consider when making comparisons between brands or types of inverters.

Three-step charging by the PROsine line of inverter/chargers will vary the charge rate and voltage depending on the type of battery electrolyte, the size of the batteries, the temperature of the electrolyte. If the incoming AC line voltage varies greatly, that too will effect the charging characteristics.

The first stage, the *bulk* charge delivers the maximum allowable charge, taking into consideration the variables noted above. It continues this bulk charge until the battery bank voltage reaches about 14.4 volts. This step will charge the batteries to about the 75 to 80 percent charged level.

The next step is the *absorption* stage where the voltage is held constant just below the gassing voltage while the current is proportioned down.

The final step is the *float* stage where the charging voltage is reduced from gassing levels to about 13.5 volts which continually tops off the charge.

A user-induced equalization charge can also be selected, if necessary, depending on the age and type of batteries in the system.

For RVers who stay connected in one place for an extended time, the PROsine inverter/charger can be left on for long periods without the fear of overcharging the batteries. The sophisticated dynamics of the three-step chargers eliminates that concern.

SIZING YOUR NEEDS: Much like sizing a generator, converter or solar array, it is necessary to evaluate which devices would be operated and powered by the inverter prior to the installation. Each manufacturer produces various models of differing wattage outputs to fit just about every need. It is simply a matter of applying basic mathematics to determine what size inverter you will require.

Here's a chart to help you calculate. Keep in mind, these figures are approximate and actual running wattage may vary between brands or models. Make sure that the inverter rating or size you choose exceeds the total wattage requirement based on your needs. There should be a 30 percent safety factor added to your exact requirements.

If your appliance or device is rated in amps, refer to the Power Law discussion earlier in this chapter, or simply multiply the amperage times the voltage, the result is power measured in watts.

Published efficiency graphs and figures can be taken as a method of comparison though real world applications supplied by you will determine an inverter's true efficiency. Try not to confuse efficiency with "effectiveness." There is a difference. Here is an illustration: A small 12,000 BTU heater installed in an auditorium-sized room may run with a high level of "efficiency." It may use very little current and consume an extremely small portion of liquid propane. It may be very quiet and non-obtrusive—very, very efficient. But, will it be "effective" in heating that room? It is doubtful. For RV inverters, an efficiency rating above 85 percent is considered exceptional.

Device	Watts
12" B/W TV	30
13" Color TV	80
19" Color TV	120
VCR or Stereo	50
Blender	300
Coffee maker	1000
Medium Microwave	900
Curling iron	60
Hair dryer	1500
Laptop computer	120
14" VGA monitor	130
3/8" drill motor	450
Jig saw	450

When the output AC is not being called for, most inverters will go into a simmer mode until the demand for current is evident again. During this "downtime" certain monitoring functions must continue. This results in a continuous draining of current from the battery bank. Obviously, the inverter that draws a low amount is preferential.

All 120-volt AC devices in North America are designed to operate at a frequency of 60 Hertz. The variable should be as low as possible. Plus or minus 0.1 Hz is usually considered good.

User maintenance on today's sophisticated inverter/chargers is minimal if at all. As with all electrical devices, though, be sure connections are clean, dry and tight. If troubleshooting procedures point the finger at the inverter as the culprit in a given situation, it will be necessary to return the inverter to the manufacturer since no repairs should be performed by the RVer.

RV GENERATORS: Once considered a luxury, auxiliary power plants, commonly called generators, are now more the norm, especially on motorhomes. For total independence, an on-board source of generating 120-volt AC is a mandate. With this accessory, you can feel confident of being able to use any of your 120-volt AC appliances at any time, free from the umbilical of a campground shoreline connection or the limits of a power inverter.

Today's RV generator sets have come a long way from the larger, noisier and not-so-reliable precursors of past years. Smaller, lighter, and using state-of-the-art electronics, today's units are extremely reliable. With proper maintenance, the power plant should provide hundreds of hours of alternating current electricity, which you will soon appreciate when you step out of a 100-degree plus desert and into the cool confines of your air conditioned bungalow, while your mate drops cubes of freshly made ice into a glass of your favorite beverage, throws a snack into the microwave and turns on your favorite TV show or plops in that movie classic video tape and... well, you get the picture.

With the sophistication of technical achievement, comes the commitment of following correct and proper preventive maintenance. Though today's RV generator requires less maintenance than in years past, it nonetheless requires some maintenance. It is far too easy to fall prey to the paradigm of "out of sight—out of mind" concerning the RV generator. It does take a concerted effort. Thankfully, many maintenance tasks can be performed by the RV owner. And some tasks are better left to the professional RV technician. Setting up the generator, for instance, requires a special load bank that usually won't be found in the RVers tool kit (in fact, not all RV service facilities have one). Let us take a look at the RV generator.

Operation – Any device that generates electricity seems somewhat mysterious to the untrained person. Auxiliary generators are probably situated at or near the top of this list. While it is not the goal of this section to delve deeply into the mechanics of the generator, a brief discussion might help in making them seem less intimidating.

The RV generator is actually a consolidated unit consisting of a small, air cooled engine and a second electricity producing section. The type of RV being equipped with a generator usually dictates whether the engine will have to run on gasoline, liquid propane or diesel fuel. All three fuel types are available.

Electricity is produced inside the generator section through the phenomenon of electro-magnetism. One of the reliable physical principles associated with living on earth is that electrons will flow on a wire whenever it passes through a magnetic field. Greater quantities of electricity can be produced by adding more wires or by increasing the strength of the magnetic field.

The engine has the responsibility of keeping these wires rotating through at least two magnetic fields at specified intervals. Every time a given winding slips past the "north" magnetic field, current flows in one direction. Continuing through the "south" field causes it to reverse direction. This represents one cycle, and is from where the term alternating current (AC) comes. Holding a predetermined engine speed produces the desired number of cycles per second in the windings. In North America, all appliances are rated for 60 Hertz (Hz), or cycles per second.

This stability of frequency is important for the proper operation of 120-volt equipment such as roof air conditioners, televisions, VCRs and computers. Damage to components is possible should the frequency vary greatly from the 60-Hz standard. Since the typical voltmeter cannot measure the frequency, it is necessary to have the frequency checked from time to time. One handy device available that monitors the generator output voltage as well as the frequency is called the "Good Governor" as produced by PowerWatch Technologies. This simple plug-in monitor can be set to measure the line voltage or the frequency at any receptacle in the RV. The center switch position will permit the voltage and frequency to alternately flash back and forth continuously. A wiring and polarity tester are also incorporated into this worthwhile instrument. Not only valuable to check the output of the on-board generator, use this device to verify the incoming line voltage from the campground power source before plugging in the shoreline. If the voltage is too high or too low, if the polarity is reversed, or if the frequency is out of kilter, damage could occur. The cost of the "Good Governor" is cheap insurance when one considers the costs of electrical damage that could happen. Add this one to the tool kit.

Good Governor by PowerWatch Technologies

Generator Engine – Alternator rotor and generator armature movement is powered by a gasoline engine. Usually, this is a four stroke engine with one or two cylinders that are cooled by air flow. Generator makers vary in how they place the cylinders (vertical or horizontal), the type of lubrication system (splash or pressurized), and the ease with which to gain access to various components. Size and weight are important factors the coach manufacturer must consider as well.

Fuel is supplied by either an electric or mechanical fuel pump. When installed in a motorhome, the fuel line is usually connected to a special draw tube in the main fuel tank. The end of this tube should be placed several inches above the bottom of the tank to prohibit the generator from emptying the fuel tank, thereby rendering the RVer stranded. It is not recommended to simply "tee" into an existing fuel line when installing a generator. This too, could rob the chassis engine of fuel and create some possible vapor lock situations.

Engine heat must be dissipated. Good air circulation and proper installation are crucial to adequate cooling. Also, the generator compartment must be sealed so that toxic exhaust gases cannot gain entry into the interior of the coach.

Most RV generator engines employ the use of a low oil pressure switch (LOP). The purpose of this switch is to shut down or prohibit the start up of a generator that is low on oil or does not have sufficient crankcase pressure to warrant the starting of the unit. Do not rely on this safety item to be the oil monitor for you. Check the oil level prior to starting the generator each time.

Maintenance – Generators are sturdy units, but extended use can take its toll. This toll is somewhat predictable, however, and manufacturers usually specify maintenance and inspection intervals based on the number of operational running hours such as every 50, 100, 200 and 500 hours. Additionally the RV owner can usually prevent troublesome operation by adopting several good habits. Foremost, is the pre-start check. Before each startup of the generator, check the oil level, as mentioned above. Then make sure the cooling air intake openings are free of debris, and be sure the generator compartment is clean and free of dirt.

The Golden Rule for all power plants is to never start or stop a generator with a load applied. For the health of the unit, make sure all AC appliances are turned off prior to starting or stopping the generator.

Also, watch for the effects of vibration. Starting, running and stopping the generator all produce vibration, as does simply driving or pulling the RV down the road. Check and tighten loose mounting bolts periodically. And remember, never use the generator compartment as a storage area. Good air circulation is critical to safe generator operation.

There are five important maintenance chores that the RV owner can perform:
- Keep the unit clean
- Change the oil at specified intervals
- Replace oil, fuel and air filters at specified intervals
- Replace spark plugs as needed or at specific interval
- Regularly check the battery electrolyte

Cleaning: Dirt, insect nests and debris blocking the cooling fins on the generator can cause overheating. There is no specific time interval for this task, but if you travel in dusty areas, you'll need to clean more often. The best rule of thumb is to simply clean the generator and inside the compartment whenever it needs it.

There should be no oily grime. If you notice a lot of oil blow-by or an accumulation of oil in a specific area or suspect a leak. Have it checked immediately.

Oil Changes: Most generator oil changes should take place between 50 and 100 hours. Different models have different requirements, so check the owner's manual for your particular model if a doubt exists. Unless you will be experiencing temperatures below freezing, use SAE30 oil for your changes. On a brand new unit, change the oil after the first five hours of operation and then every 50 or 100 hours after that. It is further recommended to change the oil filter (if so equipped), each time you change the oil.

Filters: There may be three types to track down and replace periodically: air filter, oil filter and fuel filters. Some units may also have a filter screen located inside the fuel pump. Other installations will find an in-line fuel filter somewhere in the system. There may even be a fuel filter attached to the carburetor on some generators. Check your owner's manual to be sure.

Spark Plugs: Spark plugs should be serviced about once a year or every 100 hours. Plugs provide a good indication of just what may be happening inside the cylinders. Badly blackened plugs may indicate a carboned cylinder head or an improperly adjusted carburetor or choke. Always replace the plugs with the same type and heat range. If your unit is equipped with breaker points, always replace the points and condenser at the same time you replace the spark plugs. Be sure to gap the plugs carefully prior to installing them. Check the owner's manual for plug and breaker gap measurements.

Battery: Check your generator start battery at least weekly, preferably as a pre-start check each time you operate the unit. Some generators are wired to the auxiliary 12-volt DC system, while others may be wired to the automotive start battery. All flooded lead acid batteries should have the electrolyte level checked often.

Muffler and Exhaust: A blocked exhaust pipe or damaged muffler may cause the engine to overheat. Many times the muffler and exhaust system on the generator hangs a little lower than anything else underneath the motorhome. Additionally, many installations are behind the rear axle making the generator exhaust system very prone to damage by "bottoming out" when approaching driveways or parking lots. Check your muffler system regularly to make sure you have not "bottomed out" lately. Also, see that the tailpipe extends beyond the edge of the coach. The RV code of standards calls for the exhaust pipe to extend past the vertical plane of the side or rear of an RV, but that it must not terminate under a window that can be opened.

Maintenance Log: For your convenience, use the log at the end of this section to record the tasks that are performed on the generator. It will also provide a track record for a service technician to review should you require deeper troubleshooting and repair procedures at some later point. Duplicate the log and keep it in your RV.

TROUBLESHOOTING: Prior to digging into your tool kit, take a close look inside the generator compartment. Do not overlook simple causes by missing something obvious. If it is an electrical problem such as no AC output, check your circuit breakers inside the RV prior to pointing your finger at the generator. Make sure all connections are clean, dry and tight. The first chart will list common complaints and possible causes concerning the operation of the engine portion of your generator set. The second chart pertains to the electrical problems you may encounter.

Following the prescribed maintenance items listed in the accompanying charts should provide numerous hours of reliable 120-volt AC service by the on-board generator. Periodically, however, it will be necessary to delve deeper: to have the choke, governor and carburetor adjusted. Though the adjustment points for these items are quite evident on most units, it is recommended that the generator be taken to a qualified service facility to have them checked. Tuning or "setting up" the generator requires the use of a special load bank that will tax the generator to a specific current limit and have the capability to monitor the output voltage, frequency and current draw at the same time. If, however, you would be interested in knowing exactly what takes place during a professional generator set-up, order the video tape, "RV Generator Tune-Up/Set-Up Procedures" by contacting the technical editor.

Use this maintenance schedule only as a guide. Specifications for your generator may differ slightly so consult the owner's manual to be sure.

Generator Service & Maintenance Log

Brand:			Model #	Serial #
	Operating Hours		Service Record	
Date	Hours Run	Cumulative	Task Performed	Performed By

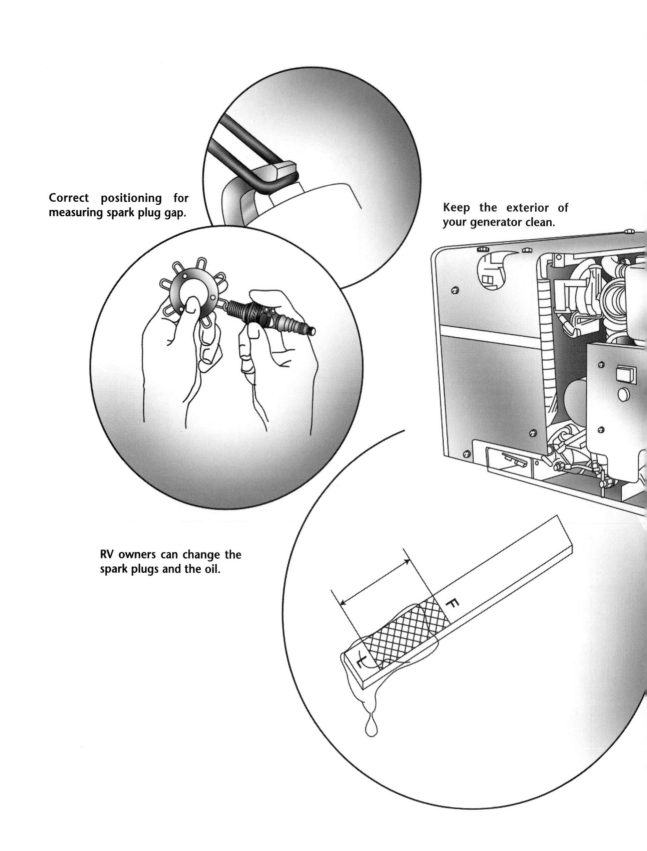

Correct positioning for measuring spark plug gap.

Keep the exterior of your generator clean.

RV owners can change the spark plugs and the oil.

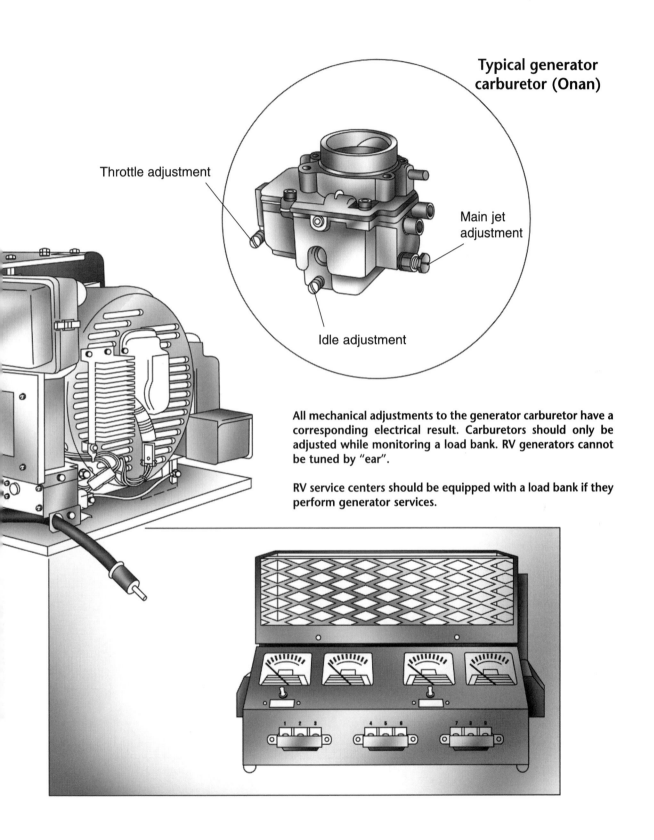

Typical generator carburetor (Onan)

Throttle adjustment

Main jet adjustment

Idle adjustment

All mechanical adjustments to the generator carburetor have a corresponding electrical result. Carburetors should only be adjusted while monitoring a load bank. RV generators cannot be tuned by "ear".

RV service centers should be equipped with a load bank if they perform generator services.

Periodic Maintenance Schedule

Use this maintenance schedule only as a guide. Specifications for your generator may differ slightly. Consult your owner's manual for exact tasks for your generator.

Maintenance Item	Operational Hours Interval				
	Daily	50	100	200	500
Check oil	✓				
Check battery electrolyte	✓				
Compartment clean	✓				
Cooling fins clean	✓				
Change oil & filter (if equipped)		✓	✓		
Clean air filter element		✓			
Clean fuel pump filter (if equipped)		✓			
Replace spark plug(s)			✓		
Replace breaker points (if equipped)			✓		
Replace air filter element			✓		
Check/tighten all electrical connections			✓		
Tighten all mounting hardware			✓		
Check exhaust/clean spark arrestor			✓		
Replace fuel filter(s)				✓	
Clean crankcase breather				✓	
Check tappet clearance					✓
De-carbon cylinder heads					✓

ENGINE SECTION	
Problem	**Possible Cause**
Engine will not crank	Dead battery
	Blown fuse
	Faulty start switch
	Faulty remote wiring
	Defective starter solenoid
Engine cranks, but won't start	No fuel (*clogged filter, pinched fuel line*)
	Clogged air cleaner element
	Fouled spark plug(s)
	Shorted or open ignition coil
	Improper ground cable
	Loose plug wire
	Weak battery
	Improper choke adjustment
	Low oil
Engine starts hard, runs rough	Stale fuel
	Clogged air filter element
	Improper carburetor adjustment
	Fouled spark plug(s)
	Weak ignition coil
	Blocked air cooling
	Improper choke adjustment
Engine stops suddenly	Out of fuel
	Clogged air filter element
	Fouled spark plug(s)
	Low oil
	Ignition control fuse blown
No power	Clogged air filter element
	Improper cooling
	Generator overload
	Improper governor adjustment
	Fouled plug(s)
	Improper carburetor setting
	Carbon build-up on cylinder heads
Engine overheats	Improper cooling
	Clogged air filter element
	Carburetor fuel mixture too lean
	Damaged exhaust components

GENERATOR SECTION	
Problem	**Possible Cause**
No AC output	Generator breaker tripped
	RV main breaker tripped
	Branch circuit breaker tripped
	Short inside RV
	Faulty internal component
Low AC output	Engine speed too slow
	Generator overload
	Faulty voltage regulator
	Faulty internal windings

Notes: _____

_____

_____

_____

_____

_____

_____

_____

_____

_____

_____

_____

_____

_____

_____

_____

_____

_____

CHAPTER FIVE

RV Plumbing Systems

Water is a vital part of RVing. It is a crucial commodity for confident self-containment and according to some, second in importance only to the 12-volt DC system. As long as there is plenty when we need it, and it tastes good, we stay happy. The system itself does, however, require a certain amount of maintenance in order for RVers to attain trouble-free usage. Certain problems can arise that cannot be ignored. Road vibration may cause fittings to become loosened or even break. Sub-freezing temperatures can burst water lines and crack fittings. Proper inspection, especially during storing and winterizing, may not only minimize, but in some cases, totally prevent many unfortunate situations from developing. All it takes is an understanding of the water systems and a few simple maintenance tasks to keep the water fresh-tasting and free-flowing during your travels.

FRESH WATER SYSTEMS

TYPES OF FRESH SYSTEMS: There are two distinct types of water systems found in RVs. The demand system is the predominant favorite of most RV manufacturers. The pressure system, commonly found in some large fifth-wheels and travel trailers, has declined in popularity over the last decade or so, yet it is still a viable system, and of course, can still be found on some of the older coaches rolling around the countryside. Let us explore the intricacies of each.

Pressure System – In this system, the entire system is pressurized. Pressure in the system forces the water through the pipes and to the fixtures. The rule here is, if the pressure diminishes, so does the volume of water that can be delivered to the faucets. Two dynamics are used to pressurize this type of fresh water system: air pressure and water pressure. Additionally, there are two methods of administering air pressure to the system.

First, understand that in the pressure system, the fresh water storage container is a rigid, cylindrical container, usually a 30-gallon capacity, and is typically located under a couch or dinette. It has a direct rigid pipe connection to the exterior fill assembly. A drain is usually located below the floor level directly under the tank. After the tank has been filled with water, air is forced into the tank. This pressurizes the tank and the system. When a faucet is opened anywhere in the system, the air pressure behind the water pushes it throughout the system.

Air is pumped into the tank through an air inlet fitting configured into the fill assembly located on the exterior of the coach. Only clean air, from a clean compressor, should be pumped into the fresh tank. It is not advisable to use "gas station air" or "shop air," since it is quite possibly contaminated. Use discretion. Avoid using pressurized air that comes from any compressor with a built-in storage tank. Contaminates will always settle in the bottom of such tanks. Compressed air produced from a compressor without a tank, one that uses the air immediately, is considered safer.

Another way of inducing air into the container is with the use of an on-board 12-volt DC air compressor. This device is permanently mounted at or near the pressure tank and is plumbed directly into the tank. The on-board air compressor ensures the RVer of two things: self-containment and a source of clean air.

The second method of pressurizing this type of container is with water pressure. Pressure is pressure, so it does not matter whether the force is water or air. A city water supply is connected directly to the fill assembly and water is forced into the system and the tank. As long as there is city (campground) water pressure present, there will be an ample amount of flow and volume at the faucets.

The on-board compressor is usually equipped with an adjustable pressure switch that allows the user to calibrate the pressure up or down depending on how much flow is needed at the faucets. While on city water, this pressure switch is usually bypassed because of the higher incoming pressure, or it is simply turned off.

Fresh Water Demand System – By far the most popular type of fresh water system is the demand system. Consisting of a non-pressurized storage tank, the water is distributed throughout the system by pumping the water, drawing it out of the tank and forcing it downstream via a 12-volt DC water pump. The various components of a demand system include:

- Water storage tank
- Demand pump
- Backflow preventers
- Hot/cold low point drains
- City water inlet
- Fixtures, including the water heater and toilet

Typical Fresh Water Demand System

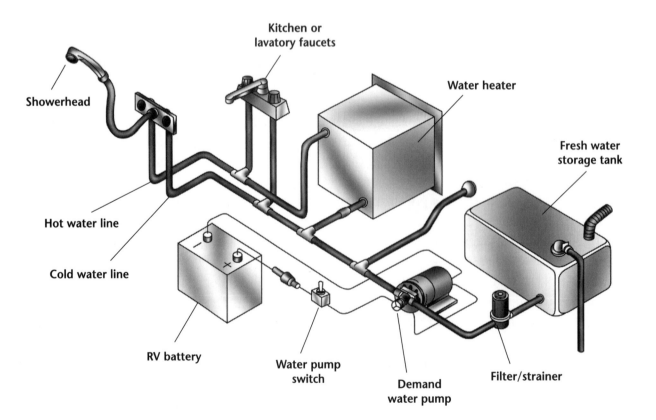

Kitchen or lavatory faucets

Water heater

Showerhead

Fresh water storage tank

Hot water line

Cold water line

RV battery

Water pump switch

Demand water pump

Filter/strainer

Fresh Water Storage Tank—Usually constructed of low density polyethylene, fresh water storage tanks are configured in many shapes and sizes to conform to the installation requirements of the coach manufacturers. Extremely durable, these plastic tanks need little in the form of maintenance. Flushing out the tanks periodically by filling, draining and then refilling, is usually all that is necessary to keep the water fresh and clean.

Water tanks have a fill inlet fitting, a drain fitting, a fill vent and an outlet fitting to draw water out of the tank. Most tanks today are outfitted with a monitor probe that provides the user with a level indication at a remote panel located in the RV. Periodically, this probe assembly may need cleaning. The probe assembly usually is inserted into the top of the tank and will have approximately five wires connected to it. If erratic operation of the level sensors is evident, simply remove this probe, wipe it down with fine steel wool and wash it clean. There may be some soft mineral deposits on the contacts or the probes that will need to be removed. Some level indicator probes may be permanently mounted on the side of the water tank and, therefore, cannot be removed for cleaning.

If a crack or leak does develop on the fresh water tank, owners are faced with either replacing the tank completely, or having the original tank repaired. The only viable method of repairing plastic fresh water tanks is by welding. Plastic welding can be performed on any structural thermoplastic such as ABS, PVC, CPVC, polypropylene and Plexiglas, among others.

Thermoplastics are unique in that they can be heated and cooled many times, over and over, without changing the chemical make-up or molecular characteristics. That is why they are so useful in the automotive and RV industries. Thermosetting plastics, on the other hand, harden when they are heated and cannot be welded.

Professional plastic welding requires an expensive piece of equipment not regularly found in an RVer's tool kit, so if cracks or leaks do develop in the fresh water storage tank, it will be necessary to schedule an appointment with a local RV service professional to evaluate the feasibility of welding the crack. If a replacement tank is days away, or if it is an obsolete design no longer available, plastic welding may be just the cure.

Miscellaneous Tips: When using sealants such as pipe dope on fresh water system fittings, be sure it is approved for such use. Some sealants may be harmful if ingested. Check the label before purchasing. It must be suitable for fresh water systems.

Never use pipe sealants on flare fittings, compression fittings or any plastic to plastic connection in the fresh water plumbing system. Sealants may be used on barbed fittings or threaded fittings other than those in the fresh water system.

Demand Pump—So named because it is constructed in such a manner that enables the pump to run only on "demand." That demand being when the RVer "demands" that water come out of the faucet by turning it on. The demand pump is wired with a pressure switch that will become activated when the pressure drops below a certain setting, as when a faucet is opened, and will continue to run until the pressure rises above a certain setting. Today's pressure switches are predominately pre-set at the factory and are non-adjustable. An interesting side note is that there are fewer problems concerning pressure switches now than when the switches were adjustable. The demand pump is wired into the 12-volt DC system. Today's demand water pump requires only simple maintenance. A later section in this chapter will detail water pump troubleshooting and repair.

Backflow Preventers—In order to keep unwanted water from back-filling into the fresh water storage tank while connected to the city water (which is usually left on during a typical campground stay), backflow preventers are installed in the fresh water system. Unchecked, city water could burst the fresh water tank and damage water lines. Backflow preventers permit water flow in one direction only.

Typically, there should be three backflow preventers, or check valves, located in the system. They should be installed:

- At the city water inlet—This keeps the water pump from pumping water from the tank and out the city water inlet when running the demand pump.
- At the demand pump—This one is usually an integral portion of the pump assembly. This check valve keeps the city pressure from back-filling the tank through the water pump.
- At the cold inlet to the water heater—This one prohibits the already heated water from being siphoned out through the cold water inlet when another faucet is opened or when the toilet is flushed. This backflow preventer may be omitted on some coaches. If so, it is recommended that one be installed.

Hot/Cold Low Level Drains—These may be situated anywhere in the fresh water system. Their purpose is to aid in draining the entire system of water, such as when storing or winterizing. They are usually located at the floor level inside a cabinet or underneath the coach. Check your owner's manual for their exact location on your RV.

City Water Inlet—Usually located on the side of the RV (some may be positioned under the coach), this inlet fitting is for connecting a hose to the campground or city water supply. Always taste the water before connecting. Caution here will minimize the chance of contaminating the entire system with foul tasting water.

It is always wise to use a pressure regulator when connecting to any city water source. Some parks and campgrounds may have unrestricted lines and such high pressures could burst fittings or rupture lines inside the RV. The city connection may "tee" into the system anywhere in the cold water side of the system. The city pressure will distribute the water equally to every fixture and appliance.

Be sure to use an approved RV water hose for making this connection to the city water supply. Other common garden hoses may impart a taste to the water that may prove to be unpleasant.

Some RVs may be equipped with what is termed a manual "quick fill" valve

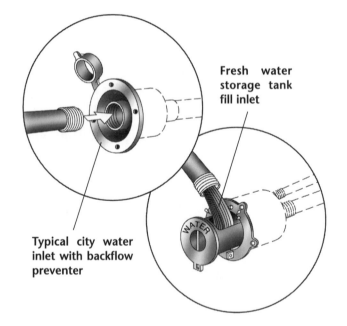

Fresh water storage tank fill inlet

Typical city water inlet with backflow preventer

to be used in conjunction with the city water inlet. This valve, when opened, will allow the city water pressure to fill the fresh water storage tank without having to disconnect the city water and fill through the tank's normal gravity fill port. Care should be exercised when using this valve. Lack of attention can cause the soft, pliable fresh water tank to expand and possibly rupture if the quick fill valve is left on too long.

Fixtures—Fixtures within the fresh water system include all hot and cold faucets located in the galley, the lavatory, and the tub/shower area. Additionally, water is fed to the toilet and the water heater.

An important fitting in the fresh water system is the anti-siphon backflow preventer associated with the tub/shower enclosure or the lavatory faucets. This fitting, which feeds the shower hose from the faucet, will normally drain all the water from inside the hose after shutting off the faucet. This is a normal occurrence. As annoying as it may be, it is a necessary safety device that will prohibit the accidental siphoning of waste water (from the toilet bowl) into the fresh water system, thereby rendering it contaminated. Do not remove or bypass this fitting.

Additional fixtures may include a water purifier and a water accumulator tank. The water purifier is self-explanatory and usually terminates at a single, dedicated spigot in the galley area. This spigot is usually used for drawing water for drinking or cooking only. It is not really necessary to purify water used for washing dishes, for instance. Some have replaceable cartridges, still others are constructed of a ceramic substance that can be scraped clean and reused many times. There are also many other types available at home improvement stores, and most can be adapted to RV use.

The water accumulator tank is used to hold a cushion of air in the system to eliminate "knocking" or "clanging" of the pipes when a faucet is abruptly turned off. We have all experienced the sensation of turning off the faucet and hearing or feeling a "banging" vibration. The accumulator tank houses a small cushion of air that acts as a shock absorber and eliminates this annoying effect.

Fresh Water System Accumulator

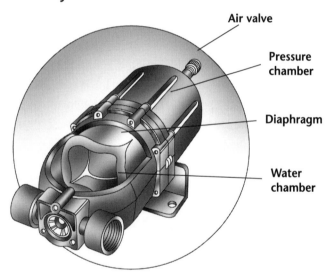

In past years, it was necessary to remove and drain the accumulator when it filled completely with water. The oxygen (air) inside became totally absorbed into the water, eliminating that cushion of air. Today, SHURflo produces an accumulator that is constructed with a flexible diaphragm that effectively isolates the air chamber from the water area negating the need to remove and drain it. The pressurized air and water never mix.

GENERAL FRESH SYSTEM MAINTENANCE: General fresh water system maintenance usually involves three items:
- Checking for leaks
- Chlorinating the water
- Cleaning/replacing the filter/strainer

Checking for Leaks: Obviously, water leaks are to be avoided. To do so, periodically check in and around all cabinets, fixtures, tank area, and behind the toilet for any indication of a leak. Seemingly small amounts of moisture can quickly escalate into a major crisis if left unattended.

Use the water pump as a troubleshooting tool. Close all faucets firmly and turn on the water pump. If the pump cycles or "burps" periodically, a leak could exist somewhere in the system. Be sure to check inside all exterior storage compartments and underneath the coach. The leak could also be internal to the pump.

Chlorinating the Water: Foul or stale tasting water can not only ruin a vacation, but may even be harmful. There is usually sufficient chlorine in most city water supply systems, but if foul tasting water persists, it may be necessary to treat the fresh water tank. Of course, the tank only stores the quality of water put in there, so be sure to taste it prior to filling up.

Drain and flush the tank with clean water. Many aftermarket products are available at your local service facility that can be added to the tank to adequately chlorinate the system. A home recipe can also be concocted that will suffice when dry camping in the middle of nowhere. Add one-quarter cup of regular bleach to the tank for every fifteen gallons of tank capacity. Do this each time the tank is filled. This step should also be performed after any period of non-use, such as during the spring shakedown.

Filter/Strainer: Most fresh water systems will usually have one filter/strainer located between the fresh water tank and the water pump. At least once a year, clean or replace the filter element or screen. This filter protects the demand pump from debris that may be inadvertently induced into the fresh tank. Plastic chips from drilling during the manufacturing process may have fallen inside the tank also. This filter can save repair dollars and more importantly, downtime, by simply keeping it clean.

Repairing the Demand Water Pump – Compared to earlier years, the modern demand water pump is a technological wonder. Today's pump manufacturers have water pumps so finely tuned that, short of blatant abuse, there is little to go wrong. Out of sight and usually out of mind day in and day out, most will faithfully continue to provide running water.

Major Components: Demand pumps, although somewhat complex internally, are very basic in function and major components. Most 12-volt DC demand pumps can be broken down into these basic components:

Flojet Water Pump

- 12-volt DC motor
- Pumping mechanism
- Pressure switch
- Check valve
- Mounting assembly

There are a few different pump designs on the market, but virtually all contain these five basic components. The method of pumping may differ, but elemental operation and the principle goal are the same—provide fresh water upon demand.

The demand principle revolves around the thought of the pump being a dormant component until we either turn on a hot or cold water faucet or flush the toilet. It is upon this call or demand for water that the pump will immediately spring to life and provide a nice steady stream of water.

The modern pump has individual components that are easily replaced. Seldom is there a need to replace the entire pump. All major component groups for each manufacturer can be individually replaced. RVers with extremely old demand pumps may want to purchase a newer style simply to upgrade the system.

The purpose of the 12-volt DC motor, the pumping mechanism and the mounting base are pretty obvious, but let us explore the reason why a pressure switch and a check valve are integral components of the demand water pump.

The pressure switch is simply an on/off 12-volt switch that has 12 volts applied to it whenever the master pump switch is on. It is a normally closed switch, which means, sitting on the bench by itself, there is continuity across the two terminals. Once pressure is applied to the switch, the contacts open and there is no continuity across the terminals. It is the purpose of this pressure switch to provide 12-volt DC current to the pump motor whenever the pressure against the switch falls below approximately 40 PSI. This is exactly what will happen when a faucet is opened or the toilet is flushed.

Unfortunately, this is also exactly what happens if a leak exists anywhere in the fresh water plumbing system. Remember, the demand for water can be either intentional or unintentional. For this reason, it is a good idea to turn off the main water pump switch if you are going to be away from the RV for any length of time.

Today's pressure switches are predominantly nonadjustable, but extremely reliable. Pressure switches of a few years ago were very temperamental and required constant adjusting and frequent replacing. Most of today's pressure switches are manufactured to keep the water pressure at or very near 40 PSI.

The built-in check valve is a necessary and required item that prohibits back-filling of the water tank through the pump while you are connected to city water. If you suddenly realize the fresh water

Modern SHURflo Pressure Switch

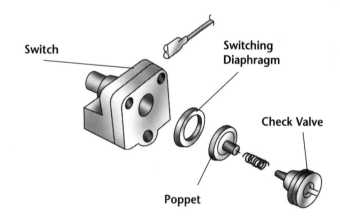

Switch

Switching Diaphragm

Check Valve

Poppet

storage tank is full or overflowing, and your rig is connected to city water, chances are the check valve inside the demand pump is defective. In most cases, the check valve assembly can be purchased separately or as part of a repair kit.

Familiarize yourself with all the repair kits available for your particular pump. There is no reason why the confident RV owner should not be able to perform all repairs to the demand water pump.

Troubleshooting: As mentioned earlier, it is possible to use the demand pump as a troubleshooting tool to pinpoint or at least narrow down possible causes for a number of plumbing ills you may encounter while enjoying the RV lifestyle.

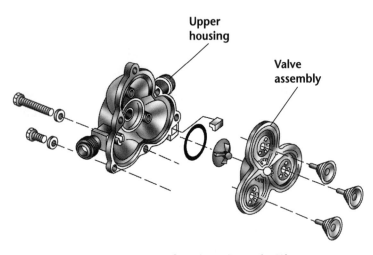

**Pumpin Mechanism Repair Kit
for the SHURflo Water Pump**

Upper housing

Valve assembly

If, for instance, you see a small puddle of water below your RV, by turning on the water pump and making sure there is plenty of water in the fresh tank, you will quickly be able to determine if the leak is from the fresh water system or the waste water system. If the pump rapidly cycles on and off, or cycles once every few seconds, it is a good sign the leak is in the fresh water system. If, however, the pump never cycles, or "burps," with the switch in the "on" position, suspect the waste water system as the source of the leak.

Here are a few typical troubleshooting scenarios.

If the pump will not run at all, open any two faucets, turn the master pump switch on, and with a 12-volt test light, pierce the red wire that is attached directly to the pump motor. Attach the negative lead of the test light to a good ground connection. If there is voltage present on the wire at the motor, check the ground wire for the pump motor. If that wire is sufficiently grounded, the motor if faulty.

If there was no voltage indicated on the red wire, touch the test light to both wires attached to the pressure switch. If one is hot, remove them both and hold them together. If the pump runs, replace the pressure switch.

Obviously, if no voltage is indicated anywhere at the pump, check that circuit until the reason for the lack of voltage can be determined. If there is no voltage anywhere in the coach, suspect the battery. If there is plenty of 12-volt DC electricity in the RV, check the pump fuse, the master pump switch, and the wires that electrically connect each of these components to the pump.

If you smell what appears to be burning wires, and you find the pump is extremely hot to the touch, remove the pump portion from the 12-volt motor and apply 12 volts directly to the motor. If it runs, but does not get hot, suspect binding components in the pump assembly. If it continues to get hot, replace the motor.

Intermittent water pump cycling has traditionally been the indicator of a water leak. The leak can be internal to the pump, but in most cases, the leak will exist somewhere in the fresh water system. A faucet may drip, the toilet ball valve may be passing water into the bowl, a fitting may be seeping, the water heater P & T relief valve may be dripping or any of a couple of dozen other possibilities.

To determine if the leak is internal to the pump, turn the pump off and disconnect the outlet water line on the pump. Plug or cap the outlet port directly on the pump. Turn the pump on. If it continues to cycle periodically, the pump has an internal leak and will need to be removed and disassembled for further repair. If the cycling vanishes, the leak is somewhere in the rest of the system.

If water is not seen readily pooling anywhere, strongly suspect the toilet. Other than the water pump, the toilet is the only other component that could possibly leak without a telltale wet spot giving away the location of the leak. Do not forget to look outside and underneath the coach as well. If the city water inlet check valve is stuck open, for instance, the same symptom will result.

Condition	Possible Cause
Pump motor will not operate	Dead battery or no voltage
	Blown fuse
	Faulty master switch
	Faulty pressure switch
	Loose or disconnected wire
	Faulty ground wire
	Burned out motor
	No demand for water
Motor runs, but is very hot	Insufficient wire size
	Low voltage
	Motor shaft binding
	Faulty motor bearings
Pump cycles periodically	Water leak in fresh water system
	Internal leak in pump
Pump runs, but is noisy	Loose screws or components in pump
	Faulty bearings in motor
	Binding components in pump
	Faulty motor windings
Pump runs, but water spatters	Low or no water in tank
	Inlet line to pump is kinked
	Water filter is dirty
	Air leak inlet to pump
	Outlet hose is kinked
	Faulty motor bearings
	Loose mechanical connections
Pump runs continuously	Pressure switch miswired
	Low battery voltage
	Stuck pressure switch
	Loose or faulty internal components

The faster the pump cycles, the larger the leak. If it only "burps" every five minutes or so, it is probably a very small leak. Large leaks should be easier to spot than small leaks. As each leak is located and repaired, run the test again. Be sure to open all cabinets and remove any access panels to water connections that may be concealed.

Some demand pumps are noisier than others, but if a pump is extremely noisy, tighten any screws that are exposed. If the noise continues, remove the pump and bench test it to determine which component may be causing the noise. Remove the pump assembly and apply 12 volts to the motor. If it continues to run noisily, replace the motor. If the motor runs fine by itself, check the

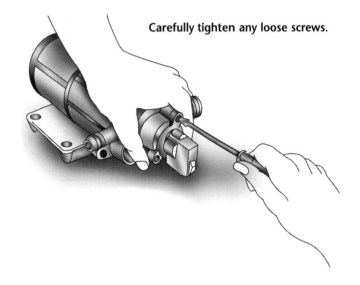
Carefully tighten any loose screws.

individual pumping mechanism components. Be sure the mounting base attaching screws are not too tight. The rubber grommets should be intact and not compressed too much.

If the pump runs, but the water simply sputters out of each faucet, suspect an air leak on the inlet side of the pump. The non-pressurized connections between the tank and the inlet to the pump are prone to having hose clamps become loosened. Tighten all clamps and make sure the hose is not kinked anywhere along its entire length. If there is an in-line filter positioned between the tank and the pump, clean it or replace it, depending on the type. In some cases the problem may be a faulty motor, but these instances are somewhat rare.

If the only way to prohibit the demand pump from running is to shut off the master switch, suspect a stuck or mis-wired pressure switch. First, make sure all the faucets in the RV are closed and the water heater is full. Then check the wiring from the master switch to the pressure switch and finally to the pump motor. The voltage should follow that same path. If the wiring appears correct, chances are the pressure switch is faulty and will have to be replaced.

By following these simple troubleshooting procedures, you should be able to quickly determine if a condition is relative to the demand pump or to the rest of the fresh water system.

Plumbing System Repairs – Modern fresh water plumbing systems have endured many changes over the years and have evolved into one of the most durable, least problematic and easiest to work with group of components found on RVs today. That is not to say repairs are never required, but when proper maintenance practices are employed, they are minimized.

Fresh water system damage is most likely to occur due to freeze damage (a lack of proper winterizing techniques) or by an errant staple or a mis-directed mounting screw piercing a water line. The good news is that regardless of the types of damage that may occur the RV owner is more than likely capable of repairing them with relative ease. Prior to attacking a repair, however, the RVer must first understand the basic differences among fresh water system components. First, let us explore the types of water lines used in RVs today.

Types of Water Lines: In years past, the most popular type of fresh water line was a semi-flexible plastic tubing called polybutylene (PB). However, recent developments concerning the manufacture of polybutylene has rendered this type extinct in new coaches being produced today. After a rash of lawsuits, Shell Chemical Company, provider of the resin for the manufacture of PB tubing abruptly withdrew the resin and their formula from the plumbing industry in early 1996, effectively stopping all production of PB tubing. The lawsuits were filed after a series of failures within some PB plumbing systems—primarily in the housing industries. That led to the adaptation and integration of cross-linked polyethylene (PEX) as the main type of tubing for RVs. As existing inventories of PB were depleted, PEX became the favored type of tubing used.

PEX is produced by three basic methods: radiation, silane and Engel. There is a difference between them, with the tubing produced by the Engel method seemingly having an advantage over the others. An example is the tubing produced by Uponor. Their "hot" cross-linked Engel-produced tubing has an inherent property called "thermal memory," which is a trait that permits kinked tubing to be repaired by simply heating the affected kink with a heat gun or a high-powered hair dryer. Thermal memory allows the tubing to return to its original shape and more importantly, its original strength. This characteristic can be handy for the RVer who discovers a kinked section under a gaucho for instance, even though it goes against the common plumbing practice of always replacing damaged tubing. Testing, however, has proven that only Engel-produced PEX has this advantage. With silane or radiation manufactured PEX, replacement is still mandatory.

Uponor's Plumb-Pex system, with its unique clamping method, allows RVers and professional service technicians an easy way to facilitate repairs and/or upgrades.

Adapter fittings are readily available for RVers splicing PEX tubing into a system previously plumbed with PB. Adapters are necessary since internal PB and PEX fittings are not compatible. The wall dimensions are thicker on PEX even though the outside diameter of the tubing is the same. On newer RVs, when making repairs to fresh water tubing, it will be necessary to ascertain if the coach is equipped with PB or the newer PEX. If it does utilize PEX, is it Engel-produced or silane produced? An inquiry to the coach manufacturer may be necessary.

Also in previous years, other types of water lines have appeared in RVs. Some still are seen today even though cross-linked polyethylene and polybutylene abound in greater numbers. Other types encountered include:

- Copper tubing
- PVC (Polyvinyl Chloride)
- CPVC (Chlorinated Polyvinyl Chloride)
- Flexible vinyl hose—may be used between the fresh water tank and the water pump.

Copper tubing connections must be either flared connections or "sweated" connections (those that are soldered with a portable propane torch). Although used extensively in the LP gas system, brass compression fitting connections should be avoided for fresh water plumbing use.

1) Slide the clamp over the tubing.

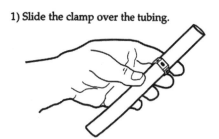

2) Slide the tubing onto the insert fitting.

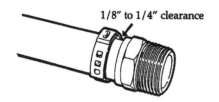

1/8" to 1/4" clearance

3) Close the clamp with the Ratchet tool.

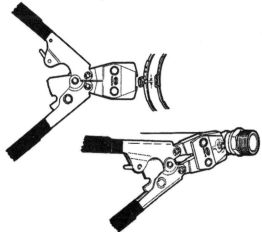

The Ratchet tool will not release until the clamp is properly closed. This insures the installer that the connection is complete.

PVC and CPVC are cemented, semi-rigid plastic pipes that are also utilized by some manufacturers. PVC can only be used for cold water lines, while CPVC is permissible for either hot or cold lines. Along with ABS fittings in the waste system, fittings for plastic piping are cemented in place.

A flexible hose-type water line is permissible, as mentioned above, between the water tank and the pump, and sometimes it is used on the outlet side or pressure side of the pump, but only for the first eighteen inches so a connection can be made to the rest of the system. This is common if semi-rigid plastic piping is used throughout the system. Pump vibration could possibly lead to a cracked fitting if a solid connection were to be made between the pump and the system. Any flexible hose utilized must be approved for RV use. This includes the hose used for the city water hook-up in the campground.

Definitions of Fittings—When purchasing or referring to the various kinds of fittings available, it is important to know the correct nomenclature for each. Even professional RV technicians become confused while pondering the different kinds of fittings and just what they should be called. Invariably, the wrong type is purchased on that first trip to the hardware store only because you thought you needed a coupling when you really needed a union. Here's a quick glossary of a few common fittings that should keep the differences clear in your mind.

Union	Two like male ends. The sizes may differ, but each end is the same type.
Coupling	Two like female ends, with each end the same type.
Elbow	Usually 45 degree or 90 degree. A variation is called a "street ell." This type has one female end and one male end of the same type.
Adapter	Always connects two different types of pipe or tubing.
Nipple	Two like male ends of threaded pipe. Similar to a union, but available in varying lengths.
Tee	A connection for three separate lines. They could all be alike or one or more may be a different type. The "branch" is always at a 90 degree angle to the "run" portion of the fitting.
Cross	Similar to the tee, but for four separate lines.
Wye	A connection for three individual lines similar to a tee, but the "branch" portion is positioned at something other than a 90 degree angle.
Bushing	Male end reduced to an always smaller female—all in the same fitting. Usually bushings are threaded, but they also may be slip fittings.
Plug	Male end method to terminate a line or pipe.
Cap	Female end method to terminate a line or pipe.
Nut	Female threaded fitting used as a method of attachment, i.e., flare nut or compression nut. An exception would be an inverted flare nut, which consists of male threads instead of female threads. The inverted flare nut is only common within the LP gas system and is not associated with the water system at all.

Common Piping Problems—If fittings are knocked loose or broken, they will have to be replaced. If a puncture occurs in a line, cut the tubing at that point and install a simple union or coupling. If damage occurs to a length of tubing, the entire length will have to be replaced, but PEX lines, remember, can be repaired if crushed or kinked.

To cut copper tubing, a special tubing cutter will be necessary. Additionally, be sure to de-burr the inside and outside of the tubing prior to attaching the fitting. Burrs left on the end of the tubing may cause an improper flare that could result in a leak.

PB and PEX tubing can be cut with a special scissors-like tubing cutter or with a common razor knife. All cut ends should be square with the tubing. It is not necessary to ream PB or PEX tubing after cutting. Tube cutting tools are readily available at local hardware stores.

If rigid piping is used such as ABS, PVC or CPVC, be sure to carefully follow the directions on the can of cement for those types of plastic pipes. For best results when cementing plastic pipe to a fitting, apply a liberal amount of cement to the fitting and to the pipe itself. Insert the pipe fully into the fitting with a quarter-turn twisting motion. In some instances, it may be necessary to hold the two pieces together momentarily, immediately after connecting them.

When replacing cemented fittings and subsequent piping, have every piece pre-cut and fitted together before cementing. If the alignment is not quite correct, changes can only be made before cementing. ABS, PVC and CPVC fittings cannot be reused.

Rigid plastic water lines are more prone to freeze damage than the more flexible polybutylene and cross-linked polyethylene. If your coach has rigid lines, and you live in the colder climates, proper winterizing procedures are mandatory.

WASTE WATER SYSTEMS

Waste systems on RVs are a necessity in order to be truly self-contained. In reality, the simplicity of the waste systems usually means not many problems actually arise. As long as a little preventive maintenance and care are employed, that is. As in any system within the RV, a certain amount of attention and prevention at varying intervals can help in minimizing any unpleasantness or worse, any downtime that takes away from the direct enjoyment of the RV.

TYPES OF SYSTEMS: There are two distinct types of waste systems: the "gray" water system and the "black" water system. The gray water system is typically waste from the kitchen sink, the lavatory sink and the shower or tub. Basically it refers to the liquid waste.

The black water system is the solid waste associated with the toilet. The black and gray systems should not be inter-connected, that is, they must each have a dedicated method of storing the waste (holding tanks), and each must have its own waste termination valve (dump valve). There are, however, a few exceptions to this rule. For instance, in some cases it is permissible to have one other fixture drain into the black water tank. For all practical purposes, however, and also for the ease of understanding, the two systems should remain separate.

Holding Tanks – Holding tanks are usually constructed of either ABS or polyethylene plastic. Polypropylene, fiberglass and metal tanks have also been used in the manufacture of holding tanks. Today's plastic tanks, however, have proven to be extremely durable and well adept for storing waste.

Location of Tanks—Most holding tanks are mounted below the floor level. Some tanks are sandwiched between the upper floor and a sub-floor, still others may be located between the floor and a belly pan on those units with sealed bottoms, such as the popular "basement" models. The coach construction and the layout of the floorplan are two of the determining factors as to where the holding tanks are situated. The black tank, however, is usually positioned directly under the toilet.

All holding tanks must be removable. That is, other components such as floors, sub-floors, under-carriage trailer hitch receiver or any aftermarket add-on device must permit the removal of the holding tanks for repair or replacement. A common occurrence is to find a damaged holding tank that needs to be removed only to find out some unknowing installer welded a permanent hitch receiver directly below the tank prohibiting its removal.

Not all RVs have both types of holding tanks. Some small camping trailers and slide-in campers may not be equipped with a gray water tank. The gray water may terminate through the side of the coach and must be connected to a sewer drain connection prior to being used, or the waste is collected in a portable bucket and then manually emptied. Additionally, some small RVs do not have a black holding tank. They may be equipped with a recirculating-type toilet that is evacuated periodically through a three-inch outlet directly into the campground sewer connection.

Size of Tanks—The size of the holding tanks vary from manufacturer to manufacturer. Often their size is dictated by the space that is available and the design of the floorplan. Obviously, the larger the better. This equates to longer intervals between evacuations which is especially appreciated when dry camping.

Dump Outlets—The outlets from the holding tanks are usually configured into a single termination assembly that is comprised of one main outlet for connecting to the campground sewer and two inlets, one from each tank. Between each tank outlet and the inlet to the termination assembly are the termination valves or "dump" valves. The gray water tank dump valve must be a minimum 1-1/4 inch diameter, while the black tank must maintain its 3 inch diameter from inlet to outlet. A flexible sewer hose with an appropriate adapter is attached to the termination assembly, connected to the campground or dump station, and the tanks are emptied.

Evacuating the Tanks—It is common practice to dump the black water tank first, then the gray tank. Dumping the gray water last will aid in rinsing any solid waste that might accumulate in the termination assembly or the sewer hose.

While in the campground, if a sewer hook-up is available, it is common to connect the flexible sewer hose and to leave the gray water holding tank termination valve in the open position. It is not advised, however, to do this with the black tank. Always fill the black tank at least three-quarters full and then evacuate it. Due to the solid nature of the waste, it will not drain properly and blockages will result if the valve is left open while connected to the park sewer. This, then, can become a truly distasteful experience.

After dumping, it is important to rinse and flush each tank thoroughly. This is accomplished by simply running fresh water through the drains and into the tank. An aftermarket holding tank rinser is ideal for cleaning the inside of the black water tank. Fill each tank until there is approximately three-quarters of an inch of fresh water on the bottom, then dump the tanks again: black tank first, then gray tank. Keeping the holding tanks flushed and rinsed will minimize or completely eliminate the common problem areas associated with the waste systems.

Odor Control—Previously, it was common practice to simply mask the odors in the holding tanks and to combat the consolidation of the solid waste by using strong chemicals. In some cases, it seemed these chemicals were more obtrusive than the odor from the waste.

Many different chemicals were formulated to aid in this dual task of masking the odor and breaking down the solids. For many years, formaldehyde-based chemicals seemed to work the best. However, as technology progressed and the dangers of formaldehyde poisoning came to be understood, other options became a reality. Today, formaldehyde and other alcohol-based chemicals are no longer recommended for use in either holding tank. Many RV campgrounds and state parks, in fact, now prohibit the dumping of formaldehyde-laced holding tanks into their waste systems.

Treating the Tanks—The safest way to protect and treat the holding tanks and to eliminate odors is to use a non-chemical, enzyme-based product, preferably one that contains live bacteria. The live bacteria actually digest the odor causing molecules and break down the solid waste. This type of bacteria was used after the Alaskan oil spill to help digest the oil and to aid in the cleanup efforts.

Tri-Synergy Incorporated has a product called RM Tank Care that has met with success in breaking down solid wastes and eliminating odors. There are many suppliers who also have produced an additive that contains no formaldehyde. Thetford Corporation has a complete line of products specifically designed for both gray and black holding tanks. Carefully read the product label before purchasing any additive for the waste system. Here is how to effectively treat RV waste tanks.

To treat both holding tanks, add four or five ounces of RM Tank Care (or equivalent), to the tanks, along with enough fresh water to cover the bottom of each tank. After subsequent evacuations of each tank during the excursion, add another four or five ounces. This will ensure the tanks remain fresh and you are doing your part to help protect the environment.

Termination Valve Maintenance—Periodically, the dump valves, especially the black water valve, will need to be serviced. Usually dump valves are bolted in place between two adapter fittings. After draining and flushing the tanks, these bolts can be taken out and the valve removed from in between the adapter fittings. If the termination valve has been cemented in place, it will be necessary to cut the pipe before and after the valve in order to remove it. To eliminate this dilemma in the future, always replace a cemented valve with one that is bolted in place.

On either side of the dump valve is an "O" ring that periodically needs to be replaced. Also, occasionally, waste will accumulate in the groove for the slide portion of the valve. To avoid crisis repairs while traveling, once a year, remove, disassemble, clean and lubricate both termination valves. This little bit of yearly maintenance will eliminate most dump valve problems encountered.

Also, during the camping season, use a slide valve lubricant such as Thetford's Drain Valve Lubricant. Two to four ounces of this water soluble additive is poured down the drain into the gray tank and flushed down the toilet into the black tank to lubricate the inside of the dump valve blades and to coat the inside of the drains and tanks to aid in complete draining and trouble-free valve operation. One of the most disagreeable RV repairs is replacing a stuck or broken dump valve with a full holding tank. RV technicians hate it and they get paid to do it. It is certainly no fun when it happens to you, miles from nowhere, in the middle of a vacation getaway. A little attention to the waste systems can avoid such scenarios.

Drain lines—The sizing of the plumbing lines and pipes varies. The connection between the toilet and the tank, as well as the outlet from the black tank to the termination valve assembly must be a three-inch pipe. The drain piping in the gray waste system from each of the sinks to the tank typically range from 1-1/4 inch to 2 inches in diameter. The tank outlet from the gray water tank to the termination assembly can be 1-1/2 inches to 3 inches in diameter. All vents from each tank must be at least 1-1/2 inches in diameter.

It is important to know where the drain lines are situated inside the RV and where each of the "P" traps are located. Periodically, "P" traps must be removed and cleaned to ensure free flowing and proper drainage from the sinks, etc. Take note that all "P" traps use threaded fittings. All traps must be accessible and removable. Never cement the "U" sections of "P" traps.

RV Holding Tank Repair – Today, virtually all RV holding tanks are made from thermoplastic. The two most common plastics used are ABS and polyethylene. Thermoplastics are extremely durable materials from which to manufacture holding tanks, and they can be formed into a myriad of specific shapes to fit into most locations. They are also highly resistant to freeze damage. Additionally, thermoplastics are relatively inexpensive, and they are readily available from an abundance of suppliers.

However, many RV waste holding tanks are located underneath the coach and as such, are susceptible to road debris, tall speed bumps and most curbs. Additionally, a not-so-careful approach to steep driveways can quickly separate the RV from its waste dump assemblies leaving a pungent, telltale trail all the way to the RV.

Holding tanks do incur periodic damage such as stress cracks, broken outlets and leaky fittings that can, for the most part, be repaired by the assertive RV owner.

Repair or Replace – This is the dilemma faced by many RVers concerning many different facets of RVing. The fine line between these two ideas, sometimes becomes difficult to discern. The predominant thought when considering repair or replacement is, "To what extent is the damage?" Clearly a holding tank with major damage, large pieces missing or simply too many cracks should be replaced.

For the most part, however, many cracks and leaks can be repaired. This is a noteworthy option, especially when traveling. You may not have the time to wait until a replacement tank can be ordered and received. Additionally, if you have an older RV, perhaps the exact tank is no longer offered. There are many obsolete components, termed "orphan parts," that are simply no longer available at any cost.

The first step in determining the damage is to completely inspect the tank. If the damage was caused by rocks or road debris, chances are the crack will be on the bottom of the tank, already exposed and easily inspected. If a collision caused a holding tank leak that appears to be coming from somewhere on top of the tank, or on the side, it may or may not be readily visible. You can try using a mirror and a flashlight to find a leak. However, to be sure, it is recommended that the tank be completely removed from the coach.

Black and gray water tanks that are installed underneath the coach are usually attached by similar methods. The only glaring difference is that the black water tank will obviously have the toilet attached to it. All toilets attach to the tank via a three-inch drain pipe. The gray water tank, on the other hand, will have a two-inch pipe as its largest possible drain entry into the tank. Both tanks will typically have a vent that protrudes through the roof of the RV. Other drains and vents may attach at any location on top of either holding tank. In most cases, the holding tank will have to be removed. For typical black water tank installations, here is how:

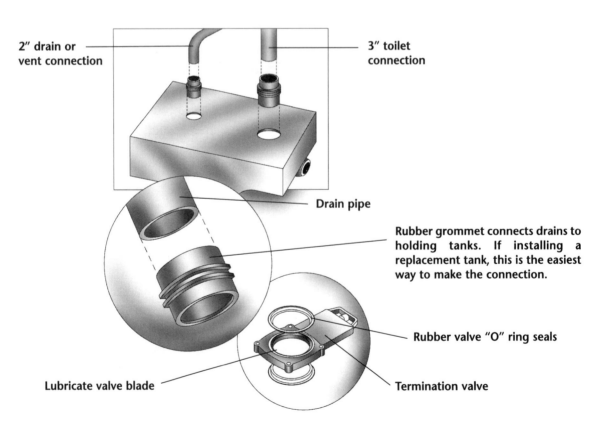

2" drain or vent connection

3" toilet connection

Drain pipe

Rubber grommet connects drains to holding tanks. If installing a replacement tank, this is the easiest way to make the connection.

Rubber valve "O" ring seals

Lubricate valve blade

Termination valve

Tank Removal –

1) First and foremost, be sure the tank has been emptied prior to even starting to think about dropping the tank. (If the damage was substantial enough to automatically empty the tank, order a replacement tank. With damage that significant, repair should not even be considered.) Flush the tank with fresh water to clean it as best as possible.

2) Turn off the water pump or the city water and disconnect the water line to the toilet.

3) Locate the closet bolts and remove the toilet. After the toilet has been removed, remove the screws that hold the floor flange in place and remove the flange. Many times the flange is threaded into the top of the holding tank. Otherwise, it just slips into a rubber grommet affixed to the top of the tank. If it is difficult to turn the floor flange, a flange removal tool can be easily made by drilling two three-eighths-inch holes into a piece of 1' x 3' wood board. The holes should correspond to the closet bolt locations on the flange. Slipping the board over the closet bolts will provide leverage as well as something to hold onto as the flange is removed. This same homemade tool can be used to reinstall the flange as well.

4) On the roof, locate the vent for that tank. Remove the vent cover and see if the vent pipe will unscrew. Keep in mind, however, not all vents go straight from the tank to the roof. Some, called "wet vents," have a drain from a sink also connected to them. Others may have 45 degree bends prohibiting them from turning. If the vent line will not unscrew, locate the point where the vent enters the tank at or near the floor level. Look inside closets, under cabinets, etc. until the ABS piping is located in an area that can be reached with a hacksaw blade. In some instances, access to the drain connection can be realized from under the coach, yet on top of the tank. The bottom line is that all drains or vents, as well as the toilet, must be removed, disconnected or cut in order to allow the tank to be dropped straight down.

5) Locate and determine just how the tank is secured to the underside of the RV. Many installations utilize mounting straps or metal bands that completely support the bottom of the tank. Some may have an upper flange that is bolted or screwed to the underside of the coach. Still others may be suspended by structural supports or angle iron. There are many methods used to attach holding tanks. Some are simply secured into the basement portion of a compartment. Look over the installation carefully to determine which method was used.

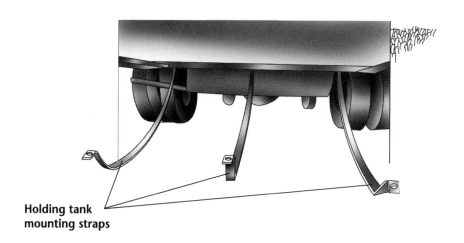

Holding tank mounting straps

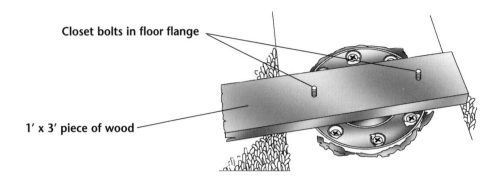

Closet bolts in floor flange

1' x 3' piece of wood

6) Remove any electrical wires attached to "well nuts," or probes that connect the monitor panel to the tank. Be sure to mark the exact location for any such wires and to note their respective colors.

7) Remove the dump assembly located at the outlet of the holding tank. Typically, the fitting or pipe is clamped, cemented, or screwed into the outlet of the tank. If the pipe is cemented, it will be necessary to cut the pipe at a convenient location. Clamped or threaded connections can be removed and reused. Many times there is only one dump outlet shared by both holding tanks, therefore, be sure both tanks are emptied in step one since both dump assemblies may have to be removed.

8) Support the tank and remove the mounting screws, supports or straps, and lower the tank to the ground. On basement installations, simply lift the tank out. Once removed, the tank can be closely inspected to determine the exact source of the leak or damage.

Removed tank with inlet and vent fittings

In some cases, it may be necessary to plug the outlet and fill the tank with fresh water in order to spot a small hairline crack or other hard-to-find leaks.

Some holding tank installations are better left to professional RV technicians. Those that are encased between the floors of an RV with a solid underbelly may prove too difficult for the average RVer to repair. Likewise, those that are "buried" in the confines of some basement model motorhomes or buses are probably a little too much to tackle. Use your own judgment.

Method of Repair—Once the crack has been located, and it is determined to indeed be repairable, next choose which method should be used to make the repair. Here are the options:
- Aftermarket patch kit
- Plastic welding
- Hot glue

Aftermarket patch kits are available for today's plastic tanks, however, they work best with tanks made of ABS plastic. They will, however, perform as a satisfactory, though temporary, patch on polyethylene tanks. They can be used anywhere on an ABS tank, but are only recommended for use on the top of polyethylene tanks.

Like the fresh water tank mentioned earlier, the only true and permanent method for repairing polyethylene holding tanks is by plastic welding. Plastic welding is also recommended for repairing ABS tanks, as well as any other type of thermoplastic, including polypropylene, PVC and Plexiglas. Plastic welding requires specialized equipment found only in well outfitted service shops. Only a small percentage of RV service facilities offer plastic welding services, so it may take some looking to find one. *(For a detailed look at plastic welding procedures, order the training video, "Plastic Welding Techniques," by contacting the technical editor.)*

The hot glue method is only recommended for very small hairline cracks around vent fittings located above the top of the tank. They can be used as a temporary cure while in the boondocks, perhaps, but repairs made with hot glue will not hold up to the test of time.

So how do you decide to use a patch kit or to have the crack welded? For ABS tanks, if the crack is in a portion of the tank that is less than three-sixteenths-inch thick, use a patch kit. If the thickness of the ABS tank is greater than three-sixteenths-inch, or if the crack is in a position of tension when the tank is installed, take the tank to a repair center proficient at plastic welding.

For polyethylene tanks, only use a patch kit if the crack is located on top of the tank or on a side within two inches of the top. Avoid using a patch kit if the crack is located at or near the bottom of the tank or near an outlet fitting, except in an emergency.

Many patch kits come with easy-to-use tubes of epoxy and strips of webbing that can be used to reinforce the area to be patched. Carefully read the instructions on the package. Be sure to take all the necessary precautions when making the repair.

A temporary patch for ABS tanks can easily be fashioned by mixing some fine shavings of ABS plastic with some ABS cement, roughing up the area around the flaw, and quickly applying a thin layer of this mixture to the crack and surrounding area. Next, work in a thin strip of cotton fabric and apply another layer or coating of ABS cement. Allow this patch to completely dry, then repeat the process again. Gradually add layer upon layer until the area over and around the crack appears thicker and stronger. Finally, allow the entire patch to cure for 24 hours before filling with water. Keep in mind that this may only prove to be a temporary fix, and it may be necessary to eventually have the crack welded by a professional.

Testing the Results—Always allow ample time for curing or drying after a repair to a holding tank. Typically, 24 hours for ABS and polyethylene tanks is sufficient when an aftermarket patch kit is employed. If either tank was professionally welding using a plastic welding machine and welding rod, the tank can be tested immediately.

It is recommended that a static leak test be performed prior to reinstalling any holding tank after a repair. Carefully support or suspend the holding tank between two saw horses and plug the outlet. An alternative to plugging the outlet is to temporarily reinstall the dump assembly and simply close the dump valve. Fill the tank with fresh water through one of the openings in the top of the tank. Allow the filled tank to sit for 30 minutes while you closely monitor the area that originally leaked. If no moisture appears during the 30-minute test, the repair was successful. If a leak persists, try the repair again. In some cases, the crack may be in a location that is under stress when installed and simply cannot be sealed. In those instances, welding may be the only viable option.

Once successful, drain the water from the tank and reinstall the holding tank in the reverse manner in which it was removed. Any ABS drain or vent pipe that had to be cut in order to remove the tank will now have to be reconnected by using ABS cement and a common ABS coupling of that particular diameter.

Connect the dump assemblies, taking care to align all parts so that both termination valves operate smoothly. Now is a good time to clean and lubricate the dump valves. Be sure each is fully closed and the sewer cap is in place.

Reconnect all monitor panel wires that were previously disconnected. Simply match the correct wire to the level indicator positions of well nut located on the side of the tank.

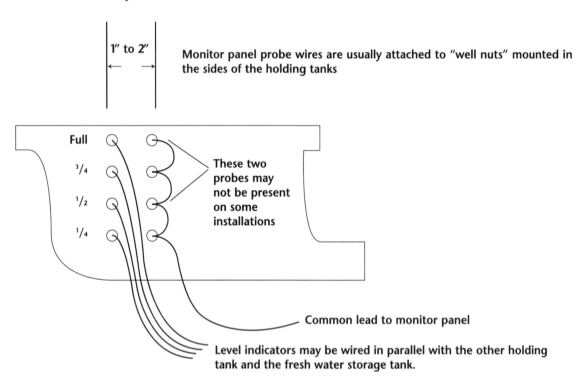

Align the toilet flange and secure it to the top of the holding tank through the opening in the floor. Be sure to use pipe sealant on any threaded fitting and ABS cement on any glue-type slip fitting. If the tank is equipped with the rubber grommet-type of connection, use either pipe sealant, tube silicone or a spray lubricant to assist in the reinstallation. Coat the inside of the grommet and the outside of the three-inch ABS down pipe.

Reinstall the toilet being certain to use a new flange gasket. Attach the water line and check for leaks at that point by subjecting the inlet fitting to city water pressure.

Once again, fill the tank through the toilet and allow the water to completely fill and back up into the toilet itself. By overfilling the tank in this manner, every component part is effectively tested. If there are no leaks, drain the tank through the dump assembly as usual.

Allow plenty of time for making holding tank repairs. Rushed jobs are often unsuccessful. Those owners who exhibit patience and persistence usually succeed.

RV TOILETS: We want our travels to be as trouble-free as possible, knowing all along that just by virtue of having a house on wheels bouncing along the highway, things are going to happen. We really do not mind washing the coach, repairing a small window leak, or even performing a lengthy winterizing procedure. Shoot, we do not even mind taking out the garbage every day, But please...! Let us not have any malfunction with the toilet!

When unforeseen problems develop, the one area we seem to dread the most is the holding tank area, or more specifically, a problem with the toilet. However, it must be realized that components with moving parts that also move down the highway are going to need periodic attention.

Though quite simple, yet functional in design, the three types of RV toilets provide us with the comforts of home while traveling. Having an understanding of the different types of toilets, along with basic knowledge of repair procedures, can prevent inconveniences with relative ease. Each RV toilet has individual characteristics and varying applications. The three types are:
- Marine toilet
- Recirculating toilet
- Portable toilet

Marine Toilet – By far the most common type of toilet in today's RV is the marine toilet. It is permanently mounted and plumbed into the fresh water piping system. Most are gravity-flushed by operating a mechanical seal that typically opens the drain and turns the water on at the same time.

The marine toilet requires a holding tank. The toilet is simply bolted to the floor flange and connected through the floor to the tank below. Although most applications mandate the toilet be positioned directly over the holding tank, Sealand Technology recently introduced a vacuum-flushed RV toilet that permits the holding tank to be as much as 20 feet away from the toilet. Marine toilets are compact and fit well into the varying RV floorplans. They are constructed without the typical back tank found on most common household toilets. Water enters the bowl directly from the fresh water system. The swirling motion of the incoming water rinses and flushes the toilet into the holding tank.

All marine toilets have a positive water seal to prevent holding tank odors from entering the coach. As an RV owner, it is important to check this water seal daily. Doing so will pinpoint potential problem areas before they actually develop. Always make sure a small amount of water actually stays in the bowl after the flushing cycle has completed.

Toilet makers employ varying mechanisms to facilitate flushing the toilet. Sealand Technology's upscale china toilets have a single foot pedal, while Thetford's popular Aqua Magic series has dual foot pedals to operate the mechanism and to open the water flow. They too, offer a china bowl toilet for those who wish to upgrade. Both are designed for minimal water consumption.

The common RV marine toilets utilize an internal vacuum breaker, which is basically a backflow device. Without the breaker, water being drawn at a distant galley sink, for instance, could theoretically create a partial vacuum that may cause water to be siphoned from the bowl of the toilet. The vacuum breaker serves as a one-way check valve of sorts.

All marine toilets mount to a standard floor flange that is secured to the RV floor. A toilet-to-flange seal or gasket is required in all instances. Additionally, all rough-in dimensions are virtually the same, which means the RVer can upgrade or otherwise replace toilets at any time. The only consideration would be the base design and the position of the flange closet bolts. Not all marine toilets have the same pedestal or base construction, so carpet, tile or linoleum cut-outs may not match.

There are two types of base-to-flange seals available: rubber and wax. It is wise to carry a spare seal. Rubber seals have the advantage because they are not drastically affected by heat. If travel is predominantly in the Sun Belt areas, a loosening of the toilet may occur in hot summer months. Ambient or radiated heat can actually melt a wax seal. In effect, as the seal collapses, it appears the toilet mounting bolts have loosened and the toilet wobbles on its base. It will be necessary to tighten the bolts periodically should the toilet be equipped with a wax seal.

Wax seals can also be quite messy when doing repairs on some specific models of toilets. The rubber seal, on the other hand, is spongier and is not as affected by hot weather. Regardless of which seal is preferred, *always* replace the seal each time the toilet is removed from the floor flange.

Recirculating Toilet – Totally self-contained, recirculating toilets do not require a holding tank or a fresh water supply, although some can be plumbed into the fresh system for ease in filling or "charging." This type is commonly found in smaller trailers and slide-in pick-up campers where design limitations prohibit the placement of a holding tank. The main benefit of a recirculating toilet is that no holding tank is necessary.

The toilet is "charged" with its own water supply of specifically treated water that circulates again and again to flush the contents from the bowl. Only the treated liquid is recirculated. A filtering device inside the main housing traps the solid waste. Recirculation is facilitated by a 12-volt DC motor attached to an internal submerged pump. A timer mechanism regulates the flush cycle.

The waste is held in an internal reservoir until full, and then the unit is flushed through a typical floor flange and flexible sewer hose into either the campground sewer connection or a standard dump station. A full-flow slide valve is usually an integral component of the recirculating toilet. Additionally, a standard three-inch termination valve will be attached to the dump assembly on the exterior of the RV. To dump a recirculating toilet, attach the flexible sewer hose to the campground sewer and to the dump assembly on the RV. Open the RV dump valve. Next, inside the coach, open the slide valve on the toilet. It is recommended to pour additional fresh water through the toilet to rinse out the drain piping and the flexible sewer hose before closing the valves.

Portable Toilet – Smaller trailers and van campers may come equipped with a portable toilet. A common design has two compartments: a fresh water storage tank and a separate holding tank. A hand operated bellows pumps fresh water from the tank into the bowl and rinses the waste (some may be battery operated as well). A foot pedal then operates the flushing mechanism to dump the bowl contents into the lower compartment. When the lower holding tank is in need of dumping, it can be easily removed and carried to the dump station. While in the RV, the toilet is attached to the floor with quick release brackets for ease of removal when dumping is necessary. As with any RV toilet, it is wise to rinse and flush the bowl and the flushing mechanism thoroughly after each evacuation at the dump station.

User Maintenance—Common sense is important when using any of the different types of RV toilets. Never flush solid objects down the toilet. Do not flush cigarette butts or gum wrappers, etc. Use only biodegradable toilet tissue.

Recirculating and portable toilets will require a treatment for odor control and solid waste breakdown. Do not use formaldehyde or alcohol-base substances. Recirculating toilets especially need a method of odor control since there is no vapor barrier or positive water seal between the stored waste and the interior of the RV in most cases.

When cleaning the toilet during the camping season, avoid using abrasive cleansers. RV toilets are constructed of either ABS plastic, ceramic, or china, so choose the cleanser that is friendly to the construction material of the toilet. Remember, most RV toilets have rubber or Teflon seals, so care must be taken not to introduce harmful cleaning agents that will damage the seals.

MARINE TOILET TROUBLESHOOTING AND REPAIR: Yearly maintenance can eliminate or at least minimize certain repairs. However, when repetitive mechanical movement of parts takes place, a certain amount of wear begins. This continues until a component fatigues or just plain gives out, and a repair is in order.

The most popular RV toilet, the marine-type is relatively free from operational troubles, but without a few maintenance items, problems can still develop. Not unlike the RV demand water pump, most toilet makers have individual replacement parts and repair kits that are readily available at most RV parts and accessory stores.

As a general rule, all repair kits come with well-written instructions along with all the parts needed for a replacement task. The only job you really have to do is to troubleshoot the symptoms correctly. First, let us look at the basic components of the RV marine toilet.

Components – Although toilet design and component construction materials may differ among the various manufacturers, the same basic components are found in each. They are:
- •Water inlet valve
- •Vacuum breaker assembly
- •Flushing mechanism
- •Flange to base attaching point
- •Bowl assembly

Water Inlet Valve—This is the fresh water connection point at the rear of the toilet. On some Thetford models it is also called a ball valve because the valve closing device is actually a small steel ball with a hole machined through that rotates in a plastic housing. Since this device could corrode or simply wear out over a period of time, it might be a wise decision for full-timers and boondockers to add an inlet valve repair kit to the spare parts inventory.

Vacuum Breaker Assembly—As mentioned earlier, the vacuum breaker prevents water from being siphoned out of the toilet bowl due to a pressure drop caused by water being used somewhere else in the fresh water system. Vacuum breakers also contain a float assembly, a seat and an assortment of seals. Some are repairable, while others must be replaced. Check with the manufacturer of your toilet to determine the availability of repair kits.

Thetford Flushing Mechanism

Ball valve water inlet

Check valve

Slide valve

Pedal mechanisms

Flushing Mechanism—Flushing mechanism designs differ, but the two most popular include Thetford's flat-blade slide mechanism and Sealand's half-round flush ball with a Teflon seal. Both are initiated by activating a foot pedal. Foot pedal flushing on these common units also automatically opens the water inlet valve and allows fresh water to enter and circulate in the bowl as it flushes the contents into the holding tank.

Both Thetford and Sealand have made it possible to add more water to the bowl after the flush, if desired. Thetford's popular models including the new Aurora model, have a separate foot pedal that opens the ball valve only, allowing more water to enter the bowl. By lifting up on Sealand's foot pedal instead of pressing down, the water inlet valve is opened and likewise, water fills into the bowl. Typically, the flushing mechanism and the water inlet valve will account for the majority of user complaints with marine toilets.

Flange Attachment—All toilets attach to a standard floor flange, which is secured to the floor of the RV. Attached to the floor flange are two or four closet bolts that secure the toilet to the flange. A gasket is positioned between the flange and the base of the toilet.

The position of the closet bolts will vary between brand and even

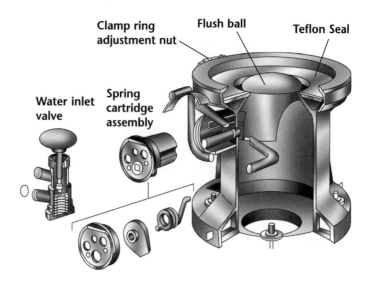

Sealland Flushing Mechanism

Clamp ring adjustment nut · Flush ball · Teflon Seal · Water inlet valve · Spring cartridge assembly

model of the same manufacturer. A popular model by Thetford uses two bolts located at the 5 and 11 o'clock positions on the floor flange. Other Thetford models have bolts positioned at 3 and 9 o'clock. Sealland, meanwhile, uses four mounting bolts, two in the front and two at the rear of the flange.

Common Complaints – Problems associated with the marine toilet are few, but over time, they do crop up occasionally. The most common complaints will center around these issues:

The rear closet bolt on this Thetford toilet is reached through an access hole under the seat by using a socket wrench, a universal joint and a 12″ extension.

• Water leaks
• Odor
• Water continues to run
• Flushing mechanism sticks

Water Leaks—There are four reasons why water may be leaking at or near the marine toilet. By checking where the water is coming from and exactly when the water appears, RVers can pinpoint which of the four main causes is the culprit.

If water drips to the floor from the upper portion of the base of the toilet, during the flushing cycle only, the problem is the vacuum breaker. Usually a float seal is not seating properly. On some units, the float can be disassembled and cleaned. Other models will require a repair kit. Still others may require a complete new vacuum breaker. To make sure, check the user's manual.

If water leaks onto the floor after the flush cycle has completed, or without flushing the toilet at all, the culprit is the water inlet valve.

Sometimes water will appear to be leaking only if the bowl is filled to capacity. There is a slight possibility the bowl is cracked at a point above the normal water level. This is not a very common situation, but it does happen occasionally and is usually caused by improper winterizing techniques. This is only possible with toilets made with plastic bowls.

Water may also be noticed around the base of the toilet with no apparent or visible dripping from above. Chances are the seal between the flange and the base assembly is faulty. Remove the toilet and replace the gasket.

Odor—Odor coming from the holding tank directly below the toilet is usually a sign there is no water being kept in the bowl, or that the water has leaked past the flushing mechanism and into the holding tank. This water seal is crucial for keeping the tank odors from permeating the interior of the RV. This situation is caused, in most cases, by foreign matter becoming trapped in the groove for the slide blade on Thetford's Aqua Magic units. On Sealand's unit, a typical cause is a worn seal or a clamp ring that is too loose.

On the Aqua Magic, fashion a hook out of a coat hanger or a bent screwdriver that will reach into the groove to scrape out the residue. Take special care not to damage the seal.

To rectify the situation on the Sealand toilet, simply tighten the clamp ring. In some cases, a complete seal kit may have to be installed in either brand if water still continues to seep past the seal and into the holding tank. It is imperative that some water stay in the bowl at all times.

Water Continues to Run—The predominant cause of this situation is a stubborn slide valve keeping the water inlet valve open. In some cases, the water inlet valve itself may be faulty, allowing water to continually enter the bowl. If the water that continues to run does not stay in the bowl but flows on through to the holding tank, the problem is usually a slide valve or flush ball that is held partially open. It is either stuck or is kept open by foreign matter wedged between the seal and the half ball or the slide. If it is obvious the slide mechanism or half ball is fully shut yet water simply continues to enter the bowl, chances are the cause is a faulty water inlet valve.

Flushing Mechanism Sticks—If the Thetford toilet is mounted too tightly to the floor flange, the base of the mechanism becomes distorted and the blade will not slide smoothly in the housing. Loosening the closet bolts and lubricating the slide blade will usually eradicate this symptom.

Occasionally, abrasive cleaners can accumulate as deposits inside the slide mechanism impeding the movement of the blade. In this instance, a complete removal and cleaning is in order. Again, be sure to liberally lubricate all slide blade components.

As previously mentioned, many repair kits and replacement parts are readily available for all RV toilets. Parts that are not available in kit form can be ordered through any RV parts and accessory store or directly from the toilet manufacturer.

GENERAL WASTE SYSTEM MAINTENANCE AND REPAIRS: Waste system problems that arise are no different than those anticipated in any other housing situation. Here are some items to check.

All drain pipes must be suspended or supported in the RV. Periodically, inspect the entire length of the drain piping system inside and underneath the coach. Look for road damage and broken supports. Also, if the configuration warrants, visually inspect the bottom of each holding tank.

Check in and around all "P" traps, sink drains, etc., for any moisture. Store only soft goods and lightweight supplies under sinks or in areas where plumbing drain pipes are run.

Pay close attention to the termination assembly area. Make sure the outlet cap is firmly attached before traveling. If liquid is present when this cap is removed prior to connecting to the park sewer, a leaky termination valve may exist. Be certain all valves are closed tight.

In cold climates, be aware of freeze damage, especially when storing the RV. Avoid using extremely caustic drain cleaners. Because of the proliferation of plastic drain pipes in the housing industry, all household-type drain cleaners used today are usually acceptable in RVs as well.

Rigid ABS drain pipes are pretty durable under normal use. However, ABS dump assemblies are no match for curbs or dips in the roadway. The most common repairs to ABS drain lines are caused by the RV bottoming out. Any impact will result in a few broken or cracked plastic fittings or dump valves. In some cases, the entire waste piping system below the floor line can be wiped out, including the holding tanks.

Unprotected waste drain plumbing must be foremost in your mind as the RV enters and departs steep driveways, crosses over speed bumps or when dodging road debris and potholes. A little too much speed, a too-steep approach angle or a too quick or too slow reaction time can all lead to an additional repair and a not-so-pleasant one at that, in an olfactory sense.

Other than "P" traps and an occasional fitting, all other ABS fittings are usually cemented throughout the RV. If a pipe or fitting needs to be replaced, it will be necessary to first cut out the bad section with a hacksaw and then to insert a new section. When making ABS pipe repairs, keep these items in mind:

- Protect the work area. Spilled ABS cement will ruin virtually any floor covering.
- Have all pieces cut and sized to fit before cementing.
- Lightly sand or bevel the edges of a cut section of pipe for easy insertion into the fitting.
- Cut the pipe square. Avoid angling the hacksaw during the cut.
- Apply the ABS cement to both pipe and fitting and insert quickly.
- Immediately after inserting the pipe into the fitting, slowly rotate the pipe 90 degrees.
- Allow freshly cemented fittings to cure before running water in the lines. Refer to the instructions listed on the side of the cement container for specific details.

The bottom line is simple: Although unpleasant as it may seem, left unattended, the RV waste systems will increasingly become more unpleasant unless a few simple preventive maintenance tasks are performed each year. Doing so, will enhance the enjoyment of the RV (and your camping neighbors will appreciate it too)!

CHAPTER SIX

Liquid Propane Systems

Liquefied petroleum gas, commonly referred to simply as LP, is a remarkable fuel. Stored as a liquid, but used as a vapor, LP is extremely proficient at satisfying our need for the creature comforts of home while traveling. Self-contained cooking, heating, refrigeration and hot water are all possible because of the direct compatibility of liquid propane with the RV design concept. One remarkable fact about LP is that a lot of it can be compressed into a relatively small container. For every gallon stored as a liquid, LP will expand to over 36 cubic feet of usable gas to be burned at the appliances. For RVing purposes alone, it is a very effective fuel.

LP USAGE AND STORAGE

The most important factor concerning LP is safety. Safety in filling, handling, storing and using must remain paramount in the minds of every RVer. LP is considered a safe and reliable product, yet it is flammable, so care must be taken at every juncture. If, when performing any procedure detailed in this handbook, you do not feel completely comfortable with the safety aspect of the situation, do not proceed. You must satisfy yourself thoroughly that neither personal nor equipment safety will be jeopardized before proceeding. Never compromise the safety factor!

Propane, butane, ethane, methane and natural gas are all classified as liquefied petroleum gases. All but natural gas are hydrocarbons, and each will give off heat as a by-product. Propane is most closely related to butane. The chemical formula for propane is C_3H_8, while butane is C_4H_{10}. Notice the two gases are very similar. Butane consists of one more molecule of carbon and two additional molecules of hydrogen, making butane a slightly heavier gas. Natural gas is also often compared to LP. For those familiar with natural gas used as a fuel, here's a chart that provides some comparisons.

Property	Propane	Natural Gas
Formula	C3H8	CH4
Specific Gravity (as a gas) air = 1.00	1.225	1.185
Boiling Point	-44° F	-258° F
Heat Output (BTU per) gallon	91,600	-----
pound	21,600	-----
cubic foot	2,520	1,000

The fact that propane has a dew point (boiling point) of −44 degrees, makes it the perfect fuel for the appliances found on RVs. In years past, butane was also used as a fuel in RVs. Its boiling point is only 32 degrees above zero, which meant it was virtually useless when the temperature dipped below freezing; not unheard of for those who enjoy winter RVing. Propane, though, is the favored choice of fuel today. Different blends do exist, but by and large, it is all propane.

LP is inherently odorless. An odorant called ethyl mercaptan is added during the distilling process. Its distinct smell leaves no doubt when LP is present. If this odorant is evident at any time during any RVing excursion, immediately extinguish all appliances and turn the LP service valve off. Have the RV thoroughly checked to be sure there are no leaks prior to operating the appliances again. Remember, never compromise the safety factor!

A clear and distinct odor does not necessarily indicate there is a LP leak, however. It is common after refilling the LP container to experience a residual odor for a while, but it should soon subside. If it persists, however, a leak test is in order. Additionally, when a container of LP is completely emptied during usage, it is also common to sense a strong smell of the odorant, which remains behind in the empty tank when it becomes accentuated due to the absence of LP.

So how is LP safely stored and carried in the RV? There are two types of LP containers used in RVs: DOT cylinders and ASME tanks. Both types must comply with rigid codes pertaining to their construction. One is built to the specifications of the American Society of Mechanical Engineers (ASME). The other conforms to the specs formulated by the Department of Transportation (DOT). Both types are subject to the codes and standards governed by the RV Industry Association (RVIA). Understanding the differences between the two types of LP storage containers and their individual components will help gain insights into using the RV effectively and efficiently.

TYPES OF LP CONTAINERS:

DOT Cylinders – The DOT cylinder is common to travel trailers and some motorhomes and pick-up campers. They are usually secured to the "A" frame on the tongue of the trailer. In some instances, they may be found in a separate compartment accessed from the exterior of the RV. Such compartments must be sealed from the living portion of the RV. They are manufactured for use in either an upright position or a horizontal position, however, an upright DOT cylinder cannot be used in a horizontal position and a horizontal cylinder cannot be utilized in an upright position. Each houses different internal components that facilitate use in one position or the other, but not both. Additionally, they should be transported in their respective positions at all times, especially when filled. Always use a safety plug in the outlet valve when transporting LP containers.

The sizing of DOT cylinders can been somewhat confusing, and the method of filling varies as well. In some parts of the country, LP is sold by the gallon (remember, it is stored as a liquid); in others, it is sold by the pound. So what may be a five-gallon container in California, may very well be a 20-pound cylinder in Illinois. In some areas, the LP is pumped into the tank and measured by the gallon. In others, the container is weighed before and after filling, and you pay for the weight in pounds of LP transferred into the cylinder. Here is a chart that also indicates the amount of BTUs available in each size cylinder.

DOT Cylinders		
Gallons of Liquid	**Pounds of Gas**	**BTU**
1.0	5	91,600
2.5	11	229,000
4.8	20	439,680
7.2	30	659,520
9.2	40	842,720

One advantage of DOT cylinders is that they can be easily removed and transported to the filling location. On a typical dual-tank setup, such as on a standard travel trailer, it is possible to remove and fill one cylinder while the RV operates off the other. ASME tanks, on the other hand, are permanently mounted and are seldom, if ever, removed. To fill an ASME tank, the motorhome must be driven to a filling location.

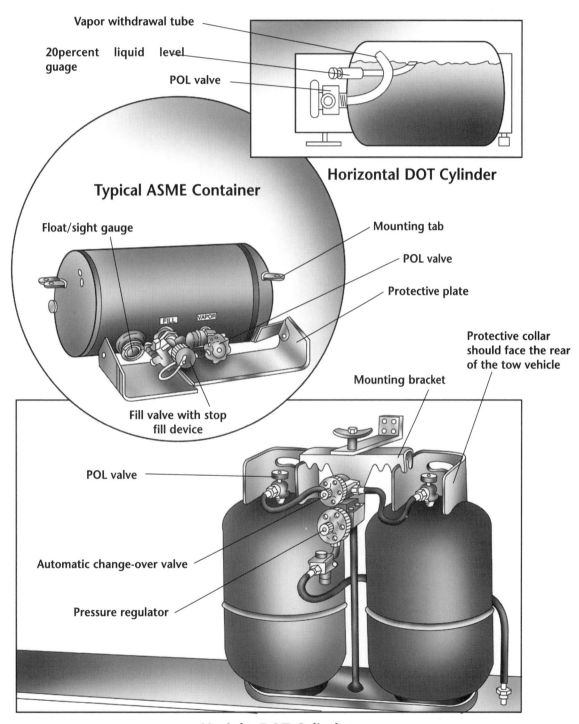

Vapor withdrawal tube

20percent liquid level guage

POL valve

Horizontal DOT Cylinder

Typical ASME Container

Float/sight gauge

Mounting tab

POL valve

Protective plate

Protective collar should face the rear of the tow vehicle

Mounting bracket

Fill valve with stop fill device

POL valve

Automatic change-over valve

Pressure regulator

Upright DOT Cylinder
Typical mounting on travel trailer

ASME Tanks – Another type of LP storage vessel found on RVs is the frame-mounted ASME container. Usually installed on motorhomes, the ASME tank is always mounted horizontally and usually permanently. Traditionally, they have a larger capacity than that of their DOT cousins, hence, they are found on the larger Class A motorhomes. RV manufacturers must comply with strict guidelines as to where ASME tanks can be located.

CONTAINER COMPONENTS: There are a few basic components found on all LP containers. Some are associated with both types, while others are unique to a particular type.

Typical ASME container

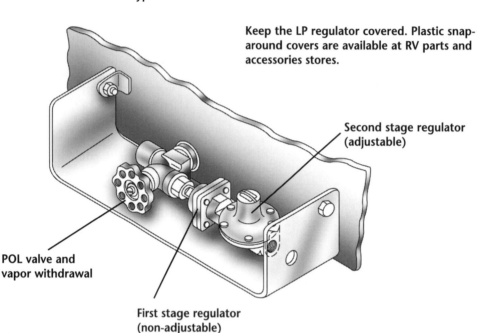

Keep the LP regulator covered. Plastic snap-around covers are available at RV parts and accessories stores.

Second stage regulator (adjustable)

POL valve and vapor withdrawal

First stage regulator (non-adjustable)

Service valve—Found on both types. It is the most used component on the container, the main outlet valve. In the past, the majority of containers were equipped with the common POL valve. The term POL has been around for a long time, but not many know its origin. Originally, POL was an abbreviation for a California manufacturer of gas-related fittings and products called Prest-O-Lite. Later, POL became known as the acronym for Put On Left since the fitting that mates with it is a left-handed threaded fitting.

Recently, however, a new industry innovation burst upon the scene. Instead of the tried and true POL-type service valve, enter the new RV Type I CGA 791 valve. The new connection features a wrenchless, swivel nut that can be tightened and loosened by hand. Additionally, the 1-5/16-inch Acme threads are right-handed threads. The new valve contains an internal, spring-loaded component that prohibits all gas flow from the container until a positive, leak-free connection has been made. The CGA 791 valve, configured with the new external Acme thread also houses the standard, internal, left-hand POL threads for adaptation to the older RVs.

The swivel nut, green in color for RV applications, has a unique bushing that if heated to 240 degrees Farenheit, will melt, permitting the spring-loaded module in the valve to move enough

Type I ASME Cylinder Valve

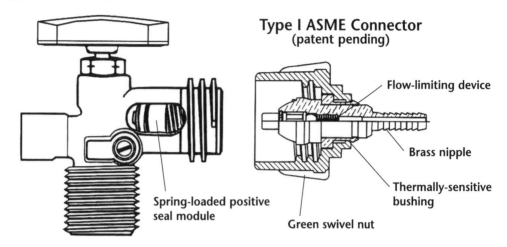

Type I ASME Connector
(patent pending)

Flow-limiting device

Brass nipple

Thermally-sensitive bushing

Spring-loaded positive seal module

Green swivel nut

to effectively stop the flow of LP from the container. This fire-related safety feature, coupled with a built-in flow limiting device in the connector, helps insure the safety of the RVer in the event a collision separates the container from the connection and/or a fire develops.

The flow-limiting device situated in the connector is also designed to sense excessive gas flow. When excessive flow is sensed, the device slows the flow to a maximum of 10 SCFH (Standard Cubic Feet per Hour). This is called the bypass flow. Why is this important for the RVer to understand? Because if the LP container valve is opened too quickly, the flow-limiting device may be activated. This is why. When all the LP appliances are turned off, the bypass flow allows the pressure to equalize within the entire system. When the pressure is equalized, normal LP flow is passed through the flow limiting valve. It takes, in most cases, about five seconds for the system to equalize. But if an appliance is left on or if a leak develops anywhere in the system downstream of the regulator, the bypass pressure will not equalize, thereby prohibiting the flow-limiting valve from opening once again. Symptoms of this condition include appliances that may light, but the flame size will be smaller than normal, or a flame that simply burns completely out. In some cases, a pilot flame may be extremely difficult to light.

To eliminate this condition, completely shut down all LP appliances and close the container valve. Wait about five minutes and then slowly open the container valve. Do not twist it open rapidly. Wait a minimum 15 minutes before lighting the appliances. If the flow-limiting condition still exists, there may be a leak somewhere in the system and a full-on leak test is in order. (Performing a system leak test will be discussed later in this chapter.)

Twenty percent liquid level gauge—Sometimes mistakenly called the 10 percent valve. It is a separate component on all ASME tanks, but is usually built into the service valve on upright DOT cylinders. It is a requirement in most states and is employed to properly fill the container. It is a virtual necessity when dispensing the LP fuel by the gallon. It lets the attendant know when the container is 80 percent full. Note: Never "top off" the tank to the maximum capacity. The tank should only be filled to 80 percent of the maximum capacity. The top 20 percent of every LP container is for the vapor area and to accommodate the expansion of the LP. By far the most common type of abuse associated with LP containers is overfilling.

Vapor withdrawal tube—Integral to horizontal containers only. It is an internal tube positioned in the upper 20 percent of the container—the vapor space. It assures that only vapor is withdrawn and processed through the regulator and into the piping system. Remember, LP is stored as a liquid, but burned in the appliances as a gas. Overfilling of the container causes liquid to fill this tube and be delivered through the regulator to the system. This condition will ruin the regulator and cause serious damage to the LP appliances. In severe cases, the entire piping system must be replaced.

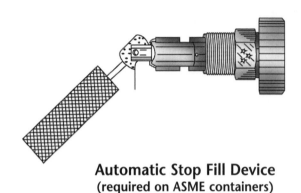

Automatic Stop Fill Device
(required on ASME containers)

Mounts permanently in ASME containers. Automatically shuts off incoming LP during the filling process once container is 80 percent full.

Safety Valve—Built into all service valves. This is a spring loaded device that monitors the interior pressure of the container. The container pressure will only get high enough to open the relief valve under the following conditions: containers not properly purged of air, container is overfilled or container is exposed to heat. All three conditions are to be avoided. The pressure relief valve on ASME containers is a separate component attached directly to the tank and is not an integral portion of the service valve.

Fill valve—On DOT cylinders, this is actually the service valve. Filling and withdrawing LP is effectuated through the same valve on DOT cylinders. On ASME containers, however, it is a separate component. A recent requirement mandates that all LP containers, ASME and DOT alike, be equipped with an overfill protection device, referred to as OPD. This listed and approved safety mechanism makes certain the tank will not be overfilled. This ruling became effective in September 1997.

Float/sight gauge—May be common to both types of containers. This device provides a visual indication of how much fuel is left in the container. Outfitted with a sending unit, it can be remotely connected to the monitor panel inside the RV. Usually only associated with ASME tanks, an aftermarket replacement service valve assembly for DOT cylinders can be installed that has a float gauge as an integral portion of that assembly as well.

Mounting brackets/collars—Protects the service valve and aperture areas from flying road debris, rocks and gravel. It also provides the method of attachment to the RV in most instances.

Data plate—Located on each container. It provides specific information regarding that particular vessel. On ASME tanks, it will be on a

Float Assembly for ASME Containers

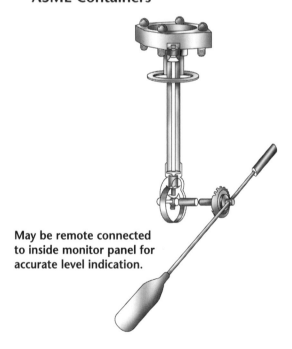

May be remote connected to inside monitor panel for accurate level indication.

plate welded to the tank; on the DOT cylinders, it is simply stamped into the protective collar. Stamped information includes tare weight (TW), which is the weight of the empty container and main shutoff valve assembly. Other data include the water capacity rating (WC), which is the capacity of the container if filled with water, the maximum it can hold. This figure, minus 20 percent, is considered the maximum LP content when properly filled.

An easy way to determine how much LP is remaining in a partially emptied DOT cylinder is to remove the cylinder and weigh. Subtract the tare weight (stamped on the collar) and divide the remaining figure by 4.2, which is approximately how much LP weighs per gallon. The resulting figure will be how many gallons are left in the cylinder.

Each gallon can provide about 91,500 BTUs of energy. To determine how long the LP will last, add up all the input BTU ratings of the four LP burning appliances. The input rating per hour can be found on the data plate of each appliance or by looking in the owner's manual of each appliance. Approximate the length of time each appliance will be operated that day and divide that figure into the 91,500. This final figure will be the approximate daily LP consumption.

Requalification of DOT Cylinders: The date of manufacture can also be found on the collar of the DOT cylinder. This is important since federal regulations now require periodic requalification of all DOT cylinders. One approved requalification method is a complete external visual inspection. When the visual inspection method is used, the first inspection and requalification is due 12 years after the original date of manufacture. Subsequent inspections and requalification are required every five years after that.

If the RV is equipped with DOT cylinders, check the date on the collar. Refilling may be refused if the cylinder is due for requalification. Do not use an older cylinder until it has been properly inspected, requalified and stamped accordingly.

The National Propane Gas Association and the Compressed Gas Association have outlined specific instructions for inspectors to follow to properly requalify DOT cylinders. What can be done to be sure DOT containers will pass the mandated visual inspection for requalification?

First, do not allow rust to build up on the LP cylinders, especially around the bottom base ring. Since the cylinders are constantly exposed to the weather, they are very susceptible to rust. Remove any evidence of rust or corrosion yearly and maintain a good covering of paint. During the visual inspection, each bottle will be scrutinized for pits caused by corrosion, so the more attention provided to this area, the more likely it will pass the inspection.

There are two terms to remember when considering the requalification inspection: condemned and rejected. Any bottle that is condemned due to its physical condition cannot under any circumstances be utilized further. It must be scrapped. If a cylinder is rejected, it simply means that it cannot be used until adequate repairs have been made. However, such repairs must be made by either the manufacturer of that cylinder or by a facility that is authorized by the Bureau of Explosives. It will, in all honesty, be easier (and more cost effective) to simply replace the cylinder with a new one should it be rejected.

The inspection includes looking for, measuring and analyzing dents, cuts or gouges in the metal of the container. Bulges or damages due to exposure to fire or abuse are also considered. Different types of corrosion will be checked: isolated pitting, line corrosion and general corrosion. In addition, close inspection around the neck area where the POL service valve is threaded into the bottle will take place. The collar and cylinder ring will also be inspected for corrosion and pitting.

There are specific condemnation rules that apply to each of the aforementioned areas of concern. RVers can eliminate early cylinder replacement and retain structural integrity by removing rust and applying a primer and coat of paint on a yearly basis.

PURGING LP CONTAINERS: All new, and in some cases used, LP containers may contain water, air or other contaminants that are not conducive to LP and appliances. All contaminates should be removed prior to placing the tank into service. This pertains to DOT and ASME containers alike. Water vapor present in the gas vapor may cause erratic regulator performance. It also makes the regulator more susceptible to freeze-ups. Additionally, it will have an effect on the odorant that is added to the LP.

Air inside the container may cause an abnormally high tank pressure, which can in turn cause the pressure relief valve to open. Poor combustion and erratic appliance operation are sure to result from either water or air being inside any LP container if allowed to stay there. If reduced performance is associated with any two or more of the appliances, it may indicate the LP container is in need of purging. Normally, purging of LP containers is performed by an LP dealer. Al RVers should, however, be aware of the procedures. They are:

- Determine if the container pressure is zero. Should it hold only air pressure (as in new tanks, which are leak-tested at the manufacturer and usually shipped containing air), it can simply be released to the atmosphere. If it is a used bottle and contains LP, the local LP retailer should be equipped with a large burner that can be connected to the container and the remaining contents burned off. NEVER release filled LP containers into the atmosphere.
- Drain any water that may have settled in the bottom of the container. This is no problem with DOT cylinders, however, ASME tanks will have to be removed from the coach in order to drain the water.
- Next, pressurize the container with approximately 15 PSI of LP vapor. Containers should never be purged with liquid. Water vapor will freeze and remain in the container if the purging is done with liquid LP.
- Vent this vapor in a safe area through the service valve.
- Repeat this vapor filling and venting process four more times.
- Methanol is then added to the container to absorb any remaining molecules of moisture. Another 15 PSI of LP vapor is then introduced into the container.
- The container is now ready for liquid filling and regular usage. Leak tests should be performed on all fittings before putting the container into service.

LP REGULATOR: All four of the major LP appliances typical of most RVs require an operating line pressure of what is measured as 11 inches of water column. Just what does this pressure measurement mean? A water column inch is a unit of measurement used for small, minute measurements of either pressure or vacuum.

The operating pressure in the RV is relatively small. How small? Eleven inches of water column is equal to about four-tenths of one PSI (0.4 PSI). To measure such small increments, it is necessary to use a device called a water column manometer. The manometer is one of the recommended RV specialty tools noted in Chapter 3. No one, under any circumstances, should adjust the LP regulator without the aid of a water column manometer. The slight amount of change that occurs in the structure of a typical burner flame when adjusting the regulator will not be readily visible with the naked eye. The increment is small, yet higher than normal pressures can be devastating to the delicate components internal to appliance gas control valves.

The liquid LP stored in the container has no specific set pressure. It will vary depending on how much fuel is in the tank, the ambient temperature and the atmospheric pressure on the outside of the tank. Suffice it to say that it is much higher than the actual 0.4 of one PSI used at the appliances. Internal container pressures exceeding 200 PSI are not unheard of. By opening the POL or service valve, the inlet side of the regulator is subjected to the existing container pressure, whatever it may happen to be at the time. Here is what happens inside a simple regulator.

As the fuel reaches the orifice of the regulator, it expands at a rapid rate and vaporizes into a gas. Remember, LP is stored as a liquid, but utilized as a gas. As LP gas enters the main body of the regulator below the rubber diaphragm, it pushes up on the expanding diaphragm. As the diaphragm moves up, the mechanical linkage moves the seat assembly away from the orifice and closer to the shut-off point at the seat.

Marshall Gas Regulator

The resistance against this upward movement of the diaphragm is provided by the main spring situated below the adjusting nut under the dust cap. As the incoming gas pressure overpowers the strength of the main spring, more LP enters the main body of the regulator. The more the diaphragm moves up, the less gas is allowed to enter the regulator until it finally shuts off completely at the seat assembly.

If a burner is lit on the stove or if the water heater cycles, or even if a leak were to develop anywhere in the system, the pressure inside the regulator will drop allowing the spring to depress the diaphragm. This, in turn, moves the linkage away from the seat allowing the LP fuel to once again enter the regulator, overpower the main spring and fill the system with LP gas.

As long as a burner is lit, the regulator continues this monitoring of outlet pressure and the regulating of fluctuating input tank pressures. When no fuel is needed anywhere in the system and the service valve is still open at the LP container, fuel flow will stop at the seat assembly inside the regulator.

Dual Stage LP Regulator

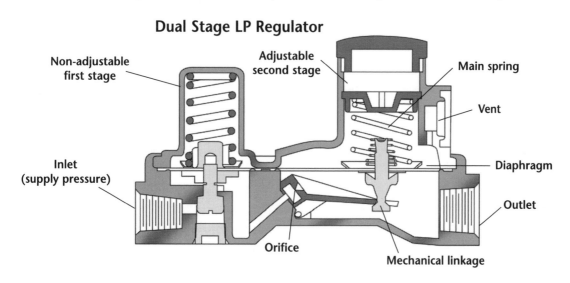

One can easily see just how much work the LP regulator actually performs, and usually under not-so-pleasant circumstances at that. It must constantly monitor tank pressures that could regularly exceed 200 PSI and yet deliver a smooth flow of LP at a pressure of 11 inches of water column, which is just 0.4 of one PSI! It is indeed a workhorse.

All newer RVs are equipped with a dual-stage regulator. This simply means that the tank pressure is reduced to 11 inches of water column in two distinct steps. The first stage reduces the tank pressure to approximately ten PSI, then the second stage reduces it further to the 11 inches of water column used at the appliances.

It is most advantageous to utilize a two-stage regulator. All newer RVs are already equipped with one. Typically dual-stage regulators last longer, deliver a smoother flow of LP and are less prone to freeze-ups. Seeing just what the regulator is up against emphasizes the need to regularly check its operation and to periodically inspect it.

Regulator Freeze-Up – Moisture inside the LP container periodically freezes in the orifice at the inlet to the regulator, stopping the LP flow. Remember, the LP is vaporizing at −44 degrees, far lower than is necessary to freeze moisture. This is why contaminated LP containers need purging. As mentioned, two-stage regulators will usually eliminate this type of regulator freeze-up since the first stage has a much larger orifice opening than a single-stage regulator. Also, heat can be transferred through the walls of two regulators instead of one. Regulator freeze-up is all but a thing of the past since two-stage regulators are now required on all newly built RVs.

Another type of regulator freezing takes place when external moisture freezes and blocks the vent portion of the regulator. The vent opening of all regulators must be pointed downward to avoid any blockage. Inspect and keep the regulator's protective cover in place.

On travel trailer installations with twin DOT cylinders, an automatic change-over valve is usually used in conjunction with a dual-stage regulator assembly. This device allows automatic switching between cylinders when one cylinder is emptied. Uninterrupted flow of LP is realized using the automatic change-over device. Additionally, the empty cylinder can then be removed and transported to the filling station while the remaining cylinder provides fuel to the system.

Always transport DOT cylinders with a POL plug or QCC1 Acme cap installed on the service valve. Also, be sure the cylinder is transported in the same position as it is utilized: horizontal cylinders must remain horizontal, upright cylinders must remain upright. This will minimize the chance of inducing liquid LP into the service valve or vapor withdrawal tube, which could damage the regulator and possibly an appliance control valve.

Setting the LP Pressure – Periodically, the LP pressure regulator may need calibration. Only the second stage of a two-stage regulator is adjustable. The first stage, which reduces the inlet pressure to about ten PSI, is not adjustable.

As previously mentioned, the regulator must be adjusted with the aid of a manometer. The water column manometer is 100 percent accurate and is recommended for setting the LP pressure. A spring gauge-type manometer is also available. It is compact and stores easily, but will require periodic calibration itself. A water column manometer, in fact, is used to calibrate the gauge type manometer.

LP LEAKS: At the same time the LP pressure is set, it is also wise to check the entire piping system for leaks. Since the manometer will already be connected to the system, the leak check task is easily accomplished. What follows explains the steps necessary to correctly measure and set the operating LP pressure in the coach to determine if a leak exists. Be sure to prepare the manometer correctly by filling the tube with water until the level on each side of the manometer is near the zero point at the middle of the scale. The scale itself will slide up or down in order to get it right on the mark. This preparatory step is crucial to the accuracy of the measurement. Filled properly, the "U" tube or water column manometer is 100 percent accurate as mentioned earlier. (It is handy to add one drop of food coloring to the water to make it easier to read the level attained.)

Manometer Test (Low-Pressure Leak Test)

1. Turn off all appliances completely, even if they are the automatic ignition type.
2. Connect the manometer to the system anywhere after the regulator. The easiest location is at a stove top burner valve, unless the stove is equipped with an in-line, third-stage regulator that is non-adjustable. Remove a burner and slip the flexible manometer tube over the burner orifice fitting.
3. Open the LP container service valve.
4. Light a stove burner to rid the system of air and to make sure that LP is indeed flowing. It is possible to have pressure in the system without flow. Leave this burner lit.
5. Slowly open the burner valve on the stove and allow gas to flow to the manometer. The incoming LP gas will force the water down one side of the manometer and up the other side. To read the manometer, simply add the numbers on each side of the manometer at the point indicated by the water level.
6. Remove the dust cover and adjust the regulator by slowly turning the adjustment screw clockwise for more pressure and counter-clockwise for less. Adjust until the manometer measures 11 inches of water column.
7. Turn off the lighted burner. There will be a slight rise in the manometer reading, but it should be no more than one full inch. Remember to add the two sides together. If the pressure continues to rise and will not stop, or stops well above the 12-inch maximum, the regulator will need to be replaced.
8. Close the service valve at the container. This traps gas in the system between the valve and the water in the manometer.
9. Bleed the pressure by lighting a stove burner again until the pressure drops to about five or six inches of water column. Immediately turn off the lighted burner. Be quick as it will drop fast. Obtain any convenient reference point on the manometer and note this measurement. Then wait for a period of 10 minutes.
10. If the pressure drops below the starting reference point, there is a leak somewhere in the LP system. If the pressure slowly rises, LP is leaking through the POL valve (it will be necessary to repair this leak first or bypass the service valve in order to verify a leak-free system). If there was absolutely no drop in pressure during the 10-minute test, the system is in fine shape.
11. Turn off all stove burners completely, remove the manometer and reassemble the stove burner. Bubble test any additional fittings that may have been disconnected.

If a leak was detected via the manometer test, it will now be necessary to locate and repair the leak prior to operating any appliance. Remember, do not compromise the safety factor.

Checking the LP pressure twice a year in this manner will guarantee the appliances are being fed a quality diet of fuel at the correct line pressure. Plus, verifying the system to be leak free is an added benefit of having the cost effective manometer as a valuable part of the tool kit.

Finding LP Leaks If the manometer leak test detected a drop in pressure during the 10-minute test, there is a leak somewhere in the LP system. It is necessary now to troubleshoot the system and pinpoint exactly which component is leaking. It could be a cracked or loose flare nut, a hole in the copper tubing or a faulty component in an appliance.

The first thing to do is to eliminate the appliances as the problem. It is possible, in some instances, to have LP leak through an appliance even though that appliance was turned off. To eliminate each appliance, remove the three-eights-inch flare nut at each appliance, one at a time, and plug the line with a flare plug. Run the test again after plugging off each appliance. If the leak disappears after disconnecting the furnace and plugging the line, for instance, then the problem is somewhere in the furnace. If the leak persists after disconnecting each appliance and plugging the incoming copper lines with flare plugs, it will then be necessary to further troubleshoot.

At this point, turn the LP back on and spray or daub a leak detector solution on each fitting and pipe joint in the system. Start at the POL fitting at the LP container and "bubble" test each fitting and joint. Although they exist, it is not necessary to purchase a special leak detector solution. Simple dish washing soap mixed and diluted with water, or better yet, a child's bottle of blowing bubbles works extremely well. Avoid using dish soap that contains ammonia products.

If bubbles appear around any fitting after a few seconds, try tightening the fitting. Always use a backup wrench when tightening any LP fitting. Daub a little more solution to verify the leak has been eliminated. Also, while going through the system, fitting by fitting, keep a sharp nose for the unmistakable presence of the LP odorant. Many times your nose will determine the culprit fitting before even applying the soap bubbles.

After checking each fitting in the system, including the test fitting, run the full ten-minute manometer leak test again. Remember, to be leak free, there should be no drop in pressure during the ten-minute test. If a water column manometer was employed and a drop in pressure was evident, a leak still exists somewhere in the system.

If the LP leak is isolated to one of the four LP burning appliances, call the local RV service center as further internal diagnosing of that appliance will be necessary. Some modern furnace control valves permit a slight but intentional LP flow through the valve even when the unit is not running. This is normal, but to be sure, call a professional RV service tech.

Periodically test the on-board LP leak detector. Be sure to follow the instructions in the owner's manual. If at any time there appears to be no LP flowing, check the operation of the leak detector. Most will have a positive fuel shut-off component located at or near the service valve. It is possible that the detector is simply doing its job and has shut off the flow of LP.

LP COMBUSTION: All four of the major LP burning appliances found on RVs require the proper amounts of air and LP gas to be mixed for optimum operating efficiency. Understanding this simple fact, and making sure it occurs, could save repair dollars and costly downtime while traveling. What follows is a brief discussion on the attributes of proper combustion as it relates to RV appliances. It will further emphasize the importance of a strong preventive maintenance program concerning the coach.

The burners in the appliances each perform the same general function. They mix specific amounts of air with the incoming LP gas prior to it being ignited or burned. This mixture is what is crucial to the operation of the appliances as it relates to efficiency. In most cases, there are no adjustments that can be made to the incoming air. Some earlier RV appliances, which were adapted from the mobile home industry, were equipped with adjustable air shutters. However, the advent of electronic ignition and the gradual decline in the use of the common pilot flame, virtually eliminated the usefulness of air adjustments. The water heater is the only exception today.

Controlling the pressure at which the LP gas is delivered to the burners of the appliances is accomplished by the LP regulator. The adjustment of the LP pressure is very critical for the proper operation of the appliances.

The amount of LP gas that enters the burner is controlled by the individual burner orifice or jet. This is a predetermined amount that defines the BTU capacity of that particular appliance. RVers have no control over how large this opening is, nor do we need to. However, we can be responsible for how small this opening can get. Dirt, dust and spider webs coagulate regularly in burner orifices. We have all heard the campfire stories of insect nests in the orifices. Well, they are very true indeed. Partially blocked orifices, in effect, restrict the flow of LP that is mixing with the air, resulting in an improper mixture that creates carbon deposits (soot) and a poor running appliance. Remember seeing that large black stain on the side of the RV above your neighbor's water heater?

To combat this situation and to get the most out of LP burning appliances, make it a point to clean the burners and check the LP pressure periodically. It should be done, at the very least, once a camping season. If travel is predominantly in dusty climates, consider cleaning the burners more often. Perhaps twice per camping season.

Flame Failure Safety Devices – With the exception of the range, most LP appliances rely on a built-in safety method that will shut off the incoming LP should the flame be extinguished. In past years, all appliances utilized a pilot flame that ignited a larger, main flame. If the pilot flame blew out, the main burner could not ignite and gas flow would cease.

A integral portion of most safety valves and pilot burners is the thermocouple. Although the industry has progressed technically by leaps and bounds, some things just never become 100 percent outdated. The typical thermocouple is one of those items.

In 1806 the inventor of the thermocouple discovered that when two different metals were heated to a certain temperature, an electrical voltage was produced. This is but one of the facets behind the principle of thermal electricity.

Twenty or so years later, a couple of inventing geniuses invented the common electromagnet. Now the thermocouple had a purpose. When combined with the electromagnet, the thermocouple could produce the voltage needed to power the magnet which in turn was used in an assortment of configurations to control the flow of gases and vapors. This was the beginning of the flame failure safety system.

Typical Thermocouple

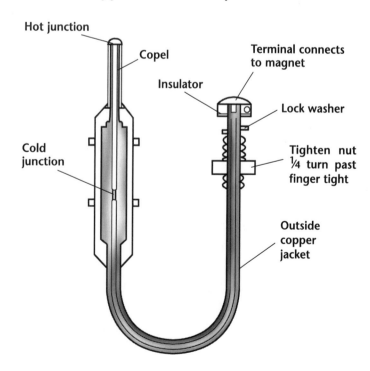

Hot junction

Copel

Terminal connects to magnet

Insulator

Lock washer

Cold junction

Tighten nut ¼ turn past finger tight

Outside copper jacket

The thermocouple as we know it consists of two unlike or dissimilar metals. Today's thermocouples utilize stainless steel and a variant of copper called copel as the two different metals. They are fused together at one end. This is called the hot junction. This is the portion that is actually in the pilot flame. In fact, to work at the optimum, only the first three-eighths of an inch of the thermocouple should actually be in the flame. In order to produce the voltage necessary, there must be at least a 400 degree temperature difference between this hot junction and the cold junction. If too much of the thermocouple is positioned in the flame, a higher temperature will be realized at the cold junction since it will be physically closer to the flame. If that condition exists, the necessary voltage difference will not be present and subsequent appliance problems will usually result, typically, pilot outages. Concerning pilot flame size, bigger is not always better.

At the opposite end of the thermocouple is the terminal attachment that screws into the flame failure safety device or gas control valve. Always use caution when tightening this terminal. Only tighten it one-quarter turn past finger tight or damage may result.

The principle of operation is this: As the tip of the thermocouple containing the two dissimilar metals is heated in a common flame, a DC voltage is produced that is sent along the insulated wire encased in the copper tube to the terminal that is attached to the electromagnet in the gas valve. The voltage produced energizes the electromagnet, which allows the gas to continue to flow to the appliance. If the pilot flame were to go out, the tip, or hot junction, cools and the voltage stops. When the voltage stops being produced, the electromagnet portion of the gas control valve becomes de-energized, the gas flow stops and the flame goes out. It is now necessary to re-light the burner.

So how much voltage are we talking about anyway? Approximately 25 to 30 millivolts are produced by the typical RV thermocouple. It will vary somewhat with its overall length. One millivolt is one one-thousandths of one volt, so it is a relatively small output voltage.

Occasionally, thermocouples become faulty and must be replaced. Less frequently, electromagnets must also be replaced. Some gas control valves have replaceable magnets while others do not. On those appliances with non-replaceable magnets, the entire gas valve must be replaced.

Thermocouples are relatively inexpensive items. It is recommended to carry an extra thermocouple for each appliance that uses one on the RV. It could very well be cheap insurance and will guarantee a smooth flowing LP gas system during the trip.

But what can you do to help extend the life of the thermocouples? Once a year use a wad of fine steel wool to brighten up the tip of the thermocouple. Carbon buildup from the open pilot flame can cause erratic temperature differences between the hot and cold junctions in the thermocouple resulting in intermittent operation of that appliance.

Inexpensive aftermarket thermocouple testers are available that can test the effectiveness of thermocouples. Also, if the VOM in your tool kit incorporates a millivolt scale, you can perform an open circuit voltage test or bench test on the thermocouples to test their output. This is how.

First, disconnect the terminal of the thermocouple from the gas valve. Attach the negative lead from the VOM to the outer copper tube casing anywhere along the length of the thermocouple. Attach the positive lead from the meter to the terminal button at the very end of the thermocouple. Apply a flame to the hot junction until the voltage reaches between 25 and 30 millivolts. If a thermocouple cannot produce that much, chances are it is faulty and should be replaced. After the test remember to only tighten the terminal one quarter turn past finger tight.

On pilot-less appliances, a printed circuit board controls the gas flow. The flame failure safety device on these "direct spark" units is considered integrated into the electronics of the board, coupled with a flame sense probe positioned in the flame much like a thermocouple. These, too, can be tested but it requires special equipment not likely to be carried by the average RVer. Therefore, testing of direct spark-ignited appliances is best left to the professional service technician.

GENERAL NOTES:

- Never overfill any LP container. Do not allow a LP retailer to fill any container more than 80 percent full. Avoid topping off the tank.
- The POL fitting is a left-hand thread. Do not use any pipe dope or sealant on this fitting. It seals with a brass-to-brass machined surface only. Adding a sealant may actually cause a leak. The newer Acme Type I fitting is to be tightened hand tight only.
- Always bubble test any fitting that has been disconnected then reconnected, including the POL fitting after filling a DOT cylinder.
- All POL fittings should be "excess flow" fittings.
- Never use a lighted flame to test for leaks. Always use a soap solution that does not contain ammonia or chlorine.
- On twin cylinder installations, such as on a travel trailer, install the cylinders with the open portion of the collar ring facing the trailer, not the tow vehicle. The closed collar will protect each tank's service valve from road debris.
- Never store LP containers indoors. Do not expose the containers to heat and always plug the POL service valve when not in use.
- Always be safety conscious. Never compromise the safety factor.
- The safest way to travel is with the service valve turned off. This is especially true when filling up at the gas station. Never have appliances lit while refueling with gasoline.
- Leak test the complete system at least once a camping season.
- Use common sense. If you smell LP, immediately turn off the supply of gas.
- If in doubt – don't. If you do not feel comfortable performing any procedure on your LP system or any of the appliances, turn the LP container off and call the local RV service center.

As crucial as the LP system is to enjoying the advantages of self-contained RVing, possessing a thorough knowledge of the system and its components will further enhance your ability to stay on the road. Next, let us explore the individual RV appliances.

THE RV FURNACE AND HEATING SYSTEM

Ahh! The comforts of home. Cold beverages, hot water, home cooked meals and a warm, cozy bungalow to take the nip out of the air. The RV furnace can particularly be appreciated during those chilly fall and spring evenings. For those who RV on a full-time basis, it can literally be a requirement on a cold winter's night. Today's RV furnace and heating system has come a long way since the early days of RVing.

Early RV furnaces were really nothing more than scaled down versions of heaters and furnaces found in mobile homes. In fact, some were the exact same unit. Those early heaters were big and bulky, as well as heavy users of LP fuel. Today, more BTUs of heating efficiency can be packaged into a much smaller unit, weighing a fraction of what the earlier units weighed, and at the same time, be installed in non-obtrusive, out-of-the-way locations within the floorplan. Additionally, today's units require only nominal preventive maintenance compared to what seemed like constant attention on

Suburban Forced-Air Furnace

Today's forced air furnaces are more efficient, lighter and more compact.

the earlier furnaces. The RV furnace and heating system has progressed both technically and functionally.

Types of Furnaces: There are three basic types of RV furnaces found in RVs:

- Forced air
- Radiant or gravity
- Catalytic

Most furnaces today are ignited by an automatic electronic principle that has come to be known as DSI, direct spark ignition. Pilot models still exist, though they are not as popular as the DSI models.

In the pilot system, a constant standing pilot must be maintained in order to ignite the much larger main burner whenever there is a call for heat. The lighting of this pilot involves manually holding a gas valve open while a small amount of LP is drawn into the pilot area. Actual ignition of the pilot flame is effectuated by a match, a flint ignitor, a glow coil or a piezo [PEE-AY-ZO] ignitor. Maintenance tasks and most troubleshooting tips will pertain to both pilot and DSI models alike with a few exceptions. The operating principle of each type of furnace, however, remains basically the same regardless of the means of ignition. The purpose of a pilot flame is solely to light the main burner when a call for heat comes from the thermostat.

FORCED AIR FURNACES: By far the most popular choice among manufacturers today is the forced air furnace. The forced air furnace draws in fresh air from outside the vehicle, mixes it with LP, burns that mixture in a sealed combustion chamber and blows air over the heated chamber and into the living portions of the RV through a system of ducts.

Most forced air furnace manufacturers use this same design strategy for their units. Some may have slightly different components and possibly a different sequence of operation, but by and large, most follow the same basic principle.

An important aspect concerning forced air furnaces that is often overlooked is the area of return air. Insufficient return air will cause the furnace to overheat and performance will be hindered. If the furnace is installed under a bed or a cabinet, there typically should be a minimum of 48 to 55 square inches of grill area in order to have enough air returned to the cabinet of the furnace. Never store supplies on or around the furnace cabinet. Refer to the specific owner's manual for a detailed explanation of a particular unit.

Components – The following basic components represent a typical RV forced air furnace. Your furnace may or may not have all these parts:

- **Thermostat**—Usually mounted on the wall, typically in the living or dining area of the coach. A built-in thermometer senses the room temperature and calls for heat when the temperature drops below the setting.
- **Relay**—The relay receives the signal from the wall thermostat and sends current to the 12-volt DC motor. This is usually called a time-delay relay. Sometimes it is also referred to as the fan switch. It is constructed with a bimetal disc that allows the furnace fan to continue running after a heating cycle in order to purge the combustion chamber of any unused gases as the furnace cools down.
- **Motor**—The 12-volt DC motor usually performs two functions. First, it will draw in fresh air from outside the RV through an internal venting system. All appliances mix air with the

LP for proper and complete combustion. The fresh air blower, attached to the shaft of the motor, draws this primary air into the combustion chamber. Once the internal conditions are right, LP will enter the chamber to be mixed with the air for burning. Another blower wheel is also attached to this motor usually at the opposite end of the shaft. This blower fan, much larger than the fresh air blower, circulates the heated air throughout the ducting system to all areas of the RV.

- **Ducting system**—Consisting typically of flexible heater duct hose, the ducting system runs throughout the RV, usually into every room or area. Some larger RVs will have a more elaborate ducting system with four or five outlets placed in or near the floor areas of the coach. All ducts begin at the furnace housing, therefore, those outlets closest to the furnace will disseminate the heat first. Care must be taken when routing the flexible ducting system. Easily crushed, some ducts can be totally cut off from the distribution network. Avoid bends or tight turns in the ducts. Blockages and obstructions may cause erratic operation of the furnace.

- **Venting system**—There are usually two segments of the venting system associated with modern furnaces: the fresh air intake vent and the hot exhaust vent. All by-products of burning LP, including carbon monoxide and other extremely hot gases, must be exhausted from the furnace combustion chamber and delivered to the outside atmosphere. A rigid piping exhaust system carries these harmful gases to the exterior of the RV. Never touch the exterior exhaust vent during furnace operation. Very high stack temperatures exist that can be dangerous. Typically, the fresh air intake and the hot air exhaust are coupled into one outside vent assembly. The fresh air intake portion must be kept separate from the exhaust portion if the two are combined into one vent. It is vital that the exhaust vent be totally sealed from the interior of the RV.

- **Sail switch**—Also called an air prover switch. This micro-switch is positioned in the direct flow of air from the blower fan. It performs two basic functions. First, it will only close if there is enough air being brought into the combustion chamber to support combustion. It "proves" there is sufficient air to mix with the LP before the fuel is allowed into the combustion chamber. Concurrently, it delivers the voltage sent from the relay on to the next electrical component.

- **Printed circuit (PC) board**—Now the standard in most LP appliances. Consisting of electronic components, the PC board performs four basic functions in the furnace:
  - Monitors a timing circuit to make sure the chamber is purged of any unused gas before allowing more LP to enter.
  - Powers the LP gas valve on the furnace, which starts the flow of LP to the combustion chamber.
  - Emits a high output voltage that creates an ignition spark that lights the burner in the chamber.
  - Creates what is termed a "lockout" condition if the flame does not ignite in the prescribed number of tries. Usually the board continually sparks until a flame is sensed. In some cases, the board may try three times to light the burner. Lockout stops any of the remaining events from happening until the wall thermostat contacts have been manually opened and reset. The fan may continue to run, but there will be no heat.

- **Limit switch**—Performs another safety function, just as its name implies. It will allow the current flow to continue through the circuit only if the internal case temperature is below a certain setting. This thermal switch will interrupt current flow to the PC board if the internal temperature rises above this preset "limit."
- **Gas valve**—Electrically controlled by the PC board, the gas valve can have one or two solenoid valves that must open in order for the LP to reach the burner area. Usually quite durable, gas valves do, however, sometimes fail.
- **Electrode assembly**—Situated in the combustion chamber, this device receives the high voltage output from the PC board and creates an electrical arc to ground. At the same time, the LP/air mixture is forced to flow through this electrical arc causing ignition of the fuel at the burner assembly. The electrode assembly also "senses" the presence of the fire and sends a micro-amp signal back to the PC board allowing the gas valve to remain open. If the flame is unstable, or if it is extinguished for any reason, the micro-amp circuit between the electrode and PC board is broken, and the board shuts off the current to the gas valve. This electrode assembly is susceptible to carbon buildup and heat stresses over a period of time. Many PC boards have been replaced in error when the cause of an outage has simply been a carboned electrode assembly.

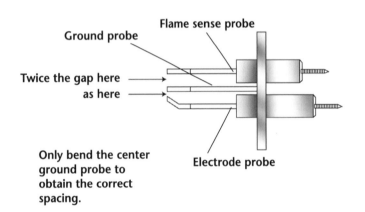

Ground probe

Flame sense probe

Twice the gap here as here

Only bend the center ground probe to obtain the correct spacing.

Electrode probe

The furnace electrode assembly is prone to carbon build-up. Careful cleaning will result in efficient operation.

- **Burner**—The LP/air mixture passes through an orifice and into the sealed combustion chamber and ultimately is consumed by the fire at the burner assembly. The burner design will vary among manufacturers, yet the purpose is the same. It will burn the fuel to create the heat that the fan then distributes through the ducting system. All main burners are situated inside the combustion chamber, therefore, it is not recommended to remove the burner. Special gaskets make sure the combustion chamber remains sealed at all times.

Sequence of Operation – Since the whole sequence is usually automatic on modern RV furnaces, here is a detailed account of what happens when the thermostat calls for heat.

If the room temperature drops below the set temperature on the thermostat, a 12-volt DC current is sent to the time delay relay/fan switch. The relay has three main components, a heater coil, a set of contacts and a thermal disc, that open and close the contacts at a certain temperature.

The relay receives the current from the thermostat and passes this current to the built-in switch inside the relay. This is accomplished by the heater coil which then actuates the bimetal thermal disc which closes the contacts.

Current is then passed to the 12-volt DC motor that spins two blower wheels simultaneously. One begins drawing fresh air into the combustion chamber from outside the RV while the other wheel begins blowing unheated air through the distribution ducting system.

The blower wheel blows against a large paddle attached to the sail switch that closes its contacts once the blower has reached approximately 75 percent of its normal speed. Once the sail switch closes, the current is next passed to the limit switch. The limit switch is a normally closed thermal switch that will only open the circuit if high casing temperatures are experienced. If a normal condition exists, the current passes through the limit switch to the printed circuit board.

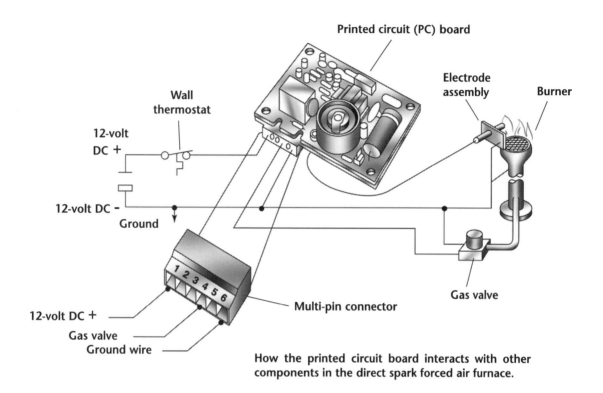

How the printed circuit board interacts with other components in the direct spark forced air furnace.

Here is where things become slightly more complicated as the PC board next performs simultaneous tasks. The PC board has a built-in timer that allows the blower fan to purge the combustion chamber of any unused gases or other by-products of combustion. After this time has elapsed, the board will then send current to the gas valve, which opens and gas flows to the burner. At the same time, a high voltage spark is produced by the board and sent along what looks like a spark plug wire, to the electrode assembly. As the gas mixture flows through the spark created by the board, it ignites and burns. The electrode then will sense this flame by sending a very small current, measured in micro-amps, back to the board confirming the presence of the flame. The flame itself acts as a conductor to complete this sense circuit. If the flame did not ignite, the circuit is opened and the board either tries for a second or third time to light the burner, or it goes into a lockout condition.

This lockout condition is a safety feature that is not alterable. PC boards, although all look identical, can actually be quite different by having shorter or longer purge times, one or more tries for ignition before lockout, etc. Using an incorrect board to remedy a faulty furnace condition may result in damage to the new board. Newer aftermarket PC boards, specifically those designed by Dinosaur Electronics, have been developed to eliminate many of the common burnout problems associated with some appliance PC boards. As an added benefit, Dinosaur boards are wired with a protecting fuse.

Sequence of Operation of the RV Forced Air Furnace

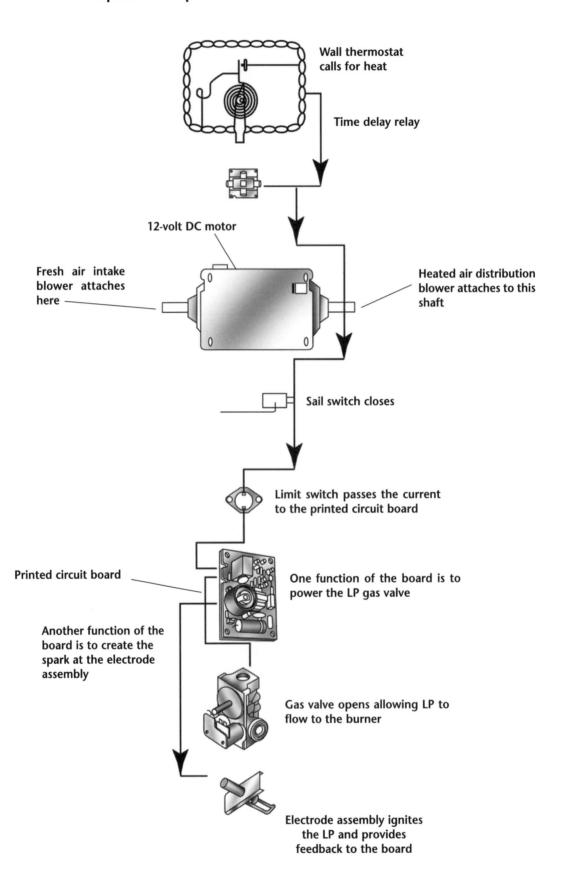

Wall thermostat calls for heat

Time delay relay

12-volt DC motor

Fresh air intake blower attaches here

Heated air distribution blower attaches to this shaft

Sail switch closes

Limit switch passes the current to the printed circuit board

Printed circuit board

One function of the board is to power the LP gas valve

Another function of the board is to create the spark at the electrode assembly

Gas valve opens allowing LP to flow to the burner

Electrode assembly ignites the LP and provides feedback to the board

If a flame ignited the main burner and the heating cycle began, the wall thermostat will open its contacts when the temperature setting has been satisfied. If the unit went into lockout, the wall thermostat contacts must be manually opened and then closed to start the process over again. In a lockout condition, the blower fan will continue to run until the thermostat contacts are manually opened.

After a normal heating cycle, the blower fan will remain running, purging the combustion chamber of unused gases and venting any remaining by-products of combustion. The fan will continue to run until the heater coil, located in the relay, cools anywhere from three to five minutes, then the contacts are opened and the blower motor stops.

Maintenance – All LP burning appliances require periodic maintenance. Some procedures are probably beyond the scope of the average RVer, so if you are not comfortable performing any maintenance task, call a nearby RV service facility. Although you may decide not to perform maintenance yourself, it still is a requirement for trouble-free operation. What follows is a generic list of tasks that are applicable to the majority of forced air furnaces found on today's RVs. Keep in mind, the model in your RV may differ slightly. Consult the owner's manual for the exact location of the components discussed.

Additionally, it will probably be necessary to remove the inner furnace assembly from the outer casing in order to clean and service the unit. Usually, only two or three screws need to be removed in order to pull the furnace. Again, consult the owner's manual for specifics.

The LP gas line and 12-volt power supply will also have to be removed. Turn off the LP at the container and plug the three-eighths-inch copper line once it is removed from the furnace. After servicing the furnace, be sure to leak-test the system prior to lighting any LP appliance.

Areas that typically need attention are:

- •Electrode assembly—Carbon deposits can be brushed off and the electrodes brightened with steel wool or emery cloth. Inspect the ceramic insulator if so equipped. Any cracks or chips will necessitate electrode replacement. It is recommended to keep a spare electrode assembly in the spare parts kit. If the electrode has three probes, make sure there is twice the gap between the center probe and the flame sense probe than there is between the center probe and the spark probe.

- •Pilot assembly—If the furnace is a pilot model, it will be necessary to clean the pilot orifice. It is recommended that the orifice be soaked in a solution of acetone and then air dried. Never insert anything into or through the orifice.

- •Main burner—Dust, lint or any other debris should be cleaned from the main burner and the main burner orifice at least once a camping season. However, most are located interior to the sealed combustion chamber. This is one job for a professional service technician. All gaskets must be replaced when removed. Due to the dangers of carbon monoxide, it is not advisable to remove any component that employs a gasket or seal.

- •Thermocouple—If the furnace is a pilot model, clean the thermocouple hot junction by lightly brushing or brightening with fine steel wool.

- •Blower wheels—Dust and lint will congregate in the corners of these "squirrel cages" if not cleaned at least once a year. In some cases, this accumulation can actually slow the fan speed so that the sail switch will not close. Disassemble and wash and clean the blower wheels thoroughly.

- **PC board**—Yearly, clean the contacts where the multi-pin connector attaches. Use a simple pencil eraser to brighten the contact strips. Be careful when handling the PC board. Dropping or mishandling can be an expensive mistake.
- **Vent tubes**—Check and clean yearly or more often if necessary. It is crucial that the exhaust vent remain clean and clear of any obstructions. Often, wasps or other insects will build nests in the vent tubes, especially during times of lengthy storage.
- **Interior casing**—Vacuum in and about the casing the furnace slides into. Reach into the distribution ducts as far as possible. Cleanliness and furnace performance are proportionally related.
- **Wall thermostat**—Clean the contacts by simply inserting a small piece of paper in-between the contacts, closing the contacts, and then slowly pulling the paper out. Never file or sand thermostat contact points. Clean only with dry, plain paper. Any typical business card will suffice.
- **Duct system**—Inspect all ductwork throughout the RV. Straighten any sharp bends or turns. Look for crushed ducts under gauchos or where ducts pass through walls or partitions under cabinets, etc. Shorten any lengths that appear too long. Many installers have simply "snaked" excess ducting under cabinets rather than taking the time to cut them to the proper lengths. This can create an overheated situation in the furnace or insufficient heat delivery in the RV.
- **LP pressure** – Be sure the LP delivery pressure is set at eleven inches of water column.

For a detailed companion video tape that shows all the various procedures for cleaning and servicing the RV furnace, please contact the technical editor.

Troubleshooting – The following chart will help determine which components may be at fault when the operation of the furnace falls below normal expectations.

Troubleshooting Notes: Lockout can occur if the gas pressure happens to fluctuate at the time the thermostat calls for heat. Pressure fluctuations can be caused by a faulty dual-stage pressure regulator located at the LP container. It could also be caused by a kink or obstruction in the delivery tubing or gas lines. Isolating the furnace from the coach piping system can determine if the LP system is the cause. Connect a separate LP bottle and regulator and run the furnace on a test bench. If the furnace performs properly on the bench, then the coach LP system should be checked. (It may be necessary, on some furnaces, to install the furnace in the outer casing and to install the fresh air and exhaust vents in order to safely bench test the unit.)

If lockout persists, check the return air flow areas. Refer to the owner's manual for the details on the minimum amount of return air space. Also, check the operation of the sail switch and be sure the electrode and burners are cleaned and free of carbon deposits. Finally, have the LP supply checked for excessive moisture. It may be time to purge the LP container.

RADIANT HEATERS: Radiant heaters, also called gravity heaters, are not as prevalent as in past years, but there are still many in use today and they, too, need periodic maintenance. Radiant heaters operate on the simple principle of convection—hot air rises, cold air falls. Normally, all radiant heaters are pilot models with the same methods of lighting as mentioned in the section above. The main burner is ignited by the pilot and the heat generated simply "radiates" to all areas of the RV. Radiant heaters are usually positioned near the floor of the coach to take advantage of the convection principle. As the hot air rises, it heats the interior of the RV.

Condition	Possible Causes
Blower does not run	No 12-volt DC at furnace connection
	Loose or faulty connections, blown fuse
	Faulty thermostat, contacts not closing
	Faulty relay
	Faulty motor
Blower is noisy	Dirty blower wheels
	Excessive voltage, must be less than 14.5 volts DC
	Reversed polarity causing motor to run backwards
	Blower wheel hitting casing
	Foreign matter in blower housing
	Worn motor bushings or bearings
	Blower wheels out of balance
Blower runs, burner does not ignite	No LP fuel reaching furnace
	Inadequate LP pressure, less than 11" water col.
	Reverse polarity
	Inadequate return air supply to furnace
	Blockage in distributing ducting
	Open limit switch
	Faulty printed circuit board
	Faulty gas valve assembly
	Inadequate gaps at electrode assembly
	Faulty electrode assembly
	Loose or disconnected wiring
Burner ignites, then shuts down	Flame sense probe not positioned in flame
	Faulty wiring
	Carboned electrode assembly
	Faulty PC board
Main burner will not shut off	Thermostat contacts not opening
	Faulty gas valve
	Shorted relay
Repeated PC board failures	Spark jumping to flame sense probe
	Board or wires shorted to furnace case
	High DC voltage spikes from converter
	Shorted or damaged electrode assembly

Sequence of Operation – When the room temperature falls below the set temperature or setting on the thermostat, (some thermostats are built in to the gas control valve mounted at the heater instead of on the wall), there is a call for heat. Air is brought in from outside the RV by a small fan located at the rear of the heater. The LP and fresh air mix in the combustion chamber, commonly called a firebox on radiant heaters, and is ignited by the constant pilot flame.

Some radiant heaters may have an additional fan that helps blow air past the firebox to aid in the distribution of heat throughout the coach. Once the room is heated to adequately satisfy the thermostat, the main burner is extinguished, but the constant pilot remains lit. A blower fan may continue to run in order to purge the firebox of any unburned fuel and other by-products that may still linger. Usually though, any unburned fuel is simply consumed by the pilot.

Maintenance – Normal cleaning and servicing procedures are followed for the radiant heater as well as the forced air furnace. The three main areas of concern are:

- Cleanliness—Clean components mean less downtime
- Correct LP pressure—Always a mandate with any LP appliance
- Venting—The exhaust vent and intake vent should be clean and cleared of any obstructions, such as a wasp nests

Radiant heaters are very simple in design. By attending to the above three items, the RVer will experience very few problems with the heater.

CATALYTIC HEATERS: Similar to radiant heaters in that they employ the convection principle, catalytic heaters are unique in the manner in which the LP fuel is burned. Catalytic heaters have a combustion process that burns LP without a flame and at uncommonly low temperatures.

Typical Catalytic Heater

Additionally, all radiant heat produced by the catalytic heater is usable. There is very little wasted energy. The heat is directed to people and to objects and only heats the surrounding air space by radiant transfer after first warming the occupants.

The catalytic process is such that it burns the LP in the air to produce infrared heat without a flame. The flameless process mixes the gas and the air within the presence of a platinum-based catalyst pad, which is the primary feature of the catalytic heater. LP enters and permeates the pad from rear to front, mixes with the air at the front surfaces and burns without a flame. Sometimes a slight flame may be visible at the heater face on the initial lighting from a cold start. This is normal during the time the catalyst pad heats up. Also, there may be a slight odor of propane during this cold start-up.

Catalytic heaters may be vented through the side wall of the RV or simply surface-mounted on any wall inside the coach with no direct vent to the outside. Some are thermostatically controlled. All heaters must be listed and approved for RV use.

In the past, non-vented catalytic heaters were allowed in RVs only under strict guidelines. As the technology has progressed and improved, safety features have been implemented; the non-vented catalytic heater has since proven itself to be an extremely efficient method of comfort heating in smaller RVs. They are now allowed to be installed anywhere inside the RV, however, since the catalytic process heats people and objects rather than air, it is best to mount the heater in an area with no obstructions, such as furniture or cabinetry.

One of the newest safety features is the oxygen depletion sensor (ODS), which will shut down the heater if the oxygen level in the RV falls below a safe level. Additionally, today's heaters are equipped with a 100 percent safety shut-off system in the event the flame extinguishes or when non-ignition occurs.

Components – Very basic in design, the catalytic heater has few parts other than the pad, a housing and the method of controlling the LP flow. Since no venting is required on some models, installation is relatively simple. Only an LP gas line is required at the mounting location.

Here are the major components of a typical catalytic heater:

- **Catalytic pad**—The main component on the catalytic heater. It is fragile and sensitive; never touch the pad itself. It is possible to experience what is called "catalytic pad poisoning" which can damage the pad by cleaning or by being exposed to impurities or physical abuse. The catalytic pad can only be used with propane. Airborne contamination from motor fuels, cooking oils and aerosol compounds can all contribute to a shortened pad life. Pads should be replaced about every three years under normal use.
- **Method of ignition**—The recommended catalytic heaters use a piezo or an electronic ignition system for lighting the fuel.
- **Thermocouple**—As a portion of the safety system, the thermocouple produces the millivolts necessary to keep the gas control valve open and the LP flowing into the unit.
- **Gas valve**—Permits the flow of LP as long as the thermocouple produces voltage.
- **Thermostat**—Models that are thermostatically controlled require a 12-volt DC source. Usually when 12 volts are required for the thermostat, the heater is equipped with electronic ignition.

Maintenance – There is very little maintenance to perform directly on the catalytic heater. The primary concern is to make sure the incoming LP pressure is maintained at 11 inches of water column, and that the surrounding area is kept clean and free from lint or other airborne contaminates. Never touch or wash the pad itself. Maintenance is limited to simply vacuuming the outer grill in front of the pad.

Since non-vented catalytic heaters consume air from inside the room, it is recommended that a window or two stay slightly opened in the RV in order to provide sufficient fresh air. The coach must have a minimum of at least one square inch of free fresh air opening for every 1,000 BTUs the heater is rated for. Do not operate the heater in coaches that are tightly sealed or closed off.

Additional Notes: Keep in mind that other than checking the LP pressure and testing the thermocouple, all repairs to catalytic heaters must be performed by the factory.

Also, be sure to read the cautions and warning in the owner's manual. Each model may have specific information that is not listed here.

Regardless of which type of furnace or heater installed in your RV, take time to record the model number, serial number and any specification number that may be pertinent to the unit. When contacting the manufacturer or service center, this information will be needed to answer questions or to order replacement parts.

The RV Water Heater

Prolonged hot showers are predominantly taken for granted by most citizens, but while traveling in a RV, a hot shower involves an interesting test of timing. It is truly an experienced RVer who is aware of just how long it takes for six to ten gallons of hot water to trickle down the drain. The goal is to have all remnants of soap suds accompany that last drop of hot water at precisely the same time. However, within less than an hour, fresh, hot water will once again be available to stream forth from that shower head.

The RV water heater has been a most welcomed appliance to the family of LP burning appliances found on most RVs. Hot water for bathing and washing dishes makes life on the road much easier. Some of the fancier rigs are even equipped with a clothes washer. Hot water has certainly been endearing to many novice RVers who would never go "camping" unless shower facilities are available.

The RV water heater, as with any of the LP-fired appliances, needs occasional maintenance to keep it in shape. Fortunately, the water heater is the easiest of the appliances on which to work. Situated at a comfortable height, most components are located on the outside of the RV, easily accessed behind the vented door. Some models have printed circuit boards and thermostats located on the rear of the unit, but for the most part, most have controls and components on the front.

Typical Water Heater

TYPES OF WATER HEATERS: The predominant model today is the automatic spark model, commonly referred to as the DSI model. This unit is fully automatic. All that is necessary for the owner to do is simply make sure the heater is filled with water and flip the switch. All components and accompanying functions are controlled by a printed circuit board.

The second most popular choice found today is the standard pilot type water heater. These units are the latest versions of even the earliest models. Simple in design and operation, they have been a mainstay for many years. Even though they are less expensive than their automatic cousins, they are slightly less popular. It appears automation wins out over economics.

Another type found on some earlier RVs is the electric version. Powered by 120-volts AC, these units are only operated when plugged into shoreline or on-board generator power. Some units today are a combination of LP gas and electric. This format allows the RVer to operate the water heater on LP while dry camping or traveling and on 120-volts AC while plugged in overnight at the campground.

Another feature that is available on some models is the motor-aid or heat exchanger kit. This kit allows the engine cooling lines to be routed through a pipe that circulates inside the water heater tank, thereby heating the stored water while driving. By the time the motorhome reaches its destination or while during a stop for lunch, hot water is already present at the faucet. This kit conserves LP fuel while traveling, also. However, the maintenance factor becomes greater with the motor-aid models. Periodically, the hoses will need to be replaced. On some of the larger Class A motorhomes or conversion buses, this could be an expensive yet necessary venture.

Components – The DSI automatic ignition water heater and the pilot water heater each have many of the same components, and some that are pertinent to just one specific type. The components that are common to both types of water heaters are:

- Inner tank
- Pressure and temperature (P&T) relief valve
- Drain
- Main burner orifice
- Mixing tube
- Primary air adjustment

The *inner tank*, usually made of aluminum and lined with glass, is surrounded with insulation and typically covered with a cardboard, Styrofoam or metal covering. Since water heaters are usually installed under a cabinet or another structure, external aesthetics are not necessarily a consideration.

The *P & T relief valve* is an interesting device. As a safety component, the P & T valve has often been viewed by RVers as an item of mystery. Many P & T valves have been unnecessarily replaced, thought to be defective because they dripped water every day. By design and intent, the P & T relief valve will usually drip some water during each and every heating cycle. This is why.

As any containerized liquid is heated, that liquid will expand, causing not only a rise in temperature, but also a rise in pressure (a percolator effect, if you will). Since the RV water heater is a tank filled with water, if there were no method to regulate or control this expansion during the heating cycle, the unchecked pressures and temperature could rupture the tank within the water heater, resulting in serious injury.

Temperatures below 210 degrees Fahrenheit are considered safe. Therefore, all P & T valves on today's water heaters are pre-set (non-adjustable) to open at 210 degrees Fahrenheit. In the small confines of the RV water heater, the water is heated very quickly with a rather inordinately large LP burner flame, so keeping up with the drastic fluctuations of both temperature and pressure is no easy task.

In RV water heaters, or any pressurized tank for that matter, there is usually a cushion of air at the very top above the water level that acts as an accumulator and buffers the water. It also allows space for the water to expand into while being heated. This air (oxygen), is eventually absorbed into the oxygen portion of the water. At this point, there is no place for the expanding water to move into since the tank is literally completely full. The P & T valve then does its job of becoming a virtual hot water faucet—it opens. Expelling hot water from the outlet of the P & T valve allows more cold water to enter the tank (lowering the temperature) and the disc valve portion of the relief valve snaps shut. Usually, draining some water from the water heater tank will reinstate this cushion of air if excessive dripping is encountered. To accomplish this, remove the water source (either turn the demand pump off or interrupt the city water flow), and open any two hot water faucets in the coach. Next, open the manual lever on the relief valve until the water flow stops. Close the valve and the faucets, then turn the pressure back on.

The fact that this dripping of the relief valve seems to be more prevalent today is justified by the design and the sophistication level of the modern water heater. Back in the good ol' days all water heaters were thermostatically controlled manually. Today, with the prominence of electronic ignition and printed circuit boards, control of the temperature of the water is taken away. On many units the thermostat is a pre-set, temperature sensing, normally closed, thermal switch that electrically turns off the water heating sequence when the pre-set temperature has been reached.

There will continue to be P & T valves that will simply fail or not seal, or otherwise become faulty, but by and large all will drip occasionally. They must, however, drip only during the heating cycle. If indeed they drip or weep during non-heating phases and the pressure within the fresh water system is less than 150 PSI, then the relief valve may be faulty.

Since heating water within the confines of a closed tank will result in the expansion of that water, and virtually all P & T relief valves will drip a little bit during the normal heating cycle most of the time, it must be determined how much is excessive. How much should it drip? And how much is a little bit? Why does it not drip every single time? Why only sometimes? There are basically seven reasons why the P & T relief valve might drip that also govern how much water it will drip. It is determined by:

1) The temperature and the pressure of the incoming water from within the fresh water system to the water heater. Once the temperature or pressure rating of the relief valve has been exceeded, the disc valve opens, expelling the hot water. As the cold water comes into the tank, how cold that water is and at what pressure it is being forced into the water heater will determine how long the disc valve portion stays open. The longer the disc valve portion stays open, the more water will drip. As the water temperature inside the water heater is cooled by the incoming water, the disc valve closes.

2) The cleanliness of the thermostat or probe portion of the relief valve. Mineral deposits and galvanic corrosion will leave a residue on the probe that could slow the temperature sensing process slightly.

3) The pressure setting of the relief valve. Although mandated at not more than 150 PSI, some replacement P & T valves are rated at 125 PSI. Though certainly not dangerous, it will tend to drip more often than one rated for 150 PSI.

4) How much of a cushion of air is on top of the water inside the tank. If most or all of the air space or expansion space has been absorbed into the water, the relief valve will drip more often. Reinstate this expansion area and the relief valve will not drip as much.

5) The age and condition of the spring assembly inside the P & T relief valve. Constant usage of the manual lever on the valve will, over time, weaken the spring or cause mineral deposits to possibly get between the seat and the disc causing excessive dripping. The manual lever is best left undisturbed.

6) The temperature rating of the pre-set thermostat found on the electronic ignition water heaters, or the positioning of the manual thermostat. Lowering the manual thermostat setting or exchanging the pre-set thermostat for one that is rated at a lower temperature will lessen the frequency of the dripping.

7) The elevation and the atmospheric pressure at which the water heater is utilized. Although very slight, it still can have an effect on how much pressure occurs.

All water heaters have a drain of some type. Located on the front of the water heater towards the bottom left corner, some drains may have an actual valve, while others may simply be a pipe plug.

Remove the plug or open the valve to drain the water heater. Open the hot water faucets inside the RV to aid in this draining. Avoid opening the P & T relief valve except to replenish the air inside the tank as described above.

The main burner orifice is threaded into either the gas control valve (in a pilot system), or the gas solenoid valve (in a DSI unit). This orifice directs the LP into the next component, the mixing tube.

The mixing tube, or "U" tube, is where the LP and the primary air are mixed just prior to burning at the main burner. This tube, though not a precision component, must be kept clean, and more importantly, properly aligned. More often than not, misalignment of the mixing tube contributes to the majority of service related ills with the LP water heater. Here is how it works:

As the LP gas is projected through the main burner orifice, air is drawn in through the openings in the mixing tube. A "venturi effect" brings in a precise amount of air that is needed to mix with the LP in order to have safe and complete combustion. The LP pressure is set at 11 inches of water column. The orifice has a specific opening, so the only variable is the amount of primary air allowed to enter. The primary air adjustment controls this.

The primary air adjustment is adjusted while the main burner flame is burning. The flame should appear mostly blue in color with some orange or yellow. The adjustment is considered correct when the flame is the correct color and also when the flame is not a loud roaring flame. If you can hear the burner from about five feet away or more, chances are the mixture is incorrect and further adjustment is necessary.

Suburban Manufacturing Company incorporates a component called an anode in their line of water heaters. The anode is a long cylindrical bar of magnesium that is threaded into the inner tank at the rear of the heater on some older water heaters. Newer Suburban models configure the anode rod as a portion of the drain plug, making annual inspections easy. Designed as a sacrificial element, it keeps electrolysis to a minimum and extends the life of the inner tank. All chemical and mineral reactions taking place inside the tank will attack the "weaker" molecules of the magnesium anode instead of the aluminum or glass lining in the inner tank. Periodically, this sacrificial anode will have to be replaced. A deteriorated anode rod will produce a less than favorable odor that permeates the water system and is released through the faucets. Most RVers assume this smell is caused by something in the fresh water tank, but rarely do they consider the water heater tank an extension of the fresh water system. If a terrible odor is present at any of the faucets in the RV, seriously consider the anode rod in the water heater as the culprit. Full-timers should add an anode rod to the spare parts kit if their water heater is equipped with one.

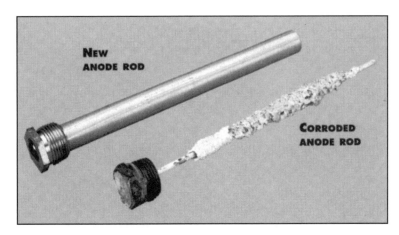

Anode Rod Comparison

Pilot Model Components – The components that are common only to pilot model water heaters include:

- Pilot assembly
- Gas control valve
- Thermocouple

The *pilot assembly* consists of the pilot orifice and the pilot burner. This is typically the location where spiders and other insects love to build their nests. The pilot orifice is one of the smallest LP components found on RVs, and since it is constantly exposed to outdoor conditions, it is most susceptible to blockages. Periodically, the pilot orifice should be removed, soaked in a solution such as acetone and simply air dried. As with any orifice, never poke anything into or through it to clean it. They are usually made from very soft aluminum or brass and are easily damaged.

In some instances, tough blockages may need a little assistance. In those cases, soak the orifice and blow through it with compressed air in the opposite direction of the normal flow of the LP. After using compressed air, always soak the orifice again in acetone and let it air dry. Avoid using compressed air alone since some air compressors contain vast amounts of moisture that may cause erratic flame characteristics at some LP burners.

Using acetone, which displaces water and quickly evaporates, will usually eliminate any moisture concerns. Take care, though, when using chemicals such as acetone. Wear proper protection for the skin and eyes. If necessary, ask for a Material Safety Data Sheet (MSDS), when purchasing any controlled chemical. MSDS forms provide safety-related information and precautionary advice.

There are two common pilot assemblies found in use today. One type has a separate thermocouple and pilot assembly (Robertshaw). The other type has a combination thermocouple and pilot assembly (Baso). They are not interchangeable.

The *gas control valve* is a complex unit that performs nine different functions for the water heater. The functions it performs and/or the components it houses are:

- Water heater thermostat
- 100 percent safety gas valve
- High temperature energy cut-off (ECO)
- Main burner LP pressure regulator
- LP gas filter
- Main burner gas valve
- Pilot burner gas valve and adjustment point
- LP pressure test tap
- Pilot burner pressure regulator

The control valve accommodates the manual knob that allows the owner to light the pilot flame, set the water temperature and shut off the appliance completely. The lower section of the gas control usually has an elbow fitting along with a threaded main burner orifice. Additionally, the incoming LP line attaches to this control as does the pilot tube and thermocouple.

The gas control valve threads into the inner tank portion of the water heater, immersing the temperature sensing tube portion into the tank of water. Internal to this temperature sensing probe is the ECO. This is a normally closed, thermally-controlled device that will open the circuit, interrupting the voltage being produced by the thermocouple when the water temperature exceeds a safe limit. When this circuit is broken, the electromagnet portion of the built-in safety device snaps shut, effectively shutting off the LP supply to the pilot and main burners.

The temperature sensing probe also houses the thermostat probe that will shut off the main burner gas supply once the temperature of the water has reached the setting established by the user. In this instance, the pilot flame will remain lit as long as the thermocouple is positioned correctly in the flame and continues to produce at least eight-millivolts (mV).

The *thermocouple* is positioned in the pilot flame and is attached to the electromagnet portion of the 100 percent safety valve located in the gas control assembly. Remember to keep the tip of the thermocouple cleaned and positioned in the pilot flame.

DSI Model Components: The following components pertain only to the automatic ignition water heaters activated by the flip of a switch from inside the RV. Aside from the common components listed above, the DSI models also have:

- Thermostat
- ECO switch
- LP solenoid gas valve
- Printed circuit (PC) board
- Electrode assembly

Suburban Water Heater

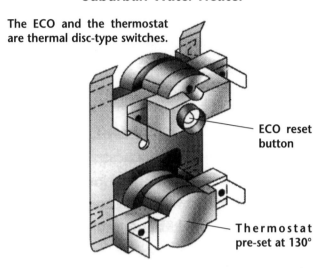

The ECO and the thermostat are thermal disc-type switches.

ECO reset button

Thermostat pre-set at 130°

The thermostat portion of the assembly is non-adjustable.

The non-adjustable thermostat is a thermal disc device secured to the front or rear of the water heater in direct contact with the inner tank. Most thermostats for DSI water heaters are pre-set for temperatures around 130 or 140 degrees Fahrenheit. Wired in line between the PC board and the solenoid gas valve is the ECO switch. Likewise, a thermal disc device affixed to the inner tank, some may contain a resettable push-button. Others will automatically reset once the water temperature drops below the pre-set temperature rating of the ECO. Effectively, the ECO and the thermostat are additional safety devices to help protect the appliance.

The LP solenoid gas valve is controlled by the PC board. The incoming gas line attaches to one end of this valve while the main burner fitting and orifice attaches to the other end. Energized by 12-volts DC from the PC board, the gas valve will remain open as long as voltage is being sent from the board. This valve will close under the following conditions:

- Water temperature reaches thermostat setting
- ECO opens the circuit to the PC board
- 12 volts DC is not supplied by the PC board

The PC board is the heart of any DSI appliance. Similar to the furnace, the PC board on DSI water heaters performs the following three functions:

- Provides 12-volts DC to the LP solenoid gas valve allowing gas flow to the main burner
- Creates a high voltage output spark that ignites the LP at the main burner
- Monitors the flame sense current from the electrode assembly and sends the unit into lockout when it fails to detect a flame; some water heaters are equipped with three-try circuit boards that will only go into lockout after three failed attempts to ignite the burner

Water Heater PC Board
(bottom view)

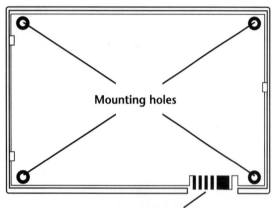

Mounting holes

Disconnect the multi-pin connector, and clean this contact strip with a common pencil eraser.

Additionally, the board permits a timed purge cycle prior to sending a spark to the electrode assembly.

The electrode assembly receives the high voltage output from the PC board and creates an electrical arc to ground. At the same time, the LP and air mixture is forced to flow through this electrical arc causing ignition of the fuel at the main burner. The electrode probe also "senses" the presence of the fire and sends a micro-amp signal back to the PC board allowing the gas valve to remain open. If the flame is unstable, or is extinguished for any reason, the micro-amp circuit between the electrode and PC board is opened and the board shuts off the voltage to the gas valve and it closes.

This electrode assembly is susceptible to carbon buildup and heat stresses over a period of time. Many PC boards have been replaced in error when the cause of an outage has simply been a carboned electrode assembly. In fact, a recent poll determined that the majority of water heater service problems are caused by the electrode assembly, more so than any other component on the water heater. For this reason, it is advisable to carry a spare water heater electrode assembly in the spare parts kit.

WATER HEATER MAINTENANCE: Once or twice during the camping season it will be necessary to clean and service the RV water heater. The water heater is exposed to the elements, therefore, road grime, dust and dirt have ample opportunity to gather in and around the various components. Periodically blowing out the front area with compressed air will help minimize this condition. Likewise, soot and remnants of the products of combustion will gather in the flue portion of the water heater. Blow through the flue occasionally with compressed air as well. Be sure to wear eye protection when performing this step. Flying debris will be present.

Aside from general cleaning and blowing off with compressed air, the following components will need periodic attention as well.

- •Electrode assembly—Carbon deposits can be cleaned off and the probes brightened with steel wool. Inspect the probes and replace the assembly when the probes become pitted or if a portion of the ceramic insulator is broken. Check the gap between the probes. If the electrode assembly has three probes, the gap between the spark probe and the ground should be half as much as the gap between the ground probe and the flame sense probe. Adjust or move only the center ground probe to achieve this spacing. Additionally, never allow the spark to jump from the spark probe to the flame sense probe. A new PC board will be needed should this occur. If the electrode assembly has only two probes, the gap should be approximately one-eighth of an inch. Take care when adjusting these probes. If any portion of the ceramic insulator becomes cracked or broken, the entire electrode assembly will have to be replaced.
- •Pilot assembly—If the water heater is a pilot model, as mentioned above, it will be necessary to disassemble and clean the orifice and the pilot burner periodically. Please refer to the pilot section above for details.

- **Thermocouple**—Clean the thermocouple tip or hot junction with steel wool or emery cloth. Keep the tip brightened and free from carbon build-up.
- **PC board**—Clean the contact strip where the multi-pin connector plugs in. Use a common pencil eraser to do this. Small amounts of corrosion, invisible to the naked eye, can prohibit proper conducting of current and strange operational characteristics may develop. Keeping the board contacts clean will minimize erratic operation.
- **Gas control valve**—Occasionally, it may be necessary to lightly lubricate the main control knob located on top of the gas control valve. Do this only when the water heater is shut off completely. Never spray cleaners or lubricants near the water heater while it is in operation. Many are flammable. A light coating of petroleum jelly or a very light white grease can be applied under the cap to the portion of the shank that revolves and can also be applied to the push button.
- **Mixing tube**—Make sure the "U" tube or mixing tube is properly centered on the main burner orifice fitting and that the alignment with the gas control valve is correct. This is one of the most common reasons for improper combustion in both types of water heaters today. The mixing tube should be straight with the flow of LP gas coming from the control valve and positioned so the orifice is centered in the opening of the mixing tube. Position the air adjustment shutter to about one-quarter open to begin with, and then adjust accordingly after lighting the main burner. The roar of the main burner should not be heard from farther than five feet away. The fire should be blue with tinges of yellow or orange at the tips.
- **LP gas pressure**—Be sure the LP line pressure is set to 11 inches of water column.

Additional Tips – If the pilot model unit is prone to pilot outage, consider adding an automatic re-ignitor kit. All pilot models can be retrofitted with an electronic kit that will automatically re-ignite the pilot flame should it be extinguished while parked. Contact the water heater manufacturer or a well-stocked parts and accessory store.

It is further advised to install a water heater bypass kit. This is especially useful when storing or winterizing the RV during cold winter months. Permanently attached to the rear of the water heater, its valve configuration allows the water heater to be closed off from the rest of the fresh water plumbing system. This is helpful when RV antifreeze is used during the winterizing procedures. With the kit, the water heater can simply be emptied and bypassed, thereby, saving a substantial amount of antifreeze.

To extend the life of the inner tank and to eliminate the build-up of mineral deposits inside the water heater, backflush the heater two or three times a year. This is especially helpful when you travel extensively and encounter various grades of water. All mineral deposits will settle to the bottom of the tank, so simply draining the tank will not rinse these deposits out. Here is a good procedure for getting them out:

1) Make sure the water in the water heater is cooled.
2) Turn off all sources of water pressure; the pump or city water connection.
3) Drain the water heater by opening the drain valve, or removing the plug, depending on how the water heater is equipped. To aid in draining, open all the hot water faucets throughout the coach.
4) If water barely trickles out the drain, remove the drain valve completely and carefully insert a straightened coat hanger into the drain opening in the tank to help break up any calcified deposits.

5) Close all hot water faucets opened earlier and turn on the city water or the water pump (the higher the pressure, the better). If a pressure regulator is normally used while traveling, temporarily remove it for this task.

6) Open the P & T relief valve and allow water to pour from the drain opening and the P & T valve simultaneously.

7) Allow this flushing to continue for five to ten minutes. This will remove any stagnant water along with any mineral deposits that typically settle to the bottom of the water heater inner tank. After about ten minutes of flushing, turn off the water source and re-install the drain valve or plug and allow the P & T valve to snap shut. Refill the tank once again with fresh water. It will be necessary to once again open all the hot water faucets inside the coach to aid in filling.

Pilot Model Water Heaters	
Condition	**Possible Causes**
Pilot will not stay lit	Faulty, weak or loose thermocouple
	Faulty magnet in safety valve
	Insufficient LP pressure
	Too large or too small pilot flame
	Dirty pilot orifice
	Faulty gas control valve
Main burner will not ignite	Dirty main orifice
	Obstruction in mixing tube
	Insufficient LP pressure
	Misalignment of mixing tube
	Improper air shutter adjustment
	Water already at thermostat setting
Erratic main burner flame	Orifice partially blocked
	Misalignment of mixing tube
	Mixing tube damaged or blocked
	Improper air adjustment
	Flame spreader mis-positioned
	Insufficient LP pressure
	Moisture in LP container
	Exhaust grill is blocked
Flashback in mixing tube	Incorrect LP pressure
	Misalignment of mixing tube
	Improper air adjustment

DSI Models Water Heaters	
Condition	**Possible Causes**
Burner will not ignite when rocker switch is activated	Low or no voltage
	Faulty rocker switch
	Open ECO switch
	Faulty thermostat
	Water already at thermostat setting
	Faulty printed circuit board
	Faulty gas solenoid valve
	Faulty electrode assembly
	Improper electrode gap
	Out of LP fuel
	Improper LP pressure
Erratic main burner flame	Orifice partially blocked
	Misalignment of mixing tube
	Mixing tube damaged or blocked
	Improper air adjustment
	Flame spreader not in position
	Insufficient LP pressure
	Moisture in LP container
	Exhaust grill is blocked
	Faulty electrode assembly
	Carboned electrode assembly
	Faulty printed circuit board
Flashback in mixing tube	Incorrect LP pressure
	Misalignment of mixing tube
	Improper air adjustment

Once fresh water is flowing from each hot water faucet in the RV, the tank is full and ready to be heated. Never operate the water heater until the tank is filled with water.

Troubleshooting – The charts above and on the previous page will help you determine the cause of many common complaints.

Additional Notes: As with all LP burning appliances, record the model number, serial number and any specification number that is included on the data plate or in the owner's manual. This information will be needed by the manufacturer or service facility when ordering parts or seeking assistance.

Remember to leak check any LP fittings which may have removed and to regularly leak-test the entire LP system using the manometer.

RV RANGE

Of all the RV appliances, the LP range, consisting typically of a combination stove top and an oven, requires the least behavioral modification for owners in their transition from home to RV. The largest hurdle to get over is simply the smaller size.

The only LP burning appliance that is not directly vented to the exterior of the RV, the range is considered so trouble-free, many owners only take the time to learn how to light the pilots, when so equipped. By learning slightly more than that, you can minimize downtime and loss of repair dollars by simply being acquainted with the sequence of operation and know how to test a couple of the components.

As mentioned, the range consists of two appliances in one. The stove top usually consists of four burners, much like a residential house range, that may or may not be lighted by a pilot assembly. Many manufacturers offer both models. The other portion of the range is the oven. Some ovens are situated above the stove top—the so called "eye level" units—while some are configured with the oven positioned below the stove. Usually, the only shared component is the incoming gas line. Some models also share a portion of the thermostat.

The pilot model stove top is the only LP appliance without a 100 percent percent safety shutoff device. Unlike all the other appliances, if the pilot flame were to be extinguished on the stove, the pilot gas would continue to flow. Granted, there would not be a great deal of gas flowing, but caution still must prevail. If the stove pilot is extinguished, turn the gas off at the LP container and wait a minimum of five minutes before attempting to light the pilot again. If the RV has been closed up for any length of time, open the windows and allow the RV to air out.

STOVE COMPONENTS: The components found on a typical pilot model stove top include:
- Third stage regulator
- Manifold
- Burner valves
- Stove burner
- Flash tubes
- Pilot burner
- Manual pilot valve
- Thermostat control assembly

On some units, a *third stage regulator* that controls the LP pressure is positioned at the point where the LP line enters the stove and connects. This third stage typically reduces the 11 inches of water column that is set at the main regulator at the LP container. The presence of this regulator means the manometer test point for checking the pressure will have to be located elsewhere. The reduced pressure at this regulator, which is non-adjustable, will not be a valid measurement for the entire system.

The regulator is secured to the *manifold* pipe. The manifold pipe is that portion of the range in which the burner valves and the thermostat are tapped or bolted. The manifold distributes the LP to each of the burners.

Each *burner valve* controls one of the three or four stove burners commonly found on RV stove tops. Each burner valve also houses the orifice for that burner as well.

The *stove burners* usually consist of the burner head, a mixing tube or venturi and the primary air inlet. The mixing tube is positioned over the orifice fitting on the burner valve. As incoming LP is passed through the orifice, it draws in primary air through the opening in the mixing tube, much

Thermostat

Today's oven thermostats are usually pre-set at the factory and are non-adjustable. Older thermostats, however, have adjustment points for the oven pilot and the stove pilot. To check yours, remove the oven control knob and look for adjustment screws as indicated. All thermostats have a thin capillary tube that extends into the oven. This capillary tube is not field repairable. If it becomes damaged, the entire thermostat must be replaced.

Range Pilot

The range burner pilot should burn with a blue flame having a slight yellow tip and extend approximately 1/8-inch above the cup so that the flame is at the centerpoint of the flash tubes. The flame also should be centered within the cup area.

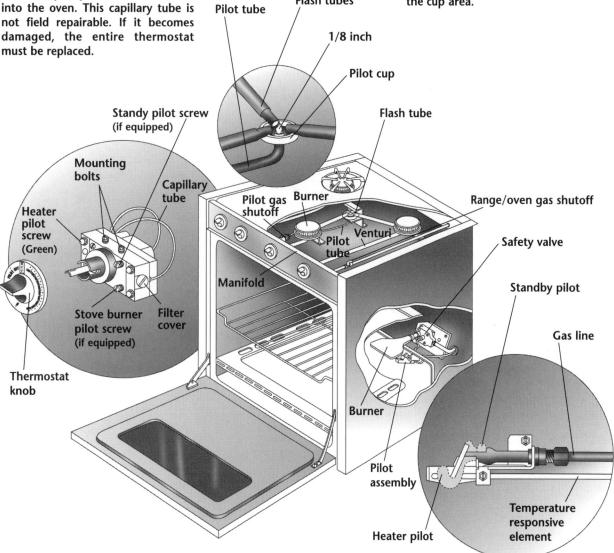

Flash tubes
Pilot tube
1/8 inch
Pilot cup
Flash tube
Standy pilot screw (if equipped)
Mounting bolts
Capillary tube
Pilot gas shutoff
Burner
Range/oven gas shutoff
Heater pilot screw (Green)
Venturi
Pilot tube
Safety valve
Manifold
Standby pilot
Stove burner pilot screw (if equipped)
Filter cover
Gas line
Thermostat knob
Burner
Pilot assembly
Heater pilot
Temperature responsive element

Oven Pilot

When the thermostat is set above zero, the constant oven pilot flame becomes larger and encompasses the element from the safety valve. The constant pilot is also called the standby pilot. The secondary pilot flame is also called the heater pilot. Once the oven has reached the set temperature, the safety valve closes and the pilot flame returns to the standby position.

like the principle of the water heater. The air and the LP are mixed in the tube and burned at the burner head. Some air openings are adjustable. If so, position the shutter so the flame is predominantly blue with a hint of orange or yellow on the tips of the flame.

Stove burner ports occasionally become clogged with cooking grease. Remove the burners and soak them in a mild solution of liquid detergent and water. Lightly scrub them with a soft bristle brush. Use a wooden toothpick for stubborn areas in and around the burner openings. Take care not to distort or otherwise enlarge the burner ports. Most are constructed of soft aluminum and are easily damaged.

Attached to the individual burners are the *flash tubes*. These tubes allow a trickle of gas to flow from the stove burner down the tube to be ignited by the pilot flame located in the center of the four burners. The gas is consumed by the pilot flame and burns back to the burner head where this "flash back flame" ignites the burner head fully. It is imperative that the flash tubes be positioned downward towards the pilot burner because LP is heavier than air, and it must flow down to the pilot flame. If a problem exists prohibiting any of the burners from being ignited by the pilot flame, chances are the flash tubes are misaligned.

The *pilot burner* is an open flame burner that is positioned equidistant from each of the four stove burners. The height of the pilot flame should be no taller than three-eighths of an inch above the rim surrounding the pilot tube.

Often, the pilot is controlled by an independent *manual pilot valve* that is attached to the manifold pipe as are the burner valves. The manual pilot valve will be a simple on/off lever-type valve with a built-in regulator or pilot adjustment point. Like the burner valves, it is accessible by lifting up or completely removing the stove top. Other times, the stove top pilot is controlled by the oven thermostat. The oven *thermostat control assembly* attaches directly to the gas pipe manifold. When the oven thermostat controls the stove top pilot the dial will be marked accordingly. Usually, there will be a "pilots off" position and another position that simply states "off." The "off" position really means "pilots on." On the typical thermostat, when the indicator only indicates "off", pilot gas is being fed to the stove top pilot and the oven pilot at the same time. With this type, when the thermostat is in the "off" position, immediately light the two pilot flames.

Other configurations for lighting the stove burners include piezo ignitors and electronic ignition sequences that are activated by simply turning on the burner valve. These two methods eliminate the necessity of a pilot flame and flash tube assembly.

The components of the range pertinent to the oven include:
- Thermostat control assembly
- Safety valve
- Pilot assembly
- Main burner assembly

The oven thermostat control assembly allows LP to flow to the stovetop pilot, the oven pilot and ultimately, to the main burner assembly in the oven. Attached to the thermostat is the temperature sensing probe, positioned inside the oven. This is the portion of the thermostat that monitors the inside temperature and allows the thermostat to ignite the main burner when more heat is called for. Many times a thermostat is wrongly accused of being faulty when, in fact, the temperature sensing probe may simply be covered with cooking oils or grease, or even oven cleaner, and is simply not sensing the temperature correctly. Keeping this sensing element clean will eliminate many problems associated with false temperatures being suspected in the oven.

Sequence of Operation – After the thermostat calls for heat, here is what happens. Assuming the pilot flame is lit in the oven, when the thermostat is set to a temperature, in most cases, the oven pilot becomes slightly larger and begins to heat a thermal bulb attached to the safety valve. This thermal bulb, which is filled with mercury, expands a bellows in the safety valve and allows the main burner gas to flow from the thermostat to the safety valve and on to the main burner. That is why there is a time delay from when the oven thermostat is first set to a desired temperature until the main burner actually ignites.

A good way to tell which component may be faulty in a situation where the main burner will not ignite at all, is to carefully watch the oven pilot. While watching the pilot flame, turn the oven thermostat knob up above 300 degrees Fahrenheit. Immediately, the stand-by pilot should expand and envelope the thermal bulb portion of the safety valve. If it fails to gain in size, replace the thermostat. If it indeed becomes bigger and engulfs the thermal bulb, then the safety valve is faulty and needs replacing. The positioning of the thermal bulb in the secondary pilot flame is crucial. It has to be in the fire in order to boil the mercury inside.

Typical Oven Safety Valve

As the mercury boils and expands, a bellows inside the valve allows LP to flow through the orifice to the main burner.

Mercury-filled thermal bulb is positioned in the secondary pilot

Main burner orifice and hood

LP inlet

After the pilot expands and heats the thermal bulb and opens the safety valve, LP fuel is then fed to the main burner assembly and is ignited by the pilot flame. The main burner varies in design between manufacturers. Some are straight tubes with burner ports on either side. Others are round, plate-like devices that configure the main flame into somewhat of a circular pattern.

In either case, the main burners will remain ignited until the desired temperature is attained inside the oven as sensed by the oven temperature sensing probe portion of the thermostat. The "broil" setting on the thermostat, bypasses the limit of the thermostat. In this setting the burner will remain ignited until the oven knob is repositioned to a different setting.

The RV oven can take a little getting used to. It has happened that the thermostat actually falls out of calibration and cooking times are not the same as in the house variety. In many instances, using the same ingredients, same recipe, same duration and the same set temperature will yield different results.

If oven problems occur, the first item to check is the oven door seal. However, some ovens found in RVs are susceptible to fluctuating LP gas inlet pressures or other phenomena that will vary the way a favorite dish will emerge from the oven. In some cases, it may be possible to compensate by calibrating the oven thermostat. It will be necessary to first determine if the thermostat can be calibrated. Not all oven thermostats have that ability. All thermostats found on RVs that can be calibrated will have a slotted screw adjustment inside the shaft, located behind the thermostat knob. Remove the knob and look into the shaft. If no slot is visible, that thermostat cannot be field calibrated.

Oven Calibration Procedures – If the oven is deemed inaccurate, measure the temperature to test the thermostat. Calibrate if the actual temperature varies more than plus or minus ten degrees of the set thermostat temperature. Be sure normal convection air flow inside the oven is not blocked by the use of wide cookie sheets, tin foil, etc.

Calibrating an adjustable thermostat requires a good, accurate mercury-type thermometer. The small cooking spring-type thermometers are neither accurate nor reliable enough for the task of calibrating.

Check to see that the oven temperature sensing bulb is positioned correctly in the oven and that no grease or oven cleaner is coating the bulb, either of which could result in abnormal operation of the thermostat as previously mentioned.

Set the thermostat to 300 degrees and cycle the oven two or three times to warm the unit. (Note: When actually setting the thermostat do not go past the desired temperature, but turn the knob just up to it.) Place the thermometer in the center of the empty oven.

Note the first measurement or reading when the main burner ignites again. You should be able to hear it come on if the oven does not have a glass panel in the door. Continue to let the burner operate. Take the second reading as soon as the main burner flame goes out and reverts back to the pilot. Again, listen closely. This completes one cycle.

The thermostat will need to be calibrated if the average temperature varies more than ten degrees from the original 300 degree setting.

To obtain the average temperature, subtract the lesser of the above readings from the greater. Add one third of that difference to the lesser number. This final average should be within plus or minus ten degrees of 300.

To illustrate: When the oven re-ignites, assume the first temperature reading is 307 degrees. After one cycle, the second reading is 319 degrees. The difference between the two is 12. One third of that difference is four, added to the lower reading (307 plus four equals 311 degrees). This thermostat exceeds plus or minus ten degrees and is in need of calibration.

To illustrate conversely: When the oven re-ignites, assume the temperature reading is 302 degrees. After one cycle, the second reading is 311 degrees. The difference between the two is nine. One third of that difference is three, added to the lower reading (302 plus three equals 305 degrees). This thermostat is within the tolerance of plus or minus ten degrees and does not need calibrating.

If the oven thermostat needs calibrating, it will be necessary to snap out the center portion of the thermostat knob (if possible) or obtain an additional knob for that range. Drill a hole in the center of the knob and install this test knob on the thermostat shaft taking care not to rotate the shaft at all. Insert a flat blade screwdriver through the knob into the adjusting slot in the shaft of the thermostat. Again be careful not to rotate the shaft. Holding the screwdriver still, rotate the knob to the average temperature recorded in the test procedure noted above. It is critical that only the knob rotate and the screwdriver and shaft remain steady. Using the above example, rotate the knob until it indicates 311 degrees.

After calibrating, test the results by again measuring the temperatures. If the thermostat is non-adjustable, it will be necessary to replace the thermostat.

Troubleshooting – The following chart will help determine the cause of some common symptoms with the RV range. Be sure to record the model number and serial number of the range for future reference when ordering parts or discussing a problem with a service facility.

Condition	Possible Causes
Stove top pilot will not stay lit	Insufficient LP supply
	Incorrect LP pressure
	Blocked pilot orifice
	Pilot flame too high or too low
Stove burners will not ignite	Incorrect LP pressure
	Incorrect gas/air mixture
	Flash tubes bent or not in position
Stove burner flame lifts off burner head	Too much LP pressure
	Incorrect gas/air mixture
Oven burner will not ignite	Incorrect LP pressure
	Incorrect gas/air mixture
	Blocked oven pilot orifice
	Temperature probe not in position
	Faulty safety valve
	Faulty thermostat

RV Absorption Refrigerator

Of all the appliances found in today's RV, the one that is probably the most perplexing to the RVer is the absorption refrigerator. Understanding the theory of absorption and contemplating why it takes heat in order to make cold can be baffling at best. Then toss in the fact that this is all accomplished with no moving parts and is done silently. Very quickly we resort to just simply shaking our heads while grabbing another cool beverage from the fridge.

However, regardless of the complexity, periodic maintenance is still a mandate concerning the LP burning appliances, including the RV absorption refrigerator—make that especially the RV absorption refrigerator. The refrigerator is the most used appliance of the four that utilizes LP gas as a fuel. Fully automatic today, it may also be the one that is most neglected.

By grasping a basic view of the theory of absorption and understanding the importance of leveling, ventilation and cleanliness, the RV refrigerator can provide many years of RVing enjoyment and untethered independence.

Basic Facts – Today's RV refrigerator uses three energy sources: 12-volts DC, 120-volts AC and LP. As mentioned earlier, the principle revolves around using heat in order to make cold. All three energy sources are utilized as heat producers. The 12-volt DC and 120-volt AC electricity are used to power a heater element, while the LP is burned at an open burner.

COOLING UNIT OPERATION: The main component of any RV absorption refrigerator is the cooling unit. The cooling unit is that item most visible at the back of the refrigerator. It consists of the pipes and coils seen when the outside service door at the rear of the refrigerator is opened. All cooling units consist of four major component parts:

- Boiler
- Condenser
- Evaporators
- Absorber

Through these four main components circulate the pressurized and sealed contents of the cooling unit in an endless cycle during the time the refrigerator is turned on. All cooling units are sealed and, therefore, are not field repairable. Specialized machinery and unique material handling make it mandatory that if a cooling unit is determined to be at fault in a non-working refrigerator, it must be replaced.

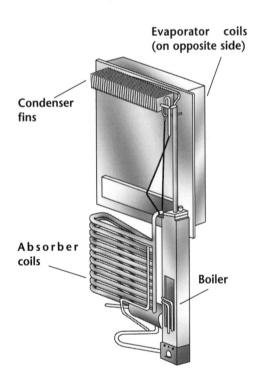

Evaporator coils (on opposite side)

Condenser fins

Absorber coils

Boiler

The cooling unit is a sealed-system component that is not field repairable. If the cooling unit is blocked or develops an ammonia leak, it must be replaced.

Contents – Inside the cooling unit, added in precise amounts during manufacture are: water, liquid ammonia, hydrogen gas and a compound chemical called sodium chromate. As temperature and pressure act on the contents, they undergo various states of evaporation and condensation, all within the confines of the sealed cooling unit. Because of the caustic nature of liquid ammonia, the sodium chromate is added to protect the insides of the pipes during the refrigeration cycle.

Refrigeration Cycle – When heat is applied to the boiler portion of the cooling unit, the ammonia and water begin to boil. Bubbles of ammonia gas are produced, which rise into the percolator tube along with an accumulation of weak ammonia and water. As the ammonia and water solution pass into the tube, the ammonia vapor continues into the water separator. Any water vapor reaching this point is condensed and falls back into the boiler section, thereby "separating" the water and leaving dry ammonia vapor to pass to the condenser. As air circulates over the condenser fins from the outside, it removes heat from the ammonia vapor inside causing it to condense into a liquid that flows to the low temperature evaporator. The low temperature evaporator portion of the cooling unit is positioned in the wall or shelf of the freezer section of the refrigerator.

The evaporator is internally supplied with hydrogen gas, which passes across the surface of the incoming ammonia and subsequently causes the vapor pressure to allow the liquid ammonia to evaporate. The evaporation of the ammonia removes heat from the evaporator section through the walls of the freezer and through the pipes, removing heat from the freezer section of the refrigerator, including any food stored there. The net result is that through the theory of absorption and its principles, the RV refrigerator is not making cold, but basically removing heat. Cold, therefore, is simply the absence of heat.

From the low temperature evaporator, any remaining remnants of liquid ammonia and hydrogen gas are passed lower into the high temperature evaporator, which is positioned in the lower section of the refrigerator. This continues to remove and transfer heat from inside the box to the outside, but not as much heat is removed. That is why it is warmer in the food section, or lower portion, than in the upper freezer section.

After the ammonia and hydrogen gas pass through the evaporator, the contents flow to the absorber section. Upon entering the upper portion of the absorber, a continuous trickle of weak ammonia solution comes into contact with the mixed ammonia and hydrogen gas, which readily absorbs the ammonia from the mixture, freeing the hydrogen gas and allowing it to rise back through the absorber coil and to the evaporator section. The hydrogen gas effectively moves back and forth between the absorber and the evaporator sections.

The strong ammonia solution produced in the absorber flows down to the absorber vessel (the large tank-looking container located below the absorber coils) where it is held, mixed with water and then fed into the boiler section; the process starts all over again.

Leveling – The motivational force in moving the liquid contents throughout the system is nothing more than gravity. From the point where liquid is first produced in the condenser section until the liquid reaches the boiler section, gravity is employed. Since liquids cannot flow uphill, the importance of running the refrigerator only while level is fully appreciated. The crucial section is the low temperature evaporator located within the freezer compartment. This is where the leveling should take place. To the refrigerator, it does not matter how level the kitchen counter, the dinette table or the outside corners of the RV are. If it does not correspond with the low temperature evaporator coils located in the freezer compartment, all leveling efforts will be for naught. With repeated operation out of level, damage to the cooling unit is inevitable.

To ensure your refrigerator is adequately level for operation, here is a handy tool recommended by Norcold. Cut a six-inch piece of 1' x 2' wood to the dimensions shown. The thickness of the material is not critical, but the long upper and lower sides should be very straight. It is best to use a hard wood for this tool.

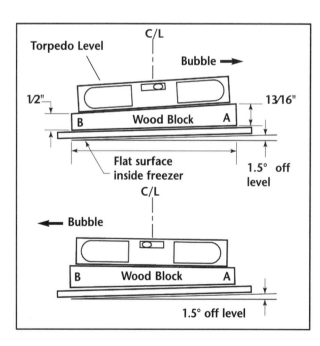

Norcold Leveling Method

The Refrigeration Cycle
Traced in Seven Steps

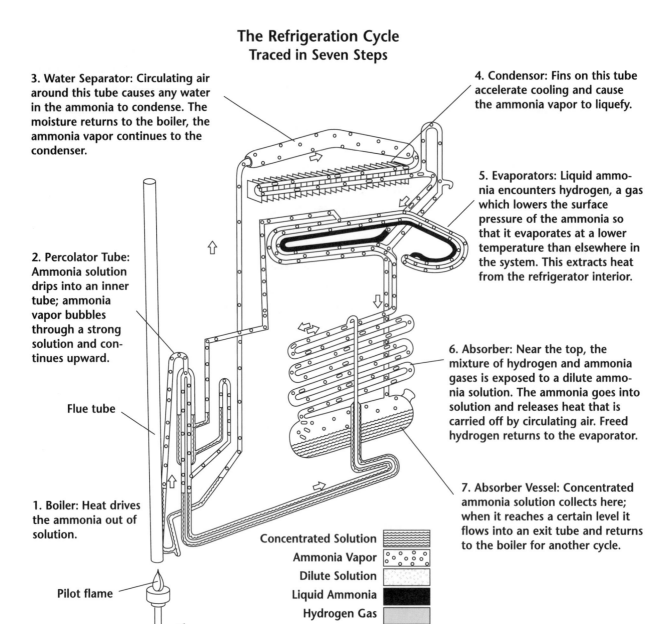

3. Water Separator: Circulating air around this tube causes any water in the ammonia to condense. The moisture returns to the boiler, the ammonia vapor continues to the condenser.

4. Condensor: Fins on this tube accelerate cooling and cause the ammonia vapor to liquefy.

5. Evaporators: Liquid ammonia encounters hydrogen, a gas which lowers the surface pressure of the ammonia so that it evaporates at a lower temperature than elsewhere in the system. This extracts heat from the refrigerator interior.

2. Percolator Tube: Ammonia solution drips into an inner tube; ammonia vapor bubbles through a strong solution and continues upward.

Flue tube

6. Absorber: Near the top, the mixture of hydrogen and ammonia gases is exposed to a dilute ammonia solution. The ammonia goes into solution and releases heat that is carried off by circulating air. Freed hydrogen returns to the evaporator.

1. Boiler: Heat drives the ammonia out of solution.

7. Absorber Vessel: Concentrated ammonia solution collects here; when it reaches a certain level it flows into an exit tube and returns to the boiler for another cycle.

Pilot flame

Concentrated Solution
Ammonia Vapor
Dilute Solution
Liquid Ammonia
Hydrogen Gas
Hydrogen and Ammonia Vapor

Set a standard torpedo level on top of the wood block. Place this assembly on a flat surface in the freezer compartment. If the unit has a freezer shelf, place the level and the wood block there. Most of the bubble should be on the "A" side of the centerline as shown In the diagram. Now, flip the assembly around, end for end. Again, most of the bubble should be positioned at the "A," or thickest end of the wood block. If this is not the case, the refrigerator is more than three degrees off level and should not be operated. If either reading shows the bubble "leaning" towards the "B" side, this too, indicates an out-of-level situation of more than three degrees.

Leveling is important during any operational mode (12-volts DC, 120-volts AC, or LP) while the RV is parked. While driving or physically moving down the road, there is enough jostling and movement to keep the liquids safely flowing through the system. It is only crucial when the vehicle is not in motion.

Leveling is one of the two most important factors to consider when using the RV absorption refrigerator. The other is ventilation.

Ventilation – Improperly vented heat is probably the singlemost cause of improper cooling of the refrigerator. As heat is removed from the interior of the unit, it is relocated to the rear of the cooling unit by the actions and reactions of the boiler, condenser, evaporators and absorber coils as described above. Heat created by the three heat sources, including the products of combustion, as well as heat generated by the condensing of the ammonia vapor, must be dissipated quickly and efficiently in order to make sure the refrigeration cycle is not hindered.

To accomplish refrigeration in an RV refrigerator, a continuous supply of free-flowing air is required to pass over the heat producing areas of the cooling unit to safely remove unwanted heat. The refrigerator installation must include a good drafting technique for evacuating this heat. A natural draft is created by installing the refrigerator into a cabinet opening with close tolerances allowing for a flue system to be employed. This flue or drafting chimney must be continuous from the bottom of the cabinet, up the back of the cooling unit and typically out the roof vent. Proper clearances must be adhered to. Check the owner's manual for the specifics and verify the installation. Some installations allow for smaller refrigerators to be vented through the side of the RV with vents placed at lower and upper locations. Each size and each brand of refrigerator may have different requirements. Check the installation against the manufacturer's requirements.

The natural draft method of ventilation induces air from outside the RV. This outside air must be at a temperature lower than the cooling unit components. A natural draft is created when the cooler intake air entering through the lower vent is heated and becomes lighter and rises up through the roof vent. The greater the difference between the removed or rejected heat and the intake air, the stronger the draft will be. This is called "thermo-siphoning."

A good installation encourages as much intake air as possible to flow over the cooling unit, thereby preventing the intake air from bypassing the heat generating components altogether. Any bypassed air tends to cool the heated air, which counteracts the draft effect.

The drafting compartment at the rear of the refrigerator should be totally sealed from the interior of the RV. It may be necessary to partially remove the refrigerator to seal all cabinet corners and joints. High temperature silicone sealant may be used for this task. Strictly adhering to the clearance guidelines for the refrigerator will indeed help its performance.

Aftermarket fans can be added to those units that do not appear to have good ventilation. Here is the bottom line: The more heat given up to the exterior of the RV in the fastest amount of time, the better the overall cooling performance. This is why the ambient heat has a direct impact on the effectiveness of the refrigerator. The inside of the refrigerator will be warmer while operating in the desert at noon, than when operating at night by the ocean. Remember, proper drafting and removing of unwanted heat occurs when the incoming air is cooler than heat removed by the components of the cooling unit.

Operating the refrigerator off level creates an inordinate amount of heat at the rear of the unit, especially at the boiler area. Coupled with improper ventilation, this extra heat can escalate very quickly into potential costly troubles. When overheating occurs over a period of time, the sodium chromate inside the pipes begins to crystallize. The percolator tube inside the boiler section can become impassable because of a blockage caused by the crystallized sodium chromate. When this happens, the cooling unit is blocked and cannot be repaired. It must be replaced.

Refrigerator Controls – So far, the cooling unit components, the theory of absorption, proper leveling and proper ventilation all pertain to virtually ever single RV absorption refrigerator ever made. The differences between brands and models is strictly in the controlling of the absorption principle. All the bells and whistles, the aesthetics of design and unique features are secondary to the basic principle of operation discussed above.

Today's refrigerators fall into two basic categories: Those that are fully automatic and those that are not. Fully automatic units only require the user to set the thermostat to the desired setting, and then tell it to go. Electronic controls will automatically choose the appropriate heat source and begin the refrigeration cycle. The priority for automatically choosing the mode of heat source is: 120-volts AC, 12-volts DC and then LP gas.

Those refrigerators that are not fully automatic require the RVer to choose the heat source. Some may even require an LP burner to be lit. All units have built-in and fully automatic safeguards to make the RV refrigerator an extremely safe appliance to operate.

MAINTENANCE: Due to the complexity of the electronics of controlling the operation of the RV refrigerator, the owner is somewhat limited in many troubleshooting and maintenance procedures. Most all ignition, operating and monitoring devices are now electronically controlled with very little the consumer can do. There still exist, however, some owner related steps to be performed.

Cleaning – Keep the rear of the refrigerator as clean as possible. Once or twice a year, vacuum in and around the burner area. Reach up to the absorber coils with the vacuum attachment, or simply wipe down the pipes with a damp cloth. Be sure to do this when the refrigerator is not operating.

From the roof, remove the roof vent and inspect the condenser fins. Because of the warmth generated by the refrigerator, many creatures, including birds, are prone to construct nests on top of the condenser, effectively blocking the flow of draft air. This can easily cause an overheated condition for the cooling unit. Plus it is a fire hazard. Stack temperatures located at the flue extension on top of the boiler are extremely hot. It is recommended to install hardware cloth or chicken wire inside the roof vent to prevent birds from entering altogether.

Like all LP burning appliances, the burner and burner orifice must be kept clean. During periods of non-use, spiders and other insects build webs and nests in and around LP burners. The refrigerator burner is no exception. Carefully remove and disassemble the burner. Refer to the owner's manual for specific instructions, but typically it is not a daunting process. Once disassembled, soak the components in acetone and let air dry. As mentioned previously in this chapter, do not insert any instrument into the orifice. Damage will result.

If the unit is equipped with a thermocouple, remove carbon deposits and brighten the tip with emery cloth. As with any thermocouple, only tighten the nut one-quarter turn past finger tight after reassembly. Position the ignitor electrode according to that model's requirements.

If the unit is equipped with a DSI board similar to the boards on the furnace and water heater, clean the multi-pin connector strip with a pencil eraser. All other PC boards may require special testing equipment, and no owner testing is recommended.

Check to make sure the flue baffle is in place above the burner and inside the flue pipe. Remove the flue baffle and clean. It will probably be necessary to remove an aluminum flue extension or cap to gain access to the flue baffle hanger. Never shorten or lengthen this hanger. Each hanger is made to a certain length for each model refrigerator. The purpose of the baffle is to draw in fresh air to aid in dissipating the heat produced by the burner flame.

Two Styles of Refrigerator Burners

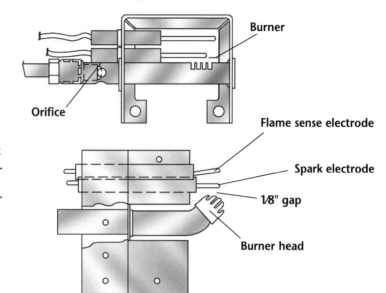

Burner

Orifice

Flame sense electrode

Spark electrode

1/8" gap

Burner head

Burner areas should be kept clean for efficient operation. Debris often falls onto the burner from inside the tube.

While the burner assembly and flue baffle are removed, clean the inside of the flue pipe with a flue brush. The flue brush is available through an appliance repair facility. Measure the diameter of the flue pipe in order to obtain the correct size brush.

After all components have been cleaned, carefully reassemble them in the reverse order from which they were removed. Take special care when tightening LP gas tubing and fittings. Always use two wrenches so components do not twist or distort from their intended position. (This is especially crucial with the older manual models.)

Leak-check any LP fittings that were removed. When it is certain there are no leaks in the area of the burner assembly, attach the manometer to the stove and check the LP pressure regulator. It may be advisable to test the pressure at the refrigerator pressure tap after the cleaning of the refrigerator if troubleshooting is also taking place. For the annual clean and service of each appliance, it is best to perform the pressure check at the easiest location, typically at a stove burner. Be sure the pressure is set to 11 inches of water column with one stove burner lit.

After verifying the LP pressure, light the refrigerator and observe the burner flame. Check again for leaks with an appropriate leak detector solution.

For information on how to order the companion video tape on refrigerator maintenance, "Cleaning and Servicing the RV Absorption Refrigerator," please contact the technical editor. This detailed account provides easy step-by-step cleaning instructions.

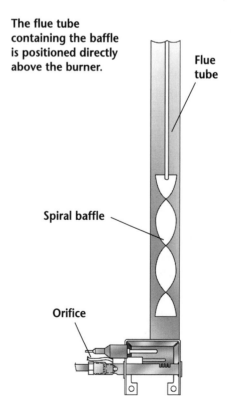

The flue tube containing the baffle is positioned directly above the burner.

Flue tube

Spiral baffle

Orifice

Other Notes – Since all brands and models differ in components, sequences of operation and troubleshooting paths, it is virtually impossible to cover all the possible scenarios within the confines of these pages. By and large, if a specific problem is in the area of refrigerator controls, i.e., the check light keeps coming on, the heat source chronically malfunctions, etc., the cause is usually PC board- or interface board-related. Today's aftermarket boards are markedly improved over earlier efforts. In some cases, tests have revealed that aftermarket replacement boards are often of enhanced quality and actually better than the original equipment board. Certainly high-quality aftermarket replacement boards should be a consideration if the cause is ultimately placed on the PC board. In any case, professional troubleshooting is required, but if a new PC board is necessary, consider the newer, improved versions that are available.

If there appears to be an operational problem such as insufficient cooling, over-cooling, or absolutely no cooling, here are a few items to check before making that appointment at the service facility.

First and foremost, be sure the refrigerator is within three degrees of level during operation. Habitually running the unit out of level, even for a few minutes, may cause a little more chromate to become crystallized. This may slowly continue until one day there will be no cooling at all. Nothing can clear a crystallized percolator tube. The entire cooling unit will need to be replaced.

Second, make sure there are no obstructions in the ventilation and drafting chimney at the rear of the cooling unit. Be sure to check the roof vent for bird nests.

Third, remember the LP pressure must be set at 11 inches of water column. By checking the pressure at a stove burner, the entire LP system can be checked for leaks.

If a problem seems to have developed, operate the refrigerator on another mode or heat source, preferably 120-volts AC or LP. The 12-volt DC operation as a heat source should not be considered as viable as the other two. Viewed typically as a maintaining heat source, the refrigerator should already be sufficiently cooled prior to switching to the 12-volt mode.

The purpose of switching modes is to try to isolate the problem area. If the cooling unit can be ruled out as a possible cause, then the RV technician will only have to concentrate on the problem mode. If the exact symptoms occur on both LP gas and 120-volt AC electricity, and there are no shared components in the controls, the problem is centered at the cooling unit.

In some instances, various control components are shared between each of the heat sources such as those models that have only one thermostat. In that case, additional troubleshooting will have to be performed by the service technician.

The goal is to eliminate the cooling unit as the cause of the problem. By doing so, typically the repair will be less costly.

Never block the rear vent opening of the refrigerator. Some owners are under the assumption that doing so will eliminate flame outage on those units that are not automatic. As discussed earlier, proper ventilation is a necessity.

Periodically check the seal on the refrigerator doors. Over time, the rubber gaskets may wear out allowing cool air inside the refrigerator to escape through the leaky gaskets around the doors. Gaskets may be checked by closing each refrigerator door on a slip of paper at various points around the gasket. If the paper can be pulled out with very little resistance or if it simply falls out, the gasket is faulty. A good sign of a faulty door gasket is an abundant formation of frost or ice on the secondary evaporator fins located inside the lower food storage section.

Proper storage of food inside the refrigerator will enable the air inside to circulate freely. Never block off a shelf with a large tray or pan. The principle of convection is employed to keep the air circulating inside the refrigerator, thereby maintaining an even temperature control throughout the entire food section. Optional fans are available that will aid in this inside air circulation. They can be purchased at any well-stocked RV parts and accessory store.

Once again, here are the four important areas to consider with the modern RV absorption refrigerator to have safe, reliable, silent operation.

- Leveling
- Ventilation
- LP gas pressure
- Cleanliness

By maintaining a watchful eye in these four areas, the RV absorption refrigerator will provide many years of reliable service.

CHAPTER SEVEN

Roof Air Conditioning

Years ago the roof top air conditioner was considered a luxury on most RVs. Many times they were only available by having the dealer install one prior to delivery of the new coach. Rarely were RVs shipped from the factory with one. If a coach did leave the manufacturer with one installed, it was usually a special order. Today, however, virtually all Class A motorhomes are shipped with at least one, oftentimes two, roof air conditioners. The same for many Class C motorhomes and travel trailers as well. RV owners have come to expect climate control as part of the whole RV-package now.

To remove heat, the air conditioner takes advantage of a natural property of liquids; namely, that whenever a liquid vaporizes, heat is absorbed. In the motor-driven compressor air conditioner, the application of this idea is sophisticated, employing a circulating refrigerant that boils at a low temperature and can be used over and over.

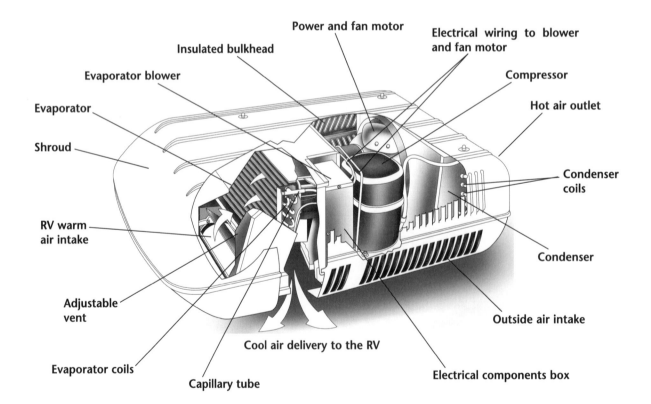

Power and fan motor

Electrical wiring to blower and fan motor

Insulated bulkhead

Compressor

Evaporator blower

Hot air outlet

Evaporator

Condenser coils

Shroud

RV warm air intake

Condenser

Adjustable vent

Outside air intake

Cool air delivery to the RV

Evaporator coils

Electrical components box

Capillary tube

Compressor-Type Air Conditioner

The RV air-conditioner is traditionally mounted on the roof. The air-conditioning cycle is a two-step operation involving evaporation (cooling) and condensation (reusing). In the compressor-type design, the refrigerant is circulated by the action of a compressor which is powered by 120-volt electricity.

The most popular air conditioner is the roof-mounted, compressor type. All compressor-type air conditioners require 120 volts AC. The electrical demand is such that the air conditioner must be wired with its own 20-amp circuit breaker. No other device can share the circuit with the air conditioner.

RV manufacturers are always searching for new ways to improve the aesthetics of their products, including air conditioners. Modern advances regarding the air conditioner include "split system" air-conditioners. Also, some models incorporate a heat pump that will both heat and cool the RV. With the proliferation of "basement" style motorhome designs, newer basement model air conditioners are on the rise. All have one thing in common: keeping the RVer cool. Roof top air conditioners, however, are still the preferred favorite among the majority coach manufacturers and retail customers.

An understanding of the components and operation of a typical root top air conditioner will assist the RVer in preventing potential problems and will further underscore the need for regular maintenance.

Components – Most RV air conditioners consist of six major component parts or groups of parts. They include:

- Compressor
- Condenser
- Evaporator
- Blower assembly
- Capillary tube
- Control devices

Typical Roof Top Air Conditioner

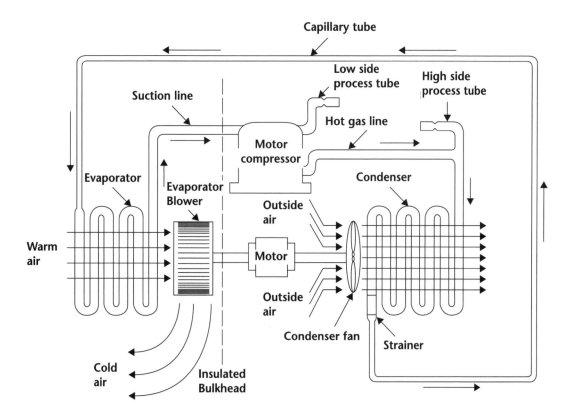

The entire system is sealed and pressurized with a refrigerant. Each refrigeration cycle starts with the compressor. Its purpose is to take in low-pressure liquid refrigerant and, just as the name implies, compress it and discharge it as a high-pressure vapor. When the refrigerant is compressed, heat is cast off, which causes the discharge line to become rather warm. Since temperature has a direct impact on pressure, on hot, sunny days, the pressure inside this discharge line can be as high as 360 PSI or more.

The next step for the high-pressure vapor is the condenser coil, which is the finned coil located on the roof and visible at the rear of the air conditioner. In the condenser, the vapor is cooled by air passing through the coil, which condenses the refrigerant into a liquid. When it leaves the condenser on the way to the capillary tube, the refrigerant stays in a liquid state.

The capillary tube is a metering device used in controlling the flow of the refrigerant. The typical roof top air conditioner is said to be capillary-tube controlled. This capillary, or "cap," tube determines the amount and the force at which the refrigerant enters the evaporator. All cap tubes are a specific length for that particular air conditioner. They must never be altered.

The high-pressure liquid refrigerant next enters the evaporator coil in a controlled amount from the capillary tube. When the high-pressure liquid enters the low-pressure atmosphere of the evaporator, the refrigerant evaporates rapidly into a gas. When this evaporation takes place, heat is absorbed from the air, which is being blown over the evaporator coil. The air with the heat removed is returned to the inside of the RV through the discharge ducts on the ceiling plate. The blower motor and fan distribute the now cool air throughout the coach. Additionally, the same motor draws air across the condenser fins with the addition of a fan attached to the opposite end of the motor shaft.

After the refrigerant passes through the evaporator, the low-pressure vapor is then returned to the compressor through the suction side or low-pressure line to begin the cooling process again. As long as there are no breaks or cracks in the tubing, joints or the various components, this process will continue as long as the compressor is running.

The various components that control the operation of the air conditioner include the following:
- **Fan switch**—Basically controls the speed of the blower fan. Different brands and models abound with various features, but most will have at least two speeds. Newer units are controlled by printed circuitry.
- **Thermostat**—Controls the operation of the compressor by sensing the need for cooling and the room temperature. The sensing element is positioned in the path of the return air being drawn back into the air conditioner. The thermostat typically has a temperature range from 90 degrees Fahrenheit to about 62 degrees Fahrenheit. That is, the thermostat will close causing the compressor to become activated only if the temperature at the sensing element is within this parameter. Rarely will a roof top air conditioner cool at temperatures below 62 degrees Fahrenheit.
- **Capacitors**—Usually there is a start capacitor (to help jump start the compressor and motor from a standing start) and a run capacitor (that takes over for the start capacitor after the unit is running) associated with the typical roof top air conditioner. They are predictably located inside the roof top shroud. All testing should be performed by a qualified air conditioner technician, but just knowing what they are and where the components are located will help the owner understand the importance of preventive maintenance. The fan motor may also have a capacitor in its circuit.
- **Compressor overload**—A thermal protective device. If the case temperature of the

compressor goes beyond a safe limit, the overload will open the circuit, thereby protecting the compressor. It is located on top of the compressor.

• **Relay** – Commonly referred to as the start relay. This device is usually located in the electrical control box near the start capacitor. This normally closed relay controls the current sent to the start capacitor. It also disconnects the start capacitor once the compressor is started, allowing the run capacitor to take over. Some relays may be classified as time-delay relays. This means that the compressor is delayed from initial start up for a short period of time to allow the head pressure to equalize in the closed refrigerant system. This greatly extends the life of the compressor.

MAINTENANCE: Periodic inspection and maintenance will keep you informed as to the condition of the air conditioner. If, at any time, a drastic decrease in cooling is noticed, or a refrigerant leak is suspected, do not operate the unit until it has been thoroughly checked by a qualified service technician. Damage to other components may result. Performing the following steps once or twice a year will permit the air conditioner to produce many years of cool air service. Be sure to perform all of these checks with the power off. The final step is the only time the air conditioner needs to be running.

1) Remove and clean the filter. The filter is usually accessible from inside the RV. Most can be rinsed out with warm water. To be sure, consult the owner's manual for that particular brand. Never operate the air conditioner with the filter removed.

2) Remove the shroud and inspect all tubing lines for cracks or splits. If any are found, do not operate the unit until a complete repair, evacuation and recharge has taken place.

3) Check all electrical wiring. Look for loose connections, wear and missing or burned insulation. Make sure all wire nuts are taped to prevent them from coming loose while enduring the vibrations that occur with roof air conditioners.

4) Check all mounting hardware and tighten the mounting bolts if necessary. Over time, rubber gaskets may need replacing. The time to replace the 14-inch gasket around the ceiling opening is before the RV is put into service for the season.

5) Inspect the fan blades and motor for free turning and to make sure the blades or squirrel cages do not rub or hit any other portion of the housing. Remove any accumulation of leaves or other debris that may have settled inside the air conditioner.

6) Inspect and clean the condenser coil and the evaporator coil. If any of the fins are damaged on the exposed condenser coil, carefully straighten them as best as possible. A fin comb can be purchased at a HVAC supply store if the condenser has sustained major denting or damage.

7) After reassembly, test run the unit and record the temperature differential. The temperature differential is the recommended difference in temperature between the cool air discharged into the room and the warmer return air that passes through the filter. The best conditions will result in a temperature differential of between 18 and 25 degrees Fahrenheit. Keep in mind, however, voltage variances, humidity and outside ambient temperatures will greatly affect this differential. The goal should be to obtain the minimum 18 degree Fahrenheit difference. Anything less might signify an operational problem and further troubleshooting may be in order.

Roof air conditioner shrouds are traditionally made of plastic and are pretty durable. However, such durability has its limits. Besides normal degradation due to the UV rays of the sun, low hanging branches or other appurtenances can literally leave their mark on the air conditioner shroud. Usually the tallest component on the roof, it can seem to act as a magnet at times. Always look before backing. Additionally, it is wise to know the overall traveling height of the RV. After loading the RV, measure to the tallest component and note this measurement on or near the dashboard. This way, when warning signs indicate a low overhead condition, a guessing game can be eliminated.

Damaged shrouds can sometimes be cemented. If the shroud is constructed of ABS plastic, patch kits are available. Replacement shrouds are usually available from the manufacturer. Another option is to replace the plastic shroud with a stronger and more durable one made of fiberglass. Bri-Rus, a West Coast company manufactures fiberglass replacement shrouds for all current and discontinued roof air conditioners. Their four basic designs will fit virtually every roof air conditioner.

TROUBLESHOOTING AND REPAIR: Because of the complicated procedures, recent changes in the environmental law and the required specialty tools and equipment needed, it is not advised that the owner perform any repairs on the hermetically sealed refrigerant system.

The troubleshooting chart on the opposite page will list many possible causes for a few conditions the air conditioner may fall into. As always, record the model number and serial number of the unit in case questions arise and parts need to be ordered.

Notes: _____

_____

_____

_____

_____

_____

_____

_____

_____

_____

_____

_____

_____

_____

_____

_____

_____

_____

_____

Condition	Possible Causes
Blower motor will not run	No voltage at air conditioner
	Circuit breaker tripped
	Open winding in motor
	Loose connection
	Faulty fan switch
	Faulty motor
Blower motor runs very slowly	Low voltage
	Loose wires or connection
	Fan or squirrel cage misaligned
Compressor will not start	Open compressor windings
	Thermostat setting already attained
	Overload device tripped
	Faulty thermostat
Compressor turns, but will not start	Low voltage
	Faulty start capacitor
	Faulty run capacitor
	Faulty compressor motor
	Defective start relay
	Unequalized pressure in system
Compressor starts, runs, then trips overload	Low voltage
	Defective start relay
	Faulty start capacitor
	Faulty run capacitor
	Overly high compressor head pressure
	Shorted compressor winding
	Internal damage to compressor
	Faulty overload device
Air conditioner short cycles	Thermostat at or near desired setting
	Partial loss of refrigerant charge
	Faulty compressor bearings
	Discharge pressure too high
	Too much refrigerant charge
	Thermostat sense probe not in position
Compressor runs continuously	Low refrigerant charge
	Refrigerant leak in system
	Dirty or blocked condenser
	Faulty thermostat
	Contaminated system
	Damaged or obstructed cap tube
	Dirty or blocked evaporator coil
	Thermostat sense probe not in position
	Coach doors and windows open
Insufficient cooling	Low refrigerant charge
	Refrigerant leak in system
	Restricted or damaged cap tube
	Blocked evaporator coil
	Faulty compressor

CHAPTER EIGHT

Hitches and Towing

Even though the equipment and techniques involved in towing are not overly complex, accurate research, thoughtful planning and the proper setup of equipment are mandates for safe and enjoyable travel. It takes a professional shop to accomplish the latter of these prerequisites, and many RV dealers and service centers are capable of performing them. It is wise, however, to shop around for the best expertise available. This is one area you do not want to choose simply by the best price.

This chapter will cover the many aspects of towing. To the uninitiated, the breadth of the information can be rather daunting unless there is some direction in your planning. The pages in this chapter are segregated into three typical towing scenarios: towing conventional travel trailers, towing fifth wheel travel trailers and finally, towing a small vehicle behind a motorhome, often referred to as "dinghy" towing. Additionally, information regarding electric brakes on travel trailers and auxiliary braking for the dinghy will also be discussed.

TOWING A TRAVEL TRAILER

When considering towing a standard travel trailer, three possibilities exist. You must either:
- Purchase a tow vehicle compatible with your existing trailer
- Purchase a trailer to match your existing tow vehicle
- Purchase the trailer and the tow vehicle at the same time

While all three are doable, the third situation is considered the best. There are simply more options available. With either of the first two, limitations exist. Let us assume you already have the trailer. Here are some key items to remember when shopping for the perfect tow vehicle.

CHOOSING THE TOW VEHICLE: To properly choose a tow vehicle, first check the trailer. Exactly what is required to safely move that trailer down the road? Think of the loaded trailer not as an RV, but rather one huge mass of poundage that you will be dragging along behind you as you cruise down the highway. The operative word here is weight. A body of weight that you must get rolling and more importantly, be able to eventually stop. Although weight figures will be located on the data plate at the left front corner of the trailer, the best advice is to have the fully loaded trailer weighed.

Chapter 9 details how to weigh your towing combination using a platform scale. Knowing your Gross Vehicle Weight (GVW) will enable you to pare down the list of potential tow vehicles. Also, towing specifications are available at your dealer for every tow vehicle along with a listing of the extra equipment needed to safely tow a travel trailer. Commonly referred to as "trailer packages," such additions include a larger radiator, a higher output alternator and larger battery, auxiliary transmission cooling and a pre-wired harness for the electrical connections. Remember, not all vehicles can safely tow a trailer. Some may actually be damaged if you attempt to tow. Ask the dealer for the manufacturer's rated towing capacity for the vehicles on your short list.

Aside from your wallet (which in itself could be a limiting factor), next ponder what you personally look for in a vehicle. Do you favor gasoline powered or diesel? What creature comforts do you need and cannot live without? Also, unless you choose to RV full-time, consider what else the tow vehicle will be doing when not hauling your belongings down the road. Will it second as a work truck? Can it be used as a family vehicle? Only you can answer these questions, as well as the question of aesthetics and accouterments.

TOWING EQUIPMENT: Once you have settled on a tow vehicle, it is imperative that you be aware of the many different types and styles of equipment available. Here is where you need some expert advice and where you will need to do a little homework. Although variations exist, some may be better than others for your particular towing combination. An examination of some of the more common options concerning towing equipment is in order, but it is important also to understand that final decisions can only be ascertained after knowing the specifics of your particular tow vehicle and trailer. It is highly advisable to develop a relationship with a local RV service facility. Make certain they are capable of installing the equipment you must consider. If necessary, contact the manufacturer of the equipment and ask them for their recommendation of a good shop in your area. More often than not they will be happy to oblige you. After all, their reputation also rides on the quality of work by the shop that installs their product.

HITCHES: Obviously, a hitch is the crucial connection between tow vehicle and trailer. As in choosing a tow vehicle, choosing a hitch is also determined by weight rating. Since you now know what your trailer weighs and what the capacity of your tow vehicle is, simply choose a hitch that falls within those parameters. Is it that simple? Just about. All good service facilities that install hitches will first ask you about the total weight you will be towing. Next, they will ask you about tongue weight. Tongue weight is that percentage of the total weight that will be placed directly on the hitch assembly. It usually amounts to approximately 12 to 17 percent of the total weight of your trailer. Any cargo stowed in the tow vehicle behind the rear axle must also be considered and added to the tongue weight when trying to determine the hitch required.

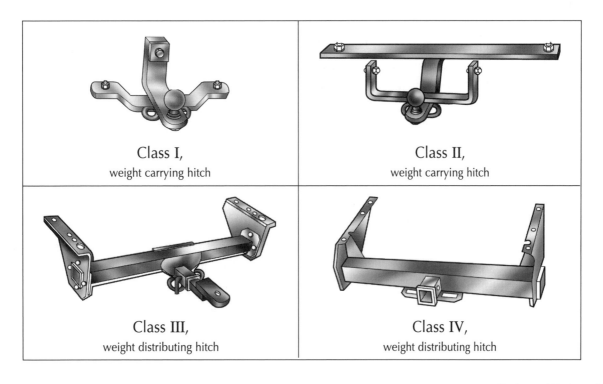

Class I,
weight carrying hitch

Class II,
weight carrying hitch

Class III,
weight distributing hitch

Class IV,
weight distributing hitch

There are two basic types of hitches: weight carrying and weight distributing. Weight carrying hitches literally carry the weight of the trailer on the hitch and rear axle of the tow vehicle. The maximum weight, or limiting factor, for weight carrying hitches is 3,500 pounds.

By far the most common type of hitch today is the weight distributing, or load equalizing hitch. Always mounted to the frame, this type of hitch, by its design, distributes the weight to both axles of the tow vehicle. Weight distributing hitches are the preferred method of towing all but the lightest forms of travel trailers. The following chart displays the differences among today's hitches.

Type	Class	Max. Trailer Weight	Max. Tongue Weight
Weight carrying	I	2,000 Pounds	200 Pounds
Weight carrying	II	3,500 Pounds	300 Pounds
Weight distributing	III	4,000 Pounds	350 Pounds
Weight distributing	IV	10,000 Pounds	1,000 Pounds

Hitch Components – What most call "the hitch," is actually comprised of several components, not including the coupler of the trailer. Weight distributing hitch assemblies include these three main components:

- Receiver
- Ball mount
- Spring bar assembly

The main component of a weight distributing hitch is the *receiver*. The receiver is, in most cases, bolted to the frame at various strategic points underneath the tow vehicle. Some may be welded. Hitch manufacturers make specific receivers for all tow vehicles that are custom designed just for that vehicle. All the bends and mounting brackets are in the correct place. It will mate perfectly with the frame of the tow vehicle. For older, obsolete vehicles, custom hitch receivers can also be fabricated by a quality hitch shop.

The *ball mount* is the link between the trailer and the tow vehicle. It, too, is available as a bolt-together unit or it can be fully welded. Installation of the ball mount is not as simple as it appears. Careful measurements must be taken on the tow vehicle and also on the trailer. Ball mount tilt angle and ball height are two important measurements that are necessary to ensure a proper hitch setup. Tilt angle is best left up to the professional hitch shop. The result of correct ball mount tilt angle will find the spring bars parallel with the bottom of the trailer coupler when fully hitched and connected.

Ball mount height, however, can be determined by leveling the trailer on a hard surface street or parking lot. The trailer must be fully loaded to its traveling weight. Measure the distance at the axle (or in between the tandem axles), from the road surface to the top of the frame. If your trailer has a solid underbelly, take it to the hitch shop for proper measuring. The top of the frame should coincide with the top of the coupler on the "A" frame. Next, add one-eighth of an inch for every 100 pounds of trailer tongue weight. The final calculation will be the correct ball height needed at the ball mount. Since ball mount height is specific to just one trailer, it is not wise to borrow someone else's ball mount. Chances are either the ball height or the tilt angle will be different.

The third component of your weight distributing setup is the *spring bar assembly*. Using the dynamics of leverage as its theory, spring bars are like the handles on a wheelbarrow. By lifting up on the bars, the weight is distributed or shifted toward the front axle. This component adds a new dimension to the handling characteristics of the tow vehicle. Steering and turning become improved and safer.

Other items located at or near your hitch include:
- **Safety chains**—in case the trailer and tow vehicle should prematurely part company
- **Break-away switch**—applies full power to all electric trailer brakes in case of premature separation
- **Electrical connector**—connects the tow vehicle lights and other circuits to the trailer

TRAILER SWAY: Not as bothersome as in years past, nonetheless, trailer sway still remains high on the list of concerns for RVers who tow trailers. Modern manufacturing techniques and advances in equipment, however, seem to have all but eliminated the nuisance of trailer sway. It has usually been attributed to poor weight distribution on the trailer frame during the construction of the RV, or to poor loading techniques by the end user. Sway can further be aggravated by passing tractor/trailer rigs, which many times is the cause of inducing the fish-tailing process. To minimize trailer sway, check your setup for:
- Proper loading
- Adequate tongue weight
- Proper equipment

Proper Loading—Proper loading and stowing of personal items and camping gear is paramount to safe towing. A balance in weight primarily between the two sides of the trailer will help minimize trailer sway.

Adequate Tongue Weight—More common in years past, inadequate tongue or hitch weight has been a significant contributor to trailer sway. With today's engineering standards being more defined, this probable cause from the past has been lessened quite a bit. Still, in terms of Class IV hitches, the ideal tongue weight should be at least 12 percent of the total weight of the fully loaded trailer. Some of the larger trailers may have tongue weights nearing 17 percent of the total. Anything less could have a tendency to be the cause of sway, should it be experienced. If necessary, move heavier objects forward of the front axle of the trailer to add to the tongue weight.

Proper Equipment—To combat trailer sway mechanically, sway control devices can be added to your hitch setup. Two types of sway controls are the most predominant: friction-type and dual cam-type. Friction-type sway controls connect from the ball mount to the side of the "A" frame coupler on the trailer. A friction pad, similar to a brake lining, rubs against a steel bar as it slides in the housing. This creates a more rigid connection between tow vehicle and trailer, thereby reducing the effects and severity of trailer sway.

Although your turning radius may be slightly reduced, the use of a friction-type sway control does not necessitate removal prior to backing up. Proper installation instructions must be followed, however, and measurements must be carefully taken. After installation, slowly try to jackknife your tow vehicle and trailer. If there is no obstruction and you are not close to hitting the sway control, then you will have no problem backing up with the sway control in place. You should, however, reduce the tension or the adjustment on the sway control while driving under slippery road conditions.

The dual cam-type sway control, uniquely manufactured and perfected by Reese Products, attaches to the trailer "A" frame and engages the spring bars directly through two cams with corresponding recesses. Once connected, like the friction-type, a more rigid structure exists that will resist trailer sway. When cornering, the cams disengage from the recessed position so as not to affect the turning radius of the tow vehicle and trailer combination. Sway control is not in effect when this occurs since the rigidity is lost when the cam comes out of the recess. However, this is not a concern. If you are making such a turn that causes the cam and the recess to become temporarily

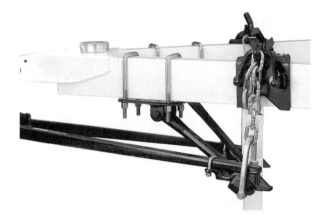

Dual Cam-type Sway Control

separated, you will be going slow enough that sway control is not needed anyway. Either type of sway controls will work with most tow vehicles and travel trailers.

Another type of hitch is available that virtually eliminates any of the effects of trailer sway. Called the Pull-Rite hitch, its unique design takes advantage of the fifth-wheel principle and puts it to use when towing a conventional travel trailer.

When towing, the location of the pivot point (the ball mount), is directly proportional to the amount of sway felt by the driver. The closer the pivot point is to the rear axle of the tow vehicle, the less sway will be evident. While the conventional hitch has its pivot point six to eight inches behind the vehicle, the Pull-Rite's pivot point is located immediately behind the rear axle of the tow vehicle, similar to a fifth-wheel hitch installation, where the pivot point is located almost directly above the rear axle in most cases. There is also a large radius bar formed into a 140 degree arc. The long draw bar glides through this arc on sealed roller bearings. Tests have shown travel trailers making a complete "U" turn on a narrow street using the Pull-Rite hitch without having to back up. Hitching up can take place anywhere along the arc. The draw bar can be positioned to the far left, for example, allowing the driver full vision of the ball mount while backing the tow vehicle under the trailer coupler.

HITCHING UP: Connecting the tow vehicle and the travel trailer involves three basic steps:
- Attaching the trailer coupler to the ball mount
- Positioning the spring bar assembly
- Connecting the electrical harness, safety chains and break-away switch

Before backing the tow vehicle under the trailer coupler, make sure there is proper clearance under the coupler. Raise the coupler with the tongue jack if necessary. Position the ball directly under the coupler. This is when it is a real benefit to have a copilot. Before lowering the coupler onto the all, measure the distance between the ground and the front bumper on the tow vehicle (the ground should be fairly level while taking these measurements). Next, measure the distance between the ground and the rear bumper (or any point of reference).

Lower the trailer onto the ball and lock the coupler. Then raise the tongue jack again while the two are connected. Raise both units above the level plane. This makes it much easier to attach the spring bars. Insert the spring bars into the sockets of the ball mount. Make sure they are locked in place. Attach the brackets to the "A" frame. To find the correct location for the brackets, hold the chain straight up, make sure there are no twists in the chain. Center the bracket on the chain and tighten the bracket screw *finger tight* only.

The next step will require a little experimentation to find the correct link in the chain to position in the brackets. Pick one and position it on the hook or in the slot. Using the assist handle, lift up on the arm of the bracket until it snaps into place, putting tension on the spring bar. Move the safety wire over the top of the arm. Repeat this procedure on the other side.

Now, lower the tongue jack until all the weight is on the hitch assembly. By adjusting the number of chain links up or down, the height of both vehicles can be regulated. The correct adjustment of the spring bars is attained when the difference between the measurements you took before connecting the trailer (from the ground to the bumpers) and the measurements you take after locking the spring bars in place, is within a half inch of each other. Also, when viewed from the side, the spring bars should be parallel with the bottom of the "A" frame and the chains should be straight up and down. It may take a few tries to identify the correct link to use. Be sure to use the same link each time.

The final step in hitching up is to connect the electrical plug for the running lights and other circuits. Be sure the contacts are not corroded. Brighten them with emery cloth or a commercially available connector cleaner. Install and adjust the sway control according to the manufacturer's recommendations. Connect the break-away switch cable to the frame of the tow vehicle or to the hitch receiver. Do not attach the cable to the ball or the ball mount. Finally, attach the safety chains. They should be crossed under the coupler so they form an "X" to catch the coupler should the hitch fail. Chains should be long enough to handle the sharpest of turns, yet short enough not to drag. After everything is connected, pull the trailer forward a few feet and check all the equipment for any adjustments that may be necessary. Adjust the mirrors to your satisfaction, and you are ready to go.

Accessories for Towing – What has been described above is considered the bare bones of towing a travel trailer. What follows is a list of various aftermarket products that will enhance your towing. As technology has progressed, so have many items of safety, efficiency and performance. The following products are simply recommended based on their ability to contribute to one or more of these three elements. There are many more products available; however, this list will give you an idea of the various areas to consider for upgrading.

- Heavy duty alternator
- High volume radiator
- Transmission cooler
- Power steering cooler
- High performance exhaust system
- Gear Vendors over/underdrive auxiliary transmission
- Turbo-charger
- Ride-Rite air springs
- Steering stabilizer
- Fuel injection

HITCH MAINTENANCE: Most hitch equipment is constructed quite sturdy. After all, there is a lot riding on the structural integrity of the hitch. Maintenance, although important, is minimal when it comes to your towing equipment. It will not take a lot of effort to check the following items, yet it is wise to perform them regularly.

Hitch Ball: Keep the ball lubricated. Many RV stores carry grease specifically designed for hitch balls, but should you choose to use a generic grease, be certain it is the high temperature variety. Lube the hitch ball each time you hook-up.

Ball Mount and Receiver: If your ball mount or hitch is the bolt-on type, periodically check the bolts and nuts for tightness. Look for any signs of rust on any component. Be sure to check inside the sockets where the spring bars slide into. Also lube the sockets.

Spring Bars: Check the chain and bar for any wear or defect. Call the manufacturer or your local dealer if a replacement is necessary. Over time, deflection of the bars may indicate a need for replacement.

Sway Controls: For friction-type sway controls, visually inspect the lining each camping season and replace it if the wear patterns expose metal. After extended trips or every 10,000 miles, remove the slide bar and clean it with emery cloth or steel wool. All that is necessary with the Reese dual-cam sway control is to inspect the bolt attachment points for tightness and to apply a thin layer of lubricating grease to the cams and their respective recesses.

Trailer "A" Frame and Coupler: Check these areas for rust. As you hitch and unhitch over a period of time, scratches may happen. Sand and touch up any scratches or nicks in the paint. Lube the locking mechanism on the coupler.

Safety Chains: Inspect each link periodically. Look closely at those links closest to the ground for wear. Do not use universal links to repair worn links. Replace the entire chain if necessary.

Electrical Connector: As mentioned earlier, look for signs of corrosion on the metal contacts. Clean them with a brush or a contact cleaner. Also, make sure the plug and the receptacle are dry. Check the length of the electrical harness for fraying or where it may have accidentally been dragged along the ground. Again, if damage is present, replace the entire harness.

Break-Away Switch: As with any electrical contact or connection, clean and dry are the operative words. Also, periodically pull the pin and check for oxidation (some pins may be plastic). Spray a shot of contact cleaner inside the switch housing and reinsert the pin fully. Check the braided cable that connects the pin. Again, replace it if any signs of damage exist.

All in all, very little maintenance is necessary for your towing equipment. However, this is one area where you would not want to take any chances. Find a routine and get into the habit of performing these inspections as you travel. You will reap many miles of safe, trouble-free RVing.

TOWING A FIFTH-WHEEL TRAILER

Most RVers do not think of having much in common with truckers other than driving the same highways, but when it comes to fifth-wheel trailers, there is much similarity and some subtle indebtedness. For instance, the fifth-wheel got its name from the trucking industry. The "fifth-wheel" being the smooth, round, hitching disk that is so easily spotted on the big tractors when their trailer is not attached.

Also the jacks the poke out from their retracted positions on semi-trailer front ends have counterparts on the RV fifth-wheel trailer, where they perform the same job of supporting the trailer when it is disconnected from the tow vehicle. And thirdly, the mechanics of joining the tandem via a pin on the trailer that locks into the jaws of a plate mounted on the truck is a direct steal from the trucking industry.

Ideas are stolen for a reason. In the case of the fifth-wheel, the plate pin arrangement provides a means for hitching and unhitching that is easy and almost maintenance free. There are some demanding aspects, some muscle is needed to pull the handle that operates the jaws or to manually crank the jacks, but both chores are no more taxing than coupling a travel trailer. And there are aftermarket products that can perform these tasks easier.

Fifth Wheel Towing

Exceptional handling and backing characteristics are two advantages of towing a fifth wheel. Hitch weight is better proportioned since the pivot point is positioned over the rear axle of the tow vehicle. Trailer sway is minimized as well.

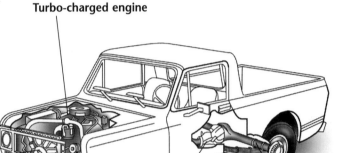

Turbo-charged engine

Large radiator

Auxiliary cooling

Under/overdrive auxilary transmission

Heavy duty suspension

Locking jaws

Plate

Crossbar

Tow vehicles must be properly equipped. Many aftermarket add-on components have been specially designed for RV towing use. The addition of such equipment will vastly improve your RV enjoyment.

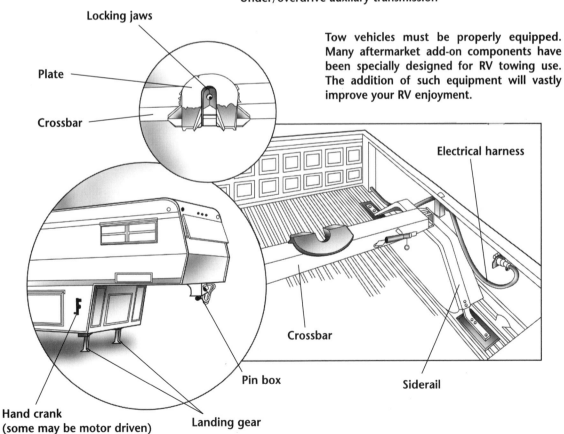

Electrical harness

Crossbar

Siderail

Pin box

Hand crank
(some may be motor driven)

Landing gear

This idea is so well accepted that there are fifth-wheel owners who would tow nothing else. They are a small but dedicated bunch bound by the much touted advantage of fifth-wheel towing, exceptional handling. It is an idea firmly rooted in reality.

With the hitch weight placed almost directly over the tow truck's rear axle, these trailers are quite stable in their tracking. Also, trailer sway is pretty much eliminated with the fifth-wheel design.

During turning and backing, a fifth-wheel develops less of an angle to the tow vehicle than would a conventional travel trailer. This allows a quick recovery after a turn, but also causes increased tire wear because the two vehicles do not round corners on the same turn radius. This forces the trailer tires to "scrub" against the pavement

For the most part, fifth-wheel towing equipment is maintenance free, and the tasks for the responsible owner are the ordinary pre-trip checks that any RVer would perform.

There are differences in hitch designs. The hitch you will purchase must match the hitch that is installed on the trailer by the manufacturer. Most trailer manufacturers install one of the different optional hitches during their manufacture of the fifth-wheel. The first time buyer has a head start on these decisions if he or she has some understanding of how fifth-wheel hitches differ and the relative advantages of each.

FIFTH-WHEEL HITCHES: There are three basic fifth-wheel hitch designs in use today:
- Crossbar or side rail design
- Pedestal or floor mount
- Inverted or gooseneck concept

The most popular designs, the crossbar/side rail and floor mount types, use many of the same components. Each has a circular plate or "fifth-wheel," mounted in the truck bed. Both require a pin protruding from a box mounted on the trailer overhang. Both have spring-loaded levers for releasing the locking jaws in the plate, and both have locking pins for preventing the lever from being accidentally dislodged from the "locked" position. They differ in the way each hitch mounts to the truck bed.

Pedestal Hitch—The advantage of the floor mount design is that the hitch takes up little space in the truck bed, and the plate is easily removable so that the truck can be put to other uses. This is accomplished with a metal framework that is bolted to the truck bed floor and to ribs that tie in to the truck frame.

Another piece welded to the base plate has channels so that a low pedestal, the mounting surface for the hitch plate, can slide in and out. A lock pin secures the pedestal. The floor mount can be mounted in practically any truck or light utility vehicle.

Crossbar/Side Rail Designs—These create a support structure for the hitch plate made up of angle iron or channel iron side pieces mounted on each side of the truck bed and a box-like crossbar that contains the plate. The bar is bolted to the side rails which are, in turn, anchored to the truck frame on either side of the wheel well and bolted to the fender to restrict any lateral movement of the support.

Side rails are either mounted over the fenders or just inside of them. The over the fender mount has the advantage of leaving more of the truck bed open for storage items, but it does not provide as firm an anchor as the inside the fender choice.

Inverted or Gooseneck Design—This hitch is a marked departure from the others since it has neither hitching plate nor pin. Instead, a larger, heavy duty coupler, similar to standard coupler found on the "A" frame of a conventional trailer, is welded onto a pin box which is mounted on the trailer.

"Gooseneck" comes from this coupler mounting which resembles the silhouette of a gooseneck.

A flat steel base plate rests on the bed of the truck and is bolted to the frame. The hitch ball, again, similar to an ordinary trailer hitch ball except larger and heavier, is welded to the base plate. The gooseneck design is popular in farming areas because a truck thus equipped can be used with farm equipment and livestock trailers.

Hitch Installation – Fifth-wheel hitches, as with all hitches, should only be installed by an experienced, qualified shop. Since some welding is recommended for typical fifth-wheel hitch installations, it should be done by a certified welder. Although all fifth-wheel hitches are bolted to the bed of the pick-up truck, it is advisable to have a corresponding strap from the first (most-forward) mounting bolt welded to the frame of the truck underneath the bed. Although it is highly unlikely that the weight of the trailer would actually cause the hitch to be ripped out of the bed, it is a viable safety feature to not rely solely on the mounting plates being simply bolted to the bed. This recommended method will find at least one bolt on each side of the hitch bolted through the bed, into a steel strap that is welded to the frame rail of the pick-up truck.

Mounting Location – Some manufacturers recommend mounting the hitch directly over the axle, some say no, it should be two inches in front of the axle. So where is the proper location to mount a fifth-wheel? While it is always prudent to follow the manufacturer's recommendations, it may not always be possible since all truck beds and fifth-wheel trailers are not exactly the same. Although only long bed trucks are recommended, bed length, overall wheelbase of the tow vehicle, design of the trailer, etc. are just a few of the areas to consider. Here is a proven method of determining where to mount the fifth-wheel hitch in your pick-up that best suits your trailer.

The first step is to measure the width of the trailer. Then divide that number by two, and add two more inches to the total. Next, measure back from the front of the bed and mark that previous total. This position is the centerline location of the hitch. Here is an example: Your fifth-wheel trailer is 96 inches wide at its widest point. Half of that is 48 inches; adding two inches equals 50 inches. Measure back from the front of the bed 50 inches (remember, not the back of the cab, but the front of the bed). This method will ensure you will have plenty of clearance on tight turns. It has happened, because of poor hitch location, that the front of the trailer and the rear of the cab have been damaged on tight turns. Where clearance is not an issue, the fifth-wheel hitch is best located directly over the axle.

HITCHING AND UNHITCHING: Crossbar/side rail and pedestal mount designs allow hitching from a range of angles. The only requirement is that the truck be maneuverable beneath the trailer overhang. Hitching involves lowering or removing the truck tailgate (a costly mistake should one forget to do so), opening the "jaws" of the plate by pulling the lever, backing up the truck until the pin is caught by the plate and seated (a loud snap will be heard) and locking the jaws by releasing the spring-loaded lever, then inserting the lever lock pin.

The trailer jacks and landing pads are raised by cranking in a counterclockwise direction. This can be done manually or, on many fifth-wheels, automatically, by simply flipping a switch. Other details include attaching the break-away switch cable to the truck frame and plugging in the electrical connector.

Unhitching is the opposite procedure. The first step is cranking down the landing gear jacks until they are firmly planted on the ground. All seasoned RVers carry wood planks to aid in this step. This is followed by disconnecting the electrical connector and break-away cable, lowering the tailgate, pulling the release lever and driving the truck out from under the trailer.

Maintenance – Fifth-wheel hitch equipment requires little attention other than keeping the hitch plate and locking mechanism well lubricated. Maintenance chores center on the peripheral items that any RVer includes in pre-trip checks including:

- Electrical connector and breakaway switch
- Tire pressure
- Mirrors
- Trailer battery (fully charge)

Lubricating the plate—Any good quality high temperature automotive grease will do this. Keep a generous amount on the plate. If it gets thin, replenish as necessary.

Electrical connector—These plugs and receptacles are generally well designed to keep grime and moisture out when they are connected. However, during period of non-use, they may corrode. Make sure the contacts are clean and dry.

Break-away switch—Examine the cable on the break-away switch and make sure that it is firmly attached to the truck. The cord must have enough slack to allow full turning.

Tire pressure—Check all tires for proper pressure and correct if necessary (see Chapter 9).

Trailer battery—Make sure it is fully charged prior to leaving.

SELECTING A TOW VEHICLE: Although some fifth-wheel trailer manufacturers produce specialty trucks that are packaged with their trailer, most owners can find a suitable tow vehicle among the stock units manufactured by the auto industry. There are, however, special considerations.

You need a hefty truck for fifth-wheel towing. There are several reasons for this. One is that, whereas the hitch weight of a travel trailer is usually about 12 to 15 percent of its gross weight, the pin weight of a fifth-wheeler generally runs about 20 to 25 percent (for a 6,000-pound trailer, that is 1,200 to 1,500 pounds!). Also, the higher profile created by the second level bedroom of the trailer causes more wind resistance and consequently, more drive train power and better cooling are needed.

Although some small fifth-wheel trailers can get by with a properly equipped half-ton pick-up, generally a three-quarter-ton truck is the minimum tow vehicle for most fifth-wheel trailers. Some larger coaches require a one-ton truck. The overall weight of the trailer is the primary concern since most fifth-wheel rigs weigh substantially more than conventional travel trailers.

All pick-up trucks used for towing fifth-wheel trailers should always be equipped with a towing package. Stock towing packages generally include any or all of the following:

- Bigger engine
- Larger radiator
- Transmission oil cooler
- Heavy duty suspension
- Specially geared rear axle
- Higher capacity alternator
- Trailer wiring harness

Another recommendation for trucks that pull fifth-wheel trailers is a Gear Vendors under/over-drive auxiliary transmission. This addition to your tow vehicle will provide an additional gear in between each of your stock gears in your existing transmission. This results in more power to the drive wheels, less wasted energy and better performance, including an increase in fuel efficiency.

ELECTRIC BRAKES: Few thoughts send stronger shudders up the spine than the thought of brake failure while towing a trailer. Fortunately, because of electric brake design, the RVer usually has advance warning and is in a great position to spot the early signs of brake trouble.

An understanding of how trailer brakes work, how to tell if they are working properly and how to recognize trouble indicators are paramount to keeping your braking system in top working condition, thus ensuring you of dependable braking power when needed. Taken as a whole, your braking system may seem complicated, however, when viewed as individual components, an understanding soon develops that will enable you to fully comprehend just how your trailer stops so effortlessly behind you. The major brake system components include:

- Electric trailer brakes
- Electrical connector
- Break-away switch
- Brake controller

Electric Brake Design and Operation – Electric brakes resemble automobile drum brakes in that two components, shoes and drums, interact to apply braking force. Shoes are curved plates with a frictional facing material affixed to the outer surfaces. There are two shoes in each brake assembly mounted on a backing plate secured to a stationary part of the axle.

The drum is a circular container that fits over the brake shoes and, since it is mounted to the rotating part of the hub, spins with the wheel. Assembled, the shoes rest inside the drum, with a small space between the relaxed shoes and the drum wall. Braking force is applied by the shoes being forced outward and pressing against the drum wall. The harder the shoes press, the greater the frictional drag exerted on the spinning wheel and quicker the stopping action.

Here, the similarity with auto drum brakes stops. Automotive drum brakes are operated hydraulically, by the pressure of fluid that moves levers and forces the shoes outward. Electric trailer brakes, on the other hand, are operated by 12-volt DC electricity originating at the tow vehicle battery.

At the heart of the electric brakes is the magnet. When the magnet is energized by the controller mounted in the tow vehicle, it is attracted to the armature, a metal disc fixed inside the drum that spins with the drum. As the magnet moves toward the armature, it is pulled in the direction of motion causing the lever to push the shoe against the drum. Both shoes are linked so that the movement of one activates the other. Braking continues as long as the magnet continues to receive the appropriate voltage from the tow vehicle.

Typical Right Side Trailer Brake Assembly

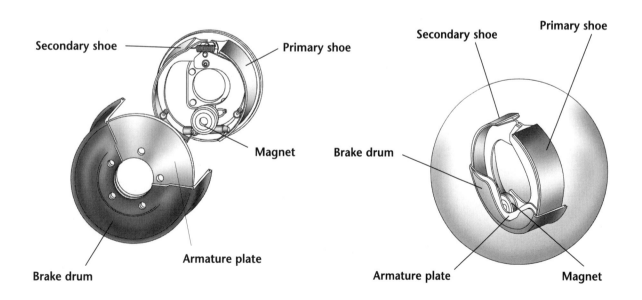

Secondary shoe — Primary shoe — Magnet — Armature plate — Brake drum — Secondary shoe — Primary shoe — Brake drum — Armature plate — Magnet

MAINTENANCE: Maintenance on electric trailer brakes involves basically three different areas: inspection, cleaning and adjustments. The informed RVer with basic mechanical ability and a few inexpensive specialty tools should have no problem performing the needed maintenance on trailer brakes.

Inspection – Your trailer brakes must be inspected and serviced at yearly intervals or more often as use and performance dictate.

Before beginning any procedure outlined here, make sure the trailer is properly raised and blocked safely with the tires completely off the ground. Remove the drum by first removing the dust cover, cotter pin and spindle nut and washer. Carefully remove the outer wheel bearing and cover it so dust does not settle on the bearing. Pull the drum away from the remainder of the brake assembly (it may be easier in some instances to first remove the tire and wheel). Look for worn shoe linings. Replace shoes if the lining is one-sixteenth of an inch thick or less. Replace them also if they are saturated with grease or oil or are cracked, gouged or if the lining has become separated from the shoes.

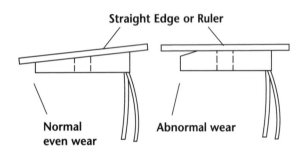

Replace the magnet if there is evidence of abnormal wear. Always replace both magnets on the same axle at the same time.

Inspect the magnet arm for any loose or worn parts. Check the shoe return springs, mounting springs and adjuster spring for deformation. Manually move the actuating arm or lever and check for any binding or rubbing. Replace the magnets if they show signs of uneven wear. Some magnets may have recessed screws. If the wear is down to the screws, the magnets should be replaced. In some instances it will be necessary to have the armature plate resurfaced. This cannot be done without a special lathe. Call your local service facility if an armature has developed a pattern of grooves due to worn or damaged magnets. It is wise to replace all the same items of the same axle even if only one side necessitates replacing. If, for instance the right side magnet is worn, but the left side is okay, replace them both. Keep all like components on the same axle, the same age.

There are two areas of the brake drum that are subject to wear and require periodic inspection. These two areas are the drum surface where the brake shoes make contact during stopping and the aforementioned armature surface where the magnet contacts. The drum surface should be inspected for excessive wear or heavy scoring. If the wear marks are worn more than 0.020 inches, or the drum has worn out of round by more than 0.015 inches, then the drum surface should be turned. If scoring or other wear is greater than 0.090 inches, the drum must be replaced.

To ensure proper contact between the armature face and the magnet face, the magnets should be replaced whenever the armature place is resurfaced.

Cleaning – Clean each brake assembly carefully with a soft, damp rag or brush. NEVER use compressed air to blow out the brake assembly. Some brake shoes may contain asbestos materials which are harmful. Make sure the brush or rag that is used is indeed damp. This will eliminate the spread of dust particles that can be inhaled. It is further recommended that a face mask filter be worn while working on electric brake assemblies. Before reassembling any parts that may have been taken apart during the inspection, apply a small dab of white lithium grease to the areas behind the shoe where the shoe rubs on the backing plate.

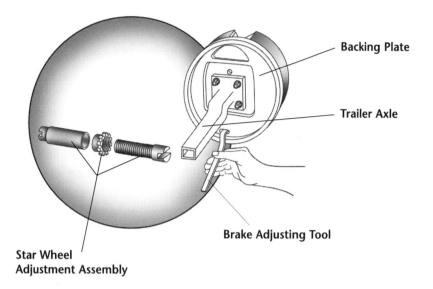

Backing Plate

Trailer Axle

Brake Adjusting Tool

Star Wheel Adjustment Assembly

Each brake assembly has an adjusting slot accessed from behind the backing plate. A rubber plug usually covers the slot. Remove the plug and insert the adjusting tool to engage the star wheel. Rotate the star wheel until the shoes prohibit the drum from turning. Rotate in the opposite direction until only a slight drag is felt.

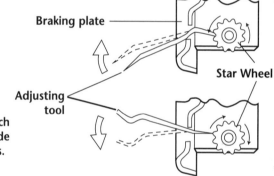

Braking plate

Star Wheel

Adjusting tool

If trailer braking is inadequate, double-check each individual adjustment. Rotating the star wheel inside the assembly tightens the shoes against the drums.

Shoe Adjustment – Unlike most automotive brakes which are self-adjusting, electric brakes require periodic adjustment to keep the shoes properly spaced. The main symptoms of brakes in need of adjustment are brakes that get hot while driving down the road (the shoes are dragging against the drum), or brakes that simply will not hold. Adjustment is simple, but important.

For shoe adjustment, jack up and properly support the trailer so that the weight is off the wheel and remove the plug from the back side of the backing plate so that an adjusting tool can be inserted through the hole. Slip the tool tip into a notch in the star wheel and ratchet and rotate the star wheel to expand the shoes against the drum (rotation may be clockwise or counter-clockwise, depending on the brake manufacturer). Expand the shoes until you cannot rotate the tire any further. This centers or seats each shoe evenly against the surface of the drum. Then back the adjustment off in the opposite direction until the wheel turns freely but has a very slight drag during rotation. Replace the plug to keep dirt and moisture out. Repeat this process on all brakes.

BREAK-AWAY SWITCH: The break-away switch is designed to apply full trailer brakes to your trailer should the trailer and the tow vehicle separate due to hitch or coupler failure. It is extremely important to remember that the break-away switch receives its voltage from the battery on the trailer, therefore, be certain your trailer battery remains fully charged at all times.

Mounted on the trailer at or near the "A" frame, it is wise to inspect and test your break-away switch regularly. As with any electrical contact or connection, clean and dry are the operative words. Periodically pull the pin and check for oxidation (some pins may be plastic). Spray a shot of contact cleaner inside the switch housing and reinsert the pin fully. Check the braided cable that connects the pin. Replace it if any signs of damage exist.

Ultima Brake Controller

A combined method to test the brakes and the break-away switch concurrently, although it takes a little longer, is to jack up each side of the trailer until the tires have been lifted off the ground. Manually spin each tire and then activate the controller. Do it again, but this time pull the pin on the break-away switch. In both instances, each tire should slam to an immediate stop. Repeat this process on the other side of the trailer. The advantage of this test is that if you only had three out of four brakes working, you would know exactly which one was not working properly.

There is no adjustment on the break-away switch. With the pin pulled, full braking occurs. With the pin in place, no braking is applied.

ELECTRICAL CONNECTOR: Look for signs of corrosion on the metal contacts. Clean them with a brush or a contact cleaner. Also, check to make sure the plug and the receptacle are dry. Check the entire length of the electrical harness for fraying or where it may have accidentally been dragged along the ground. Again, if damage is present, replace the entire harness.

BRAKE CONTROLLERS: Today's trailer brake controllers consist of two basic types: hydraulic-electric and electronic. In recent years, with the advances in the technology, the electronic brake controller has become the dominant type. Estimates of 90 to 95 percent of all brake controllers sold today are of the electronic variety… and for good reason. Much simpler to install and maintain, they are also more precise in delivering the modulated amount of current and voltage necessary to apply smooth stopping of your travel trailer or fifth-wheel. Electronic controllers are also more sensitive to the somewhat delicate electronics found in today's tow vehicles.

Though not as plentiful as in the past, hydraulic-electric versions still exist. Since this type taps into the tow vehicle's hydraulic brake line, they react to the increasing pressure in the master cylinder during braking to move an electrical contact against a rheostat inside the controller body. As more force is exerted on the tow vehicle brakes, a corresponding increase in the current is sent to the trailer brakes by the controller.

Typical electronic controllers are inertia activated or pendulum induced. They monitor the circuit through the tow vehicle stop lamp switch. This type of controller will apply a proportional amount of current and voltage to the trailer brakes as is needed and mandated by the actual force of the tow vehicle coming to a stop. All electronic controllers have a sensitivity adjustment for varying loads in the trailer. Obviously, the heavier the trailer and your gear, the more braking power is needed. Properly installed, today's smart controllers can be fined tuned to these varying loads. Likewise, a gain adjustment is included that will help prevent the trailer brakes from locking up under normal circumstances. This eliminates the need for a selective or variable resistor that sometimes needs to be added to the circuit with the older styles hydraulic-electric controllers, where selective resistors were added when the braking capacity of the controller was greater than the requirements of the trailer brakes. The electronic controllers of today automatically compensate for this. Additionally, when braking on hills, most controllers will allow a little more power to the trailer brakes while going downhill and slightly less when going uphill.

Digital electronics, nontheless, is now being employed in some of today's more sophisticated brake controllers. Jordan Research Corporation's Ultima 2020 offers true full-time, proportional braking, a feat usually reserved for the older hydraulic-type controllers. This new type of controller is actuated simply by pressure on the brake pedal. Pedal movement is transferred through a nylon coated steel cable and sensed electronically. A proportionate amount of braking is applied to tow vehicle and the travel trailer brakes.

Additional useful features include a digital ammeter, a continuity indicator, which assures the driver that the trailer and tow vehicle are indeed electrically connected, and a fully modulated manual control should the operator want just a touch of trailer brakes to compensate for a change in road condition or another corrective measure. Manual operation of the controller does not activate the stop lamps as in those controllers that monitor the stop-lamp switch.

CONTROLLER MAINTENANCE: There is very little maintenance to worry about performing concerning electronic controllers. Simply check that all electrical connections are tight, and that wires are protected where they pass through the firewall or other areas. Route wires away from exhaust components. Periodically check the 12-volt automatic circuit breaker that is used in the circuit between the vehicle's battery and the controller. Sometimes it may be necessary to clean the terminals. Electronic brake controllers are not field repairable. If a problem should arise, contact the manufacturer or your local dealer.

Troubleshooting – Most braking problems that cannot be corrected by either adjusting the trailer brakes or the brake controller can generally be traced to electrical system failures. Obviously, mechanical causes will be evident during your periodic inspections. Worn magnets, bent arms, gouged drums, worn linings, etc., are pretty conspicuous. In order to troubleshoot the brake system electrically, you will need a voltmeter and an ammeter.

Voltage—Brake system voltage is best measured at the magnets in order to check the entire system. All voltage starts at the tow vehicle battery, passes through the controller, through the electrical connection between trailer and tow vehicle, and ultimately is used at the brake magnets. Electrical integrity is crucial for safe stopping. The engine of the tow vehicle should be running when checking the voltage so that a low battery will not adversely affect the measurements.

Attach the voltmeter in parallel with any of the brake magnets. The voltage should be zero volts at the beginning of your test. As the controller is activated, or the brake pedal depressed, the voltage should gradually increase to about 12 volts DC. This slow climb in voltage is termed "modulation." No modulation means that when the controller begins to apply voltage to the brakes it immediately applies a high voltage which causes the brakes to apply instantaneous maximum power. The brakes will lock up.

The threshold voltage of a controller is the voltage applied to the brakes when the controller is first becoming activated. The lower the threshold voltage, the smoother the brakes will operate. Too high of a threshold voltage causes grabby or harsh brakes.

Amperage—System amperage is the current being drawn by all brakes on the trailer. The engine of the tow vehicle should again be running. One place to measure the current is at the brake output wire of the controller. Sometimes this is easiest at the electrical connector plug at the rear of the tow vehicle. The brake wire must be disconnected and the ammeter put in-line or in series with the brake wire. Make sure your ammeter has sufficient capacity and note the polarity to prevent damaging your ammeter (a range of 0 to 15 amps is sufficient for single or tandem axle trailers; 0 to 25 amps is needed for triple axle trailers with six brakes). The Jordan Research Ultima 2020 has a built-in ammeter as do others.

Individual amperage draw can be measured by inserting the ammeter in the line at the specific magnet you want to check. Disconnect one of the magnet wires (or simply slip the inductive-type ammeter over one of the wires) and attach the ammeter. By far, the most common electrical problem is low or no voltage at the brake magnets. Common causes for this condition can usually be attributed to one or more of the following:

- Poor connections
- Open circuit
- Insufficient wire size
- Broken wires hanging below the axle
- Improperly set up controller

Another common electrical problem is shorted or partially shorted circuits usually indicated by extremely high amperage readings. Possible causes for this symptom are:

- Internally shorted magnets
- Defective controller
- Brake wire shorted to ground somewhere in the system
- Corrosion between the ground wire and the brake wire in the electrical connector plug

All electrical troubleshooting procedures should start at the controller. Try to eliminate the controller as the problem. Make sure the controller is set up according to the manufacturer's recommendations. If the voltage and amperage are not satisfactory, proceed to the connector and then to the individual magnets to isolate the problem source. Twelve volts output at the controller on the brake wire should equate to a minimum 10.5 volts at each magnet. The voltage will be a little higher if the tests are made with the engine running as suggested. Nominal system amperage at a basic 12 volts with cold magnets and the controller gain adjustment at maximum, the current at each magnet should be as follows:

Brake Size	Amps Per Magnet
7 x 1-1/4"	2.5
10 x 1-1/2"	2.5
10 x 2-1/4"	3
12 x 2"	3

As mentioned before, some of today's electronic brake controllers come equipped with a built-in continuity tester. When the trailer is properly connected to the tow vehicle, an indicator lamp is lit on the controller. This informs the driver that there is a good connection and current and voltage can flow from the controller, through the electrical connector to the brake magnets and to ground.

Tekonsha's Commander series of electronic controllers includes a row of light emitting diodes (LEDs) that light up progressively as more braking is applied. This gives the driver a relative indication of the braking strength. It also allows for a more precise fine tuning of the gain control, which is important in adjusting the modulation for your particular trailer and brakes.

Properly adjusted electric brakes, a sound electrical path and a correctly installed brake controller all contribute to not only your safety, but to your towing enjoyment as well.

TOWING WITH YOUR MOTORHOME

Today, seemingly, more than just a few motorhome owners are adopting the practice of towing a small vehicle behind the coach. Affectionately called "dinghy" towing, this facet of RVing appears to be at an all-time high. The popularity and the attraction is evident enough; a smaller second vehicle allows for local side trips and errand running without breaking camp, unhooking the motorhome and leveling it again upon your return. It also seconds as a larger "closet" to stow supplies and camping gear while traveling. There is a long list of good reasons to opt for it.

There are some limitations, though. With a car in tow, it is difficult to back up. The RVer must be cognizant of steep driveways, as well as space limitations when searching for a parking area. The extended length of the rig necessitates longer stopping distances, and more time for lane changes, special precautions may be mandated, etc. Yet, motorhome enthusiasts overwhelmingly are willing to overlook any negatives in favor of the obvious benefits. Take an informal survey sometime and count the number of RVs you see towing a small car. It can open a whole new world of side trips to destinations you may never have though of visiting because you thought you would be limited by the length of your coach.

METHODS OF TOWING A SECOND VEHICLE: So how does one go about towing a dinghy? The single-most important aspect involving towing a car behind a motorhome is planning. Sound planning is a must. First of all, realize that there are different methods of towing a second vehicle.

Vehicles with Automatic Transmissions		Vehicles with Manual Transmissions	
Chevrolet	Blazer	BMW	All Models
	Cavalier	Chevrolet	Cavalier
	Tahoe		Metro
	Tracker		Tracker
Dodge	Dakota	Dodge	Dakota
	Ram		Durango
Ford	Explorer		Neon
	F-150 Pick-up (4wd)		Ram
	F-250 Pick-up (4wd)	Eclipse	RS
	Ranger (4wd)		GS
GMC	Jimmy		GS-T
	Yukon		3000 GT
Honda	CR-V	Ford	Contour
Land Rover	Discovery Series II		Escort
Lexus	ES 300		Explorer
	RX 300		F-150 Pick-up (4wd)
Mazda	B-Series Pick-up (4wd)		F-250 Pick-up (4wd)
Mercury	Mountaineer		Ranger

Vehicles with Automatic Transmissions			Vehicles with Manual Transmissions		
Oldsmobile	Alero		Hyundai	Accent	
	Cutlass			Elantra	
Pontiac	Sunfire			Sonata	
Range Rover				Tiburon	
Saturn	SC		Infiniti	G20	
	SL			I30	
	SW		Jeep	Cherokee	
Suzuki	Sidekick			Wrangler	
	Vitari		Kia	Sportage	
	Grand Vitari		Mazda	B-Series Pick-up (4wd)	
	X-90 SUV		Mercedes	SLK Roadster	
			Mercury	Mystique	
				Tracer	
			Mitsubishi	Mirage	
			Montero	Sport LS	
			Nissan	200 SX	
				240 SX	
				Altima	
				Maxima	
				Sentra	
				Pathfinder	
				Frontier Pick-up	
			Pontiac	Grand Am	
				Sunfire	
			Saturn	SC	
				SL	
				SW	
			Subaru	Forester	
				Impreza	
				Legacy	
				Outback	
			Suzuki	Esteem	
				Grand Vitari	
				Sidekick	
				Swift Hatchback	
				Vitari	
				X-90 SUV	
			Toyota	Camry	
				Celica	
				Corolla	
				RAV4	
			Volvo	S70	
				V70	

The three basic methods are:
- •Tow trailer
- •Tow dolly
- •Tow bar

Tow Trailer – The tow trailer is the least popular method mainly because of the bulkiness of the tow trailer itself. Also many motorhomes just do not have the towing capacity to lug a car and a full trailer behind. With the tow trailer, the entire car is positioned and secured on the trailer.

Tow Dolly – The tow dolly, however, continues to be a popular method. There are many on the road today. Its principle revolves around placing the wheels of only one axle onto a specially designed single-axle trailer. This is a preferred method by many who own front wheel drive cars. The rear axle of the car spins freely while the front end is on the dolly, so no other major equipment need be purchased. Plus the dinghy need not be further modified. Demco Manufacturing, a long time leader in the tow dolly field produces the Kar Kaddy with an interesting auto-steer feature that permits easy tracking of the towed vehicle.

Stowing the dolly while you travel and storing it at home, however, may be a nuisance. Some campgrounds have restrictions on where they may be kept during your stay. It may be wise to check ahead during the planning of your trip for any stipulations concerning a tow dolly in the campgrounds you will be visiting.

Tow Bar – The most common method of towing a small car behind your motorhome is with a tow bar. This principle permits all four wheels of the dinghy to be on the ground, which results in less tongue weight on the motorhome and easier hitching and unhitching. In most cases, however, special equipment is necessary and modifications may have to be made, but the good news, thanks to the aftermarket, is that almost any small car can now be towed in this manner.

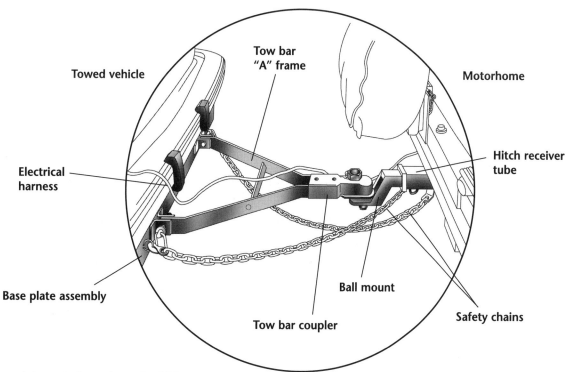

A complete motorhome/towed vehicle set-up.
Tow bar coupler should be level after hookup.

SELECTING A DINGHY: Although the previous statement may be true, there are still limitations. The limiting factor is primarily determined by the motorhome. Mainly, how much is the motorhome rated to tow? Tow capacity rating is set by the coach manufacturer and is based on many things: engine size, transmission, rear end ratio, frame structure, etc. Modifications can be made to the motorhome that will increase the towing capacity such as adding an auxiliary transmission, a high performance exhaust system and an engine turbocharger.

If your motorhome has the power and performance to tow, the limiting factor then becomes Gross Combined Weight Rating (GCWR). This is the combined weight of the RV (and everything in it) and the towed vehicle (and everything in it). Some motorhomes may be further restricted solely by their design. Many extended Class As and Class Cs have a very long overhang—a lot of coach behind the rear axle. This may diminish their capacity to tow. It only has a minimal effect if you plan to tow a vehicle with all four wheels on the ground, however. The actual tongue weight in such cases is comparatively slight.

A third limiting factor when choosing a small vehicle is the overall length of the combined units. Some states have a limit on the total length. If your motorhome is extremely long, the car you choose may push you over the combined length limit. Measure carefully.

Consider what interests you in a second vehicle. What features do you look for in a small car or pick-up truck? If you are planning to purchase a new dinghy, ask your dealer about towing it behind your motorhome. Some can be towed without any modifications, others will need special towing equipment outlined later in this chapter. Many will have speed or distance restrictions as well.

The following chart lists 1998 and 1999 produced vehicles that can be towed with all four wheels down and without major modifications. Keep in mind that, although the listed models can be towed in this manner, previous models may not. Also, this list may not be all inclusive. To be sure about a vehicle, contact that manufacturer directly.

SUPPLEMENTAL BRAKING FOR THE TOWED VEHICLE: When towing a dinghy, the braking capacity of the motorhome must also be considered. Braking capacity is rated by the chassis manufacturer so check with your dealer or the manufacturer to determine if any limitations pertain to the braking capacity of your motorhome.

Various supplemental braking devices are currently available to aid in stopping the motorhome/dinghy combination. All allow independent control of the towed vehicle's brakes. At least 10 to 12 suppliers now provide such add-on units, most of which can be installed by the do-it-yourselfer. Although no federal law exists as of yet, many states have individual laws requiring additional braking if the towed vehicle exceeds a certain weight. For instance, in Michigan, the law states that an independent braking system is required if the gross weight of the dinghy exceeds 3,000 pounds. In Delaware, supplemental braking is required if the dinghy weighs 4,000 pounds. In Texas, it is 4,500 pounds. Canada's provincial law mandates supplemental braking if the dinghy has a laden gross weight in excess of 2,000 kilograms or 4,409 pounds, or if the towed vehicle weighs 40 percent or more of the motorhome's gross vehicle weight rating. It is often emphasized that while state or local laws may be obscure or variant, the law of physics is non-negotiable. If the vehicle you are towing weighs 3,000 pounds or more, seriously consider the addition of supplemental braking. Tow trailers and tow dollies usually have electric or surge brakes, but towing with a tow bar and all four wheels down provides no additional braking. It becomes a safety issue.

Types of Supplemental Braking Systems – The available types of supplemental braking systems include those activated by hydraulic surge and mechanical means. Some utilize a pendulum-controlled air pressure system that mechanically applies the vehicle brakes. Still others use electronics coupled with an air cylinder. Other suppliers use the principle of hydraulics to activate the brakes on the dinghy. Others are vacuum-activated. Regardless of the type of system employed, it is the prudent RVer who also includes a break-away system in the event the dinghy and the motorhome unexpectedly part company. Some systems come complete with the break-away feature while it is an option on others.

Keep in mind not all supplemental braking systems are compatible with diesel-powered motorhomes, although many are. Price range varies substantially, so do your homework on which applications fit your needs based on your motorhome and dinghy. Once installed, most supplemental braking systems can be hooked up and disconnected in a matter of minutes, so ease of use rates a ten. Some units are permanently mounted in the towed vehicle, while a few can be easily transferred from vehicle to vehicle if so desired.

CHOOSING A HITCH: Unlike standard tow vehicles such as trucks and utility vehicles that have a known frame design for which the hitch makers already have a corresponding hitch, most motorhome frames have been modified or "stretched" to accommodate the RV portion. Sometimes this is done by the chassis maker and other times by the coach manufacturer. There is no design guideline. Structural integrity is the only goal. So when it comes time to install a hitch on a motorhome, you may find it necessary to have a custom hitch fabricated to fit. Many coach manufacturers offer a hitch as an optional item, so check with your RV dealer first.

When installing any hitch on any motorhome, keep in mind this important fact: All holding tanks and fuel tanks must be accessible and able to be removed. There can be no permanent structure prohibiting the removal and reinstallation of either type of tank. It is permissible, however, if the custom hitch is fabricated and then bolted to the frame of the motorhome. It cannot, however, be permanently welded in place directly below a holding tank.

TOWING EQUIPMENT:

Tow Bar – When considering tow bars, realize that different types and styles exist that may need to be analyzed prior to purchase. Also understand that you must already know which vehicle you will be towing. Like hitches, tow bars are rated by weight classification. Tow bars are available in three basic styles or types:
- Removable
- Tilt-up
- Collapsible or telescopic

Although all tow bars today are removable in the true sense of the word, there is a basic or standard tow bar available that must be removed when not in use. All tow bars today attach to the frame of the dinghy instead of the bumper. In years past, the removable bar could be attached to either the frame or the bumper. However, with today's high tech, collision-resistant plastic bumpers, it is a mandate that all tow bars attach solidly to the vehicle frame.

The tilt-up variety is similar in design except that it consists of a baseplate that is attached to the frame of the towed car and a pivotal "A" frame assembly that attaches to the baseplate. It has a mechanism that allows the "A" frame portion to be lifted vertically 90 degrees and locked into position to allow driving of the car. There may be some local restrictions on this. The contention is that the upright tow bar impedes the driver's view. Check your local codes. Newer styles allow for the tow bar to flip up against the rear of the motorhome.

The third and most popular type of tow bar is the collapsible or telescopic type. They too, consist of a baseplate mounted to the front end of the towed vehicle and a collapsible, extendible "A" frame structure that neatly trucks and folds out of the way when not needed. Likewise, it can also be totally removed from the tow vehicle during the off-season. Today's baseplates are custom designed for specific vehicles and are easily bolted to the frame using common hand tools.

Perhaps the most approved feature of this type is that it is "self-aligning." In other words, during the process of hooking up to the hitch ball on the motorhome, all you have to do is get close. The design and flexibility as the "A" frame "unfolds" from its stowed position allows off-center hook-ups. After the coupler is attached to the ball, all that is necessary is to pull forward a few feet and the car and motorhome automatically become aligned and the tow bar locks into place. Attach the safety chains, plug in the electrical pigtail and go!

Regardless of which tow bar you choose, correct ball height is essential for safe and effortless towing. Usually a drop shank ball mount is necessary on the motorhome since most are typically higher than the front end of the dinghy. Some tow bars are designed with an off-set in height. Your hitch installer will be able to advise you as to which one is best for your particular setup. Make sure that the car and motorhome are level, and that the coupler on the tow bar is parallel to the ground when hitched up for travel.

Drive Shaft Coupling – In years past, in order to tow a rear wheel drive vehicle behind a motorhome, it was necessary to remove the drive shaft completely from the car so that the rotating rear axle would not turn the transmission while traveling. All automotive transmissions and some manual transmissions require lubrication whenever the transmission is turning. Remco Manufacturing has perfected a drive shaft coupling that can disengage the drive shaft with the pull of a cable that is mounted inside the towed vehicle. When you reach your destination, simply push the cable and the mechanical clutch once again engages the drive shaft for driving.

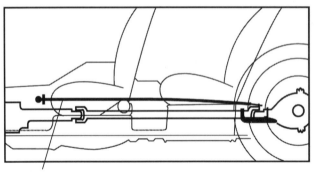

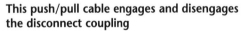

This push/pull cable engages and disengages
the disconnect coupling

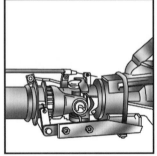

Driveshaft coupling

The existing drive shaft must be shortened to accommodate the unit, or another drive shaft must be purchased with the kit. If you plan on towing your car a lot of miles, however, this is the device to consider. With the drive shaft disconnected, no mileage will be recorded by the odometer of the towed vehicle. The coupling can also be a good anti-theft device. Installation is simple and requires only common hand tools.

Axle Lock – If your tow vehicle is front wheel drive, as many are, a whole new set of rules comes into play. The drive shaft is an integral part of the front axle assembly which also includes the transmission. For those vehicles that cannot be towed with all four wheels on the ground, Remco has produced a device called the Axle-Lock. This device mounts behind the right front tire and is activated or deactivated by hand with a one-third twist of the device. It, too, can second as an anti-theft device.

Transmission Lube Pump – The Axle-Lock solves only one part of the problem for front wheel drive vehicles. Some automatic transmissions must still be lubricated even when one of the axles is disabled. A lube pump is also needed. This device attaches to the towed vehicle but is powered by the battery on the motorhome. When activated, it pumps transmission fluid from the pan, through an in-line filter, to a selector valve that routes the fluid on a path to be cooled by the radiator and then on to the transmission and back to the pan.

Easily reached just inside the right front tire, the axle lock device is engaged with a simple 1/3 twist.

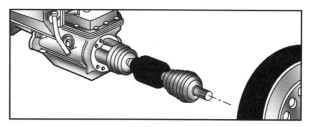

The axle-lock kit includes new replacement axle and two new boots. Permanently installed behind the right front tire, it doubles as an anti-theft device while driving solo.

Some manual transmissions must also be lubricated while turning. It may not be as simple as just putting it in neutral, hooking up and driving off. Check with the manufacturer of the towed vehicle. It is possible a lube pump may be necessary for your stick shift vehicle as well.

Speedometer Disconnect – When towing a small vehicle behind your motorhome, it is not in the best interest of the dinghy to log all the miles the RV is driving. It most assuredly will not add to the resale value of the car. Automatic Equipment Manufacturing makes a simple to install, speedometer disconnect kit that is powered from the motorhome. Using this device will eliminate an accumulation of false miles on the odometer.

Running Lights – Just as a travel trailer or fifth-wheel trailer has running lights, turn signals, stop lights, etc., so also must your towed car. Whether you choose to utilize a tow dolly or a tow bar, it is a requirement that any towed vehicle be equipped with proper running lamps (the tow trailer will have its own lights). There are a couple of options here. You can use the towed vehicle's existing lights by tapping into the wiring, or you can install a temporary light bar that attaches to the rear of the towed vehicle by suction cups. The light bar method does not modify the existing lamps on the towed vehicle. All power for the light circuits will come from the motorhome and terminate at a plug near the hitch. An electrical umbilical (pigtail) attaches to the towed vehicle to complete the circuit.

Almost all imported small cars and trucks, as well as most domestics, have amber turn signals which cannot be used for stop lamps. Special converter boxes are necessary to transform what is termed a "three-wire system" to a "two-wire system." There are complete kits available in RV stores that minimize such wiring conversions to a relatively easy task. If, however, you opt for the temporary light bar, then no modification to the towed vehicle is necessary. Simply attach the light bar to the rear of the towed vehicle, route the wiring harness over the car and plug it into the motorhome.

Tow Bar Maintenance—As with any device with moving parts, chemical action or anything attached to a RV, tow bars require a small amount of attention and periodic maintenance. The main focus in tow bar maintenance is lubrication. Each time you hook-up the tow bar, make sure the hitch ball is properly lubed. Also check the coupler on the tow bar. The locking mechanism periodically needs lubricating spray. On telescopic tow bars, keep the machined surfaces free from road grime and dirt that can scratch the sliding parts. Apply a thin amount of household lubricating oil.

Weekly, take a close look at the motorhome hitch, ball mount, safety chains, etc. If chain links become damaged, replace the entire chain. Avoid the use of "master" links. If painted surfaces become scratched or nicked, sand and repaint. Check the hitch mounting bolts for tightness at lease once every camping season.

Check the electrical connector plug and pigtail for corrosion. As always, keep electrical equipment clean and dry. Regularly check the operation of the running lamps on the towed vehicle. Have someone verify that the turn signals, stop lamps and clearance markers are in working order. Test the supplemental braking system daily if so equipped.

TOWING TIPS: You have chosen your dinghy, outfitted the motorhome, added all the necessary equipment to tow your front wheel drive automatic, and you are ready to go. But before you do, here are some tips suggested by experts who regularly tow a small car behind the motorhome.

Carry an extra set of tow bar attaching pins – All tow bars attach to the base plate with steel pins that are secured in place with a special clip. Periodically these pins and clips become damaged or lost. Never use a common bolt to attach your tow bar.

Be aware of state laws concerning towing—Some states prohibit using tow dollies without a special permit or special licensing. The contention is that it is "triple towing," three distinct vehicles attached to one another. Check with the highway patrol of the states you plan to travel to avoid any unnecessary obstacles. AAA publishes a yearly book, *Digest of Motor Laws*, which lists all traffic and towing requirements, road rules, etc., for each state and Canada. It is a wise investment if you plan to travel the breadth of North America. Call your local AAA office for additional information regarding availability.

Call your insurance agent – Let the agent know you are towing a car behind your motorhome. A special insurance rider may be necessary. A discounted rate may even apply since your car will not actually be driven much at all. Better to be safe than sorry should something unfortunate happen.

Avoid backing up – Plan ahead as you drive. Carefully consider gas stations, parking lots, etc. It is best to avoid those circumstances that require backing up when towing a second vehicle. You can, however, always unhitch in order to get out of a jam. Also, know your exact overall combined length and approximate turning radius.

Remember to unlock your steering wheel – It may be necessary to leave the ignition key in the dinghy to keep the wheel unlocked. It is also a viable trick to attach bungee straps to the steering wheel to keep the wheel centered. Some small vehicles may have a steering wheel with a tendency to "stick" after a hard left hand turn.

Have the front end aligned on the tow vehicle – This will minimize adverse tire wear as the car tracks behind the motorhome.

Utilize a "bra" or rock guard – Road debris, gravel, pebbles, etc., all have a detrimental effect on the front end of anything being towed. Ever wonder why travel trailers always have rock guards covering the front window? Avoid mounting wide mud flaps or full width devices on the motorhome. Wide objects that block off the area between the motorhome and the road surface actually trap heat under the motorhome as it travels. High heat can cause numerous types of damage to various components on the motorhome.

To get the most out of your recreational enjoyment by towing a dinghy behind your motorhome, carefully analyze your requirements based on the vehicles you choose. Try to preview the towing devices and equipment discussed in this chapter. Most well stocked service facilities will have a display area depicting the various tow bars and accessories that are available. Ask questions, take your time, then equip yourself and go!

CHAPTER NINE

RV Tires

Tires and safety—two words congruent to bacon and eggs or salt and pepper—are words that just go hand in hand. Understanding that safety includes having the correct tire at the proper inflation pressure is crucial to reliable RVing. The vitality of tires on any motorhome, tow vehicle or trailer cannot be understated. Many thousands of safe RVing miles can be realized when the RVer is cognizant of the role of tires and knows what to look for while RVing. Diligence in use and periodic inspections can lengthen the life of RV tires and help guarantee a safe ride.

Advances in design and technology have also markedly increased tire life. Tires are becoming a more valuable asset to RVers than merely a means for rolling the vehicle along the pavement. Evolving tread designs and overall construction improvements contribute to better fuel economy and safer handling of the RV. However, as dependable as they may be, tires do wear out and an improperly loaded tire can even fail. A basic understanding of tire construction, load capacity, inflation pressures and differing applications can help the RV owner select the best tire replacement when the original tires become worn.

Typical RV Tire

Tire Construction

If a typical tire were to be dissected, it would reveal various layers or plies beneath a thick outer layer, which also bears the tread. The entire tire may be made of various combinations of:
- Rubber, reclaimed rubber or synthetic rubber
- Polyester, nylon or steel cord plies
- Rayon, fiberglass or steel belts

Regardless of which materials go into the construction, tires are classified into one of the following categories based on how the belts and/or cords are applied during the manufacturing process.
- Diagonal or bias
- Belted bias
- Radial

Although applications may vary according to manufacturer's recommendations, all three types can be found on trailers, motorhomes and tow vehicles.

Diagonal- or bias-ply tires may have two or four or more body plies that cross the center line of the tread at nearly a 35 degree angle. Both the sidewall and tread are strengthened by this design involving alternating plies.

Belted bias-ply tires are similar to diagonal-ply tires in construction, except that belted bias-ply

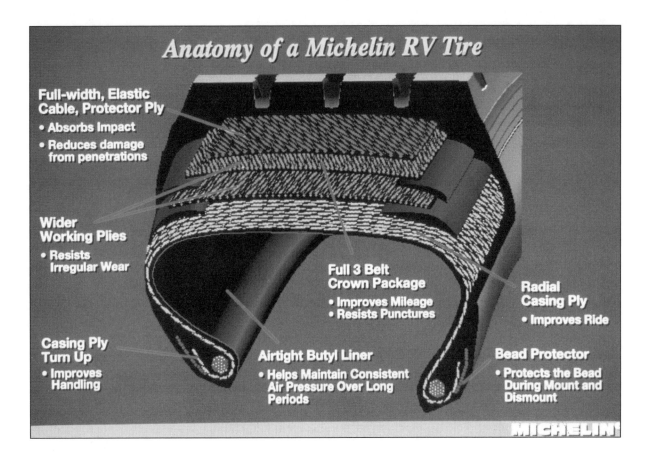

Anatomy of a Michelin RV Tire

Full-width, Elastic Cable, Protector Ply
- Absorbs Impact
- Reduces damage from penetrations

Wider Working Plies
- Resists Irregular Wear

Full 3 Belt Crown Package
- Improves Mileage
- Resists Punctures

Radial Casing Ply
- Improves Ride

Casing Ply Turn Up
- Improves Handling

Airtight Butyl Liner
- Helps Maintain Consistent Air Pressure Over Long Periods

Bead Protector
- Protects the Bead During Mount and Dismount

MICHELIN

tires have two or more belts under the tread to provide greater stability. Additionally, the belts reduce tread movement during contact with the road. This, too, improves tread life and traction.

Radial tires differ from either bias-type tire in that the body cords run perpendicularly across the center line of the tread from bead to bead (the bead is that point where the tire meets the wheel rim). Belted plies under the tread run nearly parallel to it, constricting the radial ply cords and giving additional rigidity to the tread. The belts also give greater strength without reducing the flexibility of the sidewall. As in the belted bias tire, the belts restrict tread movement on the road and improve tread life.

TIRE LOAD: The load that any tire can carry safely depends on several variables, including the tire size, the load range or ply rating of the tire and the inflation pressure. The older method of rating the load capacity utilized a "ply rating." The current method called "load range," uses a simple letter designation. See the chart below for a direct comparison.

Ply Rating (Old Method)	Load Range (Current Method)
4	B
6	C
8	D
10	E
12	F
14	G

TIRE SIZES: Although tires have many different sets of measurements available, the tire size designation can provide the most practical information to RVers, especially when related to other information embossed on the tire sidewall. Generally expressed as a grouping of letters and numbers or as two linked sets of numbers, the tire size designation gives information about cross-sectional size, load range capacity, construction and the diameter and contour of the wheel rim. Because of the degree of detail embedded into the information on the sidewall, obtaining a matching or replacement tire is a fairly simple task in most cases.

Diagonal-ply tires have designations such as 7.75-15, where 7.75 indicates bias construction as well as a cross-section approximately 7.75 inches wide at the widest point. The number 15 indicates a rim diameter of 15 inches with a five degree tapered bead ledge.

There are typically just two rim taper angles. The aforementioned five degree taper and a 15 degree taper. The 15 degree taper can be recognized by the designation as a "half-size" increment such as 15.5 for a light truck tire or 19.5 for a larger motorhome. The "0.5" indicates the rim has a 15 degree taper. Even though it is possible to stretch a 15-inch tire over a 15.5 rim or a 19-inch motorhome tire over a 19.5 rim, it is not recommended. The bead will not quite properly fit the taper of the rim. This could easily result in tire failure. It is important that the types of rims are not mixed on the same vehicle. Any professional tire shop will know the difference, but some RV dealers may not. Tire and rim combinations must be matched for diameter *and* taper angle.

Although diagonal-ply tires also use an alpha-numeric designation, this is more commonly found on belted bias tires. The belted bias equivalent of the 7.75-15 diagonal-ply tire used in the example above would be either an F78-15 or an F70-15. The term "equivalent" is used in the sense of load carrying ability rather than size.

These tires use a series size number, such as "78," "70" and "60", to indicate the tire's profile; a height-to-width ratio. For instance, a 70 series tire is approximately 70 percent as high as it is wide. The letter in front of the series number ranges from A to N and marks the relative size and load capacity of the tire at its designed load pressure. Simply stated, an A78-14 tire is smaller and is rated for lighter loads than a B78-14 tire at the same air pressure.

Radial tires use the same designation system as that for belted bias tires, but an "R" is added to the number such as, FR78-15. Some radials are marked with metric sizes, such as 195/75R-15 with 195 being the cross-sectional width in millimeters. This method of marking is commonplace today.

Although corresponding sizes of different types of tires may have the same load limits, they are not interchangeable because of differences in dimensions, load ratings, fender clearances, rim sizes, ride characteristics and other factory recommendations. These differences may seriously affect vehicle handling characteristics. Never mix different sizes or constructions (bias or radial) on the same axle except for temporary use, perhaps when used as a spare tire.

LOAD RANGE: As demonstrated in the earlier chart, tires were formerly rated by the number of plies in their construction, but are now designated by the load range they are designed to carry. Load ranges are closely linked to inflation pressures and the load limits within a given range are determined by the pressure. The higher the load, the more air pressure is required, up to the maximum inflation for the load range of the specific tire and rim. This emphasizes the importance of knowing how much the RV actually weighs.

INFLATION: Proper inflation is paramount for maximizing tire safety, vehicle handling characteristics, and improving mileage. It is also one area over which the RVer has direct control on a daily basis. Correct tire inflation provides proper sidewall deflection and safe operating temperatures

Tires

Modern design and materials have created tires that are dependable and long-lived, as well as important components for better handling and fuel economy. Yet, in order to perform properly, a tire's construction, load capacity, inflation pressure, and application must be matched to the vehicle.

Tire profiles

70 series
60 series
Height is approximately 60% of width
60 series
Width
78 series
50 series

PR8
FOR DOT TEST AND NORMAL HIGHWAY USE IN NORTH AMERICA AND AUSTRALIA
MAX. LOAD SINGLE 2780 LBS
MAX. LOAD DUAL 2640 LBS
TREAD 4 STEEL PLIES
SIDEWALLS 1 STEEL PLY
AT 70 PSI
AT 70 PSI
COLD
COLD

for the tires. Under-inflation causes excessive tire deflection and heat build-up, excessive wear on the outer tread ribs and can lead to premature tire failure. Over-inflation causes tires to ride hard and makes them more vulnerable to impact damage and an overall weakening of the tire body.

Air pressure should be checked when the tires are cold. A "cold" tire has been defined as 68 degrees Farenheit or cooler, or before being driven one mile. Heat generated by friction temporarily increases air pressure anywhere from 10 to 20 percent, so never release pressure from a presumably over-inflated, hot tire. Check for correct inflation at the beginning of a trip and recheck periodically when the tires are cold. Just before pulling out of the campsite after breaking camp is the ideal time to do it. It should become a function of the RVer's daily routine.

As stated earlier, incorrect inflation pressures can lead to tire failure, handling problems, overheated brakes, shortened tire life and premature breakdown of other related components on the chassis; any of which may contribute to a disabling delay or even worse, an accident. Most RVers know that the maximum inflation rate is molded into the sidewall of all tires. It is a federal law. Also, many know that this number represents the maximum amount of air for that size tire at that load range. It is the astute RVer, though, who is aware that perhaps not all tires will require the maximum amount.

So how much air pressure should the tires actually hold? Since all RVs are loaded and used differently, and each tire location may carry varying weights, there is really no definitive textbook answer to the question of inflation pressure that can generically fit all situations. Like many things within the RV realm, the amount of air required in each tire is subjective and unique to that tire as it carries a specific load, or at the very least, unique to that axle. Therefore, to know exactly how much air to put in each tire, the RV must be weighed as it is fully loaded for travel—the complete traveling weight. This includes all the canned goods, camping gear, personal effects, fishing poles, etc. Prior to weighing, have the fuel tanks and fresh water tank completely filled as well as the LP container, but leave the holding tanks empty. Don't forget to include all passengers or at least remember to approximate the weight of each person traveling in the RV. The more accurate the weight measurement, the more precise the inflation pressure can be determined.

Public scales that can accommodate RVs are available in many areas. Some truck stops and auto recycling yards may have platform-type scales available to the public. Moving companies are another good source to call when looking for a set of scales. Quarries, gravel pits or concrete plants are also usually equipped with scales. The facility may charge a fee for each weight recorded, but knowing the individual weight measurements is too important to be concerned about a minimal cost.

So how is an RV accurately weighed on a platform scale? Before the specifics are offered, here are some definitions and some facts that will provide a better understanding of RV weights and measurements.

RV WEIGHTS, DEFINITIONS AND WEIGHING FACTS

GROSS VEHICLE WEIGHT RATING (GVWR): Maximum permissible weight of the RV. It should be equal to or greater than the sum of the UVW plus the NCC, defined next.

UNLOADED VEHICLE WEIGHT (UVW): Weight of the coach as built at the factory. If a motorhome, it includes full fuel tanks, engine oil and coolants. The UVW does not include cargo, fresh water, liquid propane, passengers or any of the various dealer/aftermarket installed accessories.

NET CARRYING CAPACITY (NCC): Maximum weight of all passengers, personal belongings, cargo, fresh water (including a filled water heater), LP, tools, installed accessories and, if a motorhome, the tongue weight of any towed vehicle.

GROSS COMBINATION WEIGHT RATING (GCWR). If a motorhome, the value specified by the manufacturer as the maximum allowable loaded weight of the motorhome along with its towed vehicle. If a travel trailer or fifth-wheel trailer, it is the value specified by the tow vehicle manufacturer as the maximum allowable loaded weight of the tow vehicle and the towed trailer combined.

GROSS AXLE WEIGHT RATING (GAWR): Maximum total weight for which that particular single axle is designed.

Additional Facts
- An RV in a 10 percent overloaded condition reduces tire life by 15 percent.
- An RV in a 50 percent overloaded condition reduces tire life by 60 percent.
- To be accurate, the platform scales must allow positioning of the RV for weighing a single side and yet remain level.

- Cargo includes all contents of storage pods, roof racks, bicycles or motorcycles on carriers, food, canned goods, galley equipment, clothing, refrigerator contents, personal effects, etc. Virtually everything on board while traveling.
- Liquid weights include:
  - Water—8.33 pounds per gallon
  - LP—4.25 pounds per gallon
  - Gasoline—6.00 pounds per gallon
  - Diesel Fuel—7.00 pounds per gallon

WEIGHING THE RV USING A FULL PLATFORM SCALE

The following instructions are general in design and intent. Not all of the measurements will apply to every RV. For example, for a typical Class A motorhome with just two axles, only measurements 1, 2, 3, 8, 9 and 10, respectively, are required. Only record the measurements that directly apply to your particular RVing configuration.

Measurements 1 through 7 are taken with the RV laterally centered on the scales. Measurements 8 through 13 pertain to only one side of the RV and are taken while an imaginary centerline is aligned with one edge of the scale platform.

Measurement	Instructions
#1	Pull straight onto the scales until only the front axle is on the platform. Record this weight: GAW (front).
#2	Pull further onto scales until all the axles on the RV (or tow vehicle) are on the platform. Record this weight: GVW.
#3	Pull forward until only the rear axle, (or rear axle and tag axle, if so equipped) is on the platform. Front axle is off the scales. Record this weight: GAW (rear or rear and tag).
#4	If a motorhome with a tag axle, pull forward until only the tag axle is on the platform. Record this weight: GAW (tag).
#5	If towing another vehicle, pull forward until only the towed vehicle is completely on the platform. Stay connected to the tow vehicle. Record this weight: GVW (towed vehicle).
#6	If the towed vehicle has three axles, pull forward until only the middle and rear axles are on the scales. Record this weight: GAW (axles 2 and 3).
#7	Pull forward until only the rear axle of the towed vehicle is on the platform. Record this weight: GAW (rear).
#8	Keeping the imaginary center line at one edge of the scale, pull forward as in measurement #1. The vehicle must be level from side to side. Record the weight: single side (front axle).

#9	Pull forward as in measurement #2. Record this weight: Single Side (all axles).
#10	Pull forward as in measurement #3. Record this weight: Single Side (rear axle[s]).
#11	If a motorhome with a tag axle, pull forward as in measurement #4. Record this weight: Single Side (tag axle).
#12	If towed vehicle has three axles, pull forward as in measurement #6. Record this weight: Single Side (axles 2 and 3).
#13	Pull forward as in measurement #7. Record this weight: Single Side (rear axle).

Once all the pertinent measurements are recorded, actual loads can be calculated for each tire position by simply doing the math. The actual weight each tire position is carrying can now be compared to published inflation pressure guides. Tire inflation guides are compiled by each tire manufacturer and are available at all retail tire shops or directly from the manufacturer. It is advisable to contact a professional tire shop rather than to rely on the advice administered by a typical RV dealer.

While inflation pressure is considered the single-most important area to consider with RV tires, there remains other important facets to also contemplate.

Proper Blocking Techniques – RVers are aware that for the refrigerator to operate properly while standing still, the coach must be leveled. Oftentimes the tires are run up on homemade or aftermarket leveling blocks. Harm is caused to the tires when the blocks are not sized correctly. Over time, uneven distribution of weight while using leveling blocks can damage the steel cables, the casing and especially the sidewall of a tire. Maximum support is mandated in order to avoid warranty discrepancies and premature tire failure. All leveling blocks should be wider and longer than the individual tire footprint it supports. In rear dual-tire applications, both tires must be fully supported by the blocking material. If multiple blocks are used to gain additional height, the uppermost block, the one in direct contact with the tire, must still be wider and longer than the footprint.

Tire Inspection – Inspect tires regularly for signs of excessive or uneven tread wear. Bulges, fabric breaks, cuts, weather checking (dry rot) and any other damage should be addressed immediately. Anything embedded in the tread, such as stones or other road debris, should be removed. Tires should be replaced when the tread is worn to one-sixteenth of an inch in two or more adjacent grooves, or when the tread wear indicators, which are molded into the bottom of the tread grooves on some tires, are flush with the tread ribs. Again, if in doubt, have a questionable tire checked by a reputable tire dealer.

How often should tires be inspected? A thorough inspection should be made at least once a year at a bare minimum. When stored for lengthy periods, try to inspect them at least once a month. While camped, inspect the tires once a week and, as previously mentioned, every day as you travel.

Alignment – Misalignment symptoms usually appear as uneven tread wear although a small amount of misalignment can be detected by careful measurements. Potholes, extremely rough roads, bumps and curbs are all detrimental to wheel alignment which, if not corrected by a qualified service shop, will shorten tire life and may lead to a dangerous driving or towing situation. Have the alignment checked annually or every 10,000 miles of normal highway driving but more frequently if much rough road driving is done.

Wheel Balance – No tire or wheel assembly is absolutely round, nor is every tire in balance as it comes off the assembly line. Once mounted on a rim and inflated, a tire must be balanced by adding lead wheel weights to the rim as indicated by sophisticated balancing equipment. If the tire assembly is not balanced, stresses from centrifugal force will lead to uneven tread wear and premature tire failure will result.

All new tires should be balanced immediately after mounting. Tires should also be balanced again when remounting after repairs or after rotating. Once balanced by a service station or tire dealer, tires should not need additional balancing unless they become damaged or a wheel weight is dislodged or lost. Be sure to note where the balance weights are on each tire.

Storage – For seasonal storage, it is best if the RV can be raised so the majority of the vehicle's weight is removed from the tires. Hydraulic levelers make this task relatively easy on so-equipped motorhomes. If it is not possible to raise the RV during long storage periods, an alternative plan would be to periodically move the coach forward or backward a few feet so the contact point between the tire and the ground is varied. It is also wise to cover the tires during the storage period to help block the ultraviolet rays from the sun.

Ultraviolet (UV) and Ozone Damage – According to a major tire manufacturer, ozone and UV radiation are the principal enemies of uncovered tires. UV radiation travels freely in the air and is harmful to all plastics, rubber and fiberglass. Tire makers add a level of prevention by using carbon black during the manufacturing process. Carbon black is an UV stabilizer that actually absorbs the damaging rays and converts them to a simple by-product of heat. That is the good news. The bad news is that all UV stabilizers are eventually used up during the protection process and must be replenished periodically. As a competitive absorber, carbon black eventually loses its ability to protect against the never-ending assault of the UV rays. The other bad news is that there is no such thing as a permanent UV blocker.

Ozone is an atmospheric gas, found in the free air that attaches to other oxygen-related chemicals. The combined chemicals in ozone have an extra oxygen molecule that attacks tires and causes damage that cannot be restored or reversed. During the making of tires, manufacturers blend ozone resistant rubber compounds into the mix to help combat ozone. These ozone-resistant protective waxes form a barrier of sorts. To be effective, these waxes must constantly be brought to the surface of the tire. This is usually accomplished by the normal flexing and movement of a tire during travel. A fresh layer of combative waxes is always kept at the surface. When RVs are stored for lengthy periods, the tires do not receive enough "exercise" to allow the waxes to migrate to the surface, therefore, ozone has a virtual picnic on any exposed areas, especially on the vulnerable sidewalls. Ozone and UV damage can be reduced with the proper application of a treatment such as 303 Protectant or an equivalent.

Proper sizing, proper loading, proper maintenance, proper usage and periodic inspections of the RV tires can all contribute to safe, trouble-free traveling. Do not underestimate the importance of each. RV tires seldom wear out, so diligence in these areas will reap thousands of safe RVing miles. For additional or specific information, contact one of the technical service facilities listed below:

Bridgestone 800-847-3272   Firestone 800-356-4644

Michelin 800-433-6838   Uniroyal/Goodrich 800-521-9796

or write to: Tire Industry Safety Council, P.O. Box 3147, Medina, OH 44258

CHAPTER TEN

Water Damage

It first appears as an unobtrusive small speck and you pay it no attention; maybe just a bit of dirt on the wall. Later you notice an innocent spot and you make a mental note to check it out; tomorrow would be ideal because you will be doing some maintenance on the water heater anyway. A few weeks later you think you see a stain and wonder who spilled the coffee, and you make a written note to yourself to see if you can clean it when you winterize the coach next month. The next time you think about it is when you begin your spring shakedown and you notice that half a sheet of interior paneling has delaminated and peeled away, and the musty smell almost knocked you over when you opened the door.

While fumbling through the kitchen junk drawer looking for the outside storage compartment keys, you come upon the note you wrote last summer. Then your mind takes you back even further and you suddenly remember that morning when you made that mental note to check out that spot tomorrow. Hmmmm.

An over-dramatization? Perhaps. Realistic? Happens every camping season. Unfortunately, many RVers ignore the early warning signs of water leaks and consequently end up paying the price for a more costly repair later. Spotted early, water damage can be minimized and repair costs limited to simply the purchase of the supplies needed. Virtually all water leaks can be addressed by the RV owner and rectified, if action is taken as soon as the evidence appears.

An assertive preventive maintenance program can even eliminate unnecessary repairs caused by seeping water. The antithesis is the very real fact that, left unabated, water damage can be one of the most costly repairs an RVer may face if the damage spreads to wooden frame members or the floor and destroys the structural integrity of the coach.

So how can RVers prevent such unwelcome damage? Keep alert to any tell-tale signs of moisture. Regularly inspect various key points in and around the roof area. Check and even periodically test the sealants around the windows and doors by spraying them with a garden hose. Order a spare roof air conditioner gasket. Ideas abound, but the pivotal, proactive decision must be regular inspection.

If the RV is equipped with a roof rack and a ladder, it probably has a solid, laminated roof that will support an individual during the roof inspection. If, however, the coach has hollow wall construction and a soft roof, take the necessary precautions to protect the roof while on it.

THE ROOF

Once up on the roof (an extension ladder is needed—never use a step ladder to gain access to the roof of the RV), it will be necessary to place boards or plywood across two or more rafters to protect the roof while moving around. More damage and leaks can result if pressure is administered between the rafters. Never try to walk on the rafters without the boards. Do not take chances while on the roof of the RV. Remember, never compromise the safety factor.

Ideal walking boards can be made from a single sheet of three-eighths-inch plywood. Cutting a four-foot by eight-foot sheet of shop grade three-eighths-inch plywood in half, the long way, will yield two two-foot wide pieces to work on while on the roof. There will always be one on which to work and one to move to the next area on the roof. These boards are also helpful when crawling around under the coach for inspections or repairs as well. Wear athletic shoes or another type of soft-soled shoes.

ROOF INSPECTION AREAS: Closely inspect all areas of the roof. Look for low areas that may collect or pool water. This is one reason to avoid stepping between the rafters on a soft or hollow roof.

Seam – If the rolled roofing has locking seams every so many feet, inspect the entire length of each cleat and seam. Gently push down on each side of the seam to see if it may open up slightly. Apply silicone sealant directly into any voids or cracks.

Edges – Visually inspect that portion of the roof that is folded over the sidewalls and behind the molding. Many times the aluminum roof material cracks at this 90 degree bend. Apply silicone sealant to any openings or cracks that are discovered. Additionally, EPDM rubber roofing may sometimes tear at this bend. Rubber roofing requires a specific lap sealant for repairs in this area. Silicone sealant will not work.

Trim Moldings – While at the edges, closely inspect the drip railing or corner molding depending on how the coach is constructed. There may be an awning rail on the passenger side of the RV. Look especially for open areas behind the flange of the rail or trim pieces. If there is a vinyl or rubber insert molding that covers the screw heads, remove it and look at each screw head. Is there any evidence of rust? Replace the insert molding if it is cracked and weathered or if it simply will not stay put.

If many screws show evidence of rust, remove that entire piece of trim and probe into the framework with an ice pick or small knife. If moisture is evident or the wood is soft, further investigation is in order.

If the framework is steel or aluminum, simply scrape off the old sealant and apply fresh putty tape and reinstall the molding. Be sure some of the putty tape squeezes out whenever tightening a screw. Check to make sure there are no voids behind the molding where water may seep. Seal any voids or gaps with clear or white silicone sealant. If any screws in the molding appear stripped and will not tighten properly, it is imperative that another larger screw be installed. This simple step can prevent a leak from developing in the future.

Sewer Vents – Here is an item that many owners tend to overlook when considering water entry into the coach. Most owners do seal around the base of the vent, which is good, but many forget to seal around the actual vent pipe that extends up through the roof. All sewer vents must have removable covers, so remove and inspect inside the vent base around the vent pipe.

Many manufacturers use a two inch or 2-1/2-inch hole saw to cut the opening in the roof for the pipe. It is easier to install the vent pipe that way. Then they install a one and one-half inch vent pipe through this two and one-half inch hole, leaving a huge gap between the pipe and the perimeter of the hole—plenty of room for water, holding tank odors to gain entry into the ceiling area.

Plug this gap with putty tape or, if necessary, a piece of aluminum with an opening the exact size as the outside diameter of the vent pipe. This aluminum piece can be sealed and screwed in place, all under the protection of the sewer vent base assembly. Then use silicone sealant around the vent pipe before reinstalling the vent cap.

Fourteen-Inch Roof Vents and Escape Hatches – Roof vents are regularly opened and closed many times during a camping season. This movement, coupled with normal expansion and contraction, can loosen the mounting screws, or crack the sealant. Closely inspect around the flange area for such conditions. Again, plug any gaps or crevices with silicone sealant or an equivalent. Also, keep in mind many vent flanges are molded plastic that may deteriorate with constant exposure to the UV rays of the sun. If flaking of the plastic is evident, it may be time to replace the entire vent assembly. Additionally, check the 14-inch vent lid itself. Some are prone to cracks at the corners caused by the sun and pressure. Replace the lid if any cracks have developed. The crack can be sealed temporarily with silicone; however, replace it as soon as possible.

Front and Rear Caps – Most modern RVs, especially Class A motorhomes, have large molded fiberglass or plastic front and rear end caps that extend from the bumper to the roof. Typically, the cap is secured to the roof and sidewalls with screws, and this seam or joint is covered with a molding. As the sun manipulates the molded cap and roof through normal expansion and contraction, gaps or cracks may develop in this area. Closely inspect and seal any problem areas with silicone.

Roof Air Conditioner – Though not technically attached to the roof (the air conditioner actually "sandwiches" the roof between the inside plenum and main unit on top), it can still be a moisture entry point. All roof air conditioners have condensation drain holes strategically located in the bottom pan situated on the roof. If pine needles, twigs or dust and debris are allowed to collect in the pan, effectively blocking the drain holes, water will enter the roof area. Usually it will drip into the air distribution box inside the coach and be quite evident from inside. Other times it may simply seep into the roof area around the 14-inch square opening that the air conditioner is installed over.

Periodically remove the inside plenum of the air conditioner and visually check the gasket situated around the opening. If it appears crushed, cut or mispositioned, replace it. Typically, this gasket is only visible from inside the RV and only after removing the plenum.

Rubber Roof – Most new RVs are manufactured with an innovative one-piece rubber roofing material. This is one of the best methods available to minimize the chances of developing water leaks. In fact, it is recommended that after any major roof repair, a rubber roof be installed as an upgrade on any older RV as well. This will also add trade-in value to the RV.

Should tears or cuts develop in the rubber roofing, they are easily repaired with a simple patch kit such as the Dicor "Patchit," which comes complete with peel and stick patches and lap sealant. Only use repair materials recommended by the manufacturer of the rubber roof.

Rubber roofs can be retrofitted on virtually any of the older RVs, even those with soft, hollow beam construction. It will be necessary, however, to completely remove every item from the roof and cover the entire roof area with plywood decking before cementing on the rubberized roofing material. Check with a reputable and knowledgeable RV body shop for estimates. For more details, see Chapter 11.

Miscellaneous Items – Storage racks, solar panels, refrigerator roof vents, storage pods, TV antennae, satellite dishes and any number of other aftermarket devices may also be attached to the roof. Whenever any item is secured to the roof, there exists a potential for water leaks. Check the mounting techniques used to install any of these items. Look for cracked or deteriorated sealants, caulking, etc. Also check for loose or rusted mounting hardware. Be sure to seal any problem areas immediately. Silicone sealant is the preferred method to plug any holes, cracks or deteriorated caulking. Be sure to scrape and remove any old caulking prior to applying the new silicone.

It is further recommended that all roof seams, vent flanges and other miscellaneous mounting hardware be covered with a roof coating. Even after applying silicone sealant, brush on a protective coating such as Plas-T-Cote or a product called Liquid Roof. Though designed specifically for rubber roofs, Liquid Roof has proven effective over virtually any roof surface. Additionally, many coatings and sealants are available in reflective colors that help keep the interior of the RV cooler. In some areas with extremely high temperatures, it may be advisable to coat the entire roof with a reflective coating.

SIDEWALL INSPECTION AREAS: After verifying the roof is sealed against any possible water entry, inspect the sides of the RV. Here are the important areas to investigate.

Windows and Entry Door – If neglected, all windows and the entry door can become areas where water can easily enter the RV. Check the putty tape closely all around them. If any portion shows signs of deterioration, it is recommended that the entire window or door be removed and resealed with new putty tape. Over time, all putty tape will harden and crack. Sealing only with silicone will help, but eventually new butyl caulk will have to be applied.

Be sure to remove all of the old sealant before applying the new. Keep in mind, different sidewall "skin" patterns have deeper recesses and may require more than one layer of putty tape. It is recommended that a liberal amount be applied and allowed to squeeze out when the screws are reinstalled. Remember, if the screws do not tighten properly, replace them with the next larger size.

After the door or window is secured to the sidewall, trim the excess putty with a sharp razor knife for a nice, crisp finished seal. Be careful not to cut through the siding. The exposed edge of the putty tape can be smoothed easily by moistening a shop towel with a spray of Protect All protectant. This helps close any pores that may be evident in the putty. Additionally, a small, thin bead of clear silicone sealant can be applied over the putty on the top edges of the windows and entry doors.

Remember that most sliding windows for RVs have drain slots or "weep" holes cut into the bottom edge of the extruded frame. Sometimes these drain holes become plugged and water may gather in the slide track and run down the interior walls. Check to make sure these holes are clear. Some drain holes may have small plastic caps covering the slots. You will need to remove these in order to check the drain. Louvered and awning windows will not have drain holes.

Storage Compartments – Treat storage compartments the same as the entry door and windows. All are secured to the sidewall in much the same manner. The common point being that wherever a screw or rivet penetrates the sidewall, there also is the potential for a leak to develop.

Take special note if there is moisture noticed inside the storage compartment. Investigate its source without delay. It could be simple condensation, common with some metal enclosures, or it could be a leak. Do not make any assumptions. Treat any moisture as a possible leak from somewhere, then try to disprove it. The inspections will be more thorough that way.

Appliance Exhaust Vents – All LP appliances are vented to the exterior with the exception of the range. Indirectly, the range is also. The exhaust fan above the stove exits through the sidewall. Inspect these closely, especially the furnace exhaust. The high heat factor associated with the furnace exhaust vent rapidly dries out the sealants placed behind it. Sealants and putty tape at this location will require replacement sooner than at other locations.

Miscellaneous Areas – Much like everything attached to the roof, any item connected to the sidewalls should also be closely scrutinized. Check all items such as wheel skirts, city water inlet, window awnings, fresh water storage tank fill and drain, shoreline cord door, fuel tank fill doors, moldings at the floor line or any vertical seams in the siding. Seal any discrepancies using a thin bead of clear or white silicone. A little more attention to aesthetic detail should be taken when applying silicone on the sidewalls, since most areas are readily visible.

Often overlooked as potential points of entry for moisture are the lag screws that attach the upper arms and brackets for the RV patio awning. They usually are drilled and mounted through the awning rail and into wood blocking at or near the roof line. Many installers forget to seal these lag screws. This is how:

1) Extend the awning in order to gain access to the lag heads.
2) Carefully remove one lag screw at a time.
3) Squeeze silicone sealant directly into the vacated hole, then reinstall that lag screw. Repeat this process with each of the mounting lag screws, one at a time.
4) As a final precaution, squeeze some silicone inside the awning rail next to each lag. Rain water can enter the rail at any location and run inside the rail to any point of entry such as the lag screws. Water can then seep into the sidewall by "following the threads" of the lag screw.
5) Do not overlook the bottom bracket mounting screws. Typically they are secured to the sidewall at the floor line. A leak here could damage the flooring or a support structure over a period of time.

Another often overlooked situation involves the add-on screen rooms that accompany many RV awnings today. Some end panels to such rooms attach to the sidewall of the RV with snaps or twist latches that are permanently installed on the RV. It is important that these are also carefully waterproofed as well.

Cracks in the fiberglass or plastic front or rear end caps that penetrate the entire thickness may be patched with INSTA-GLAS, a premixed, multi-purpose patch kit.

INTERIOR REPAIRS

Usually any type of moisture absorbed by interior walls and the ceiling, especially if the drainage is in an advanced stage, precipitates replacement of the panels. By and large, saturation of plywood or veneered paneling results in permanent stains, splitting or separation of the layers. Most glues simply cannot hold up after constant exposure to even small amounts of moisture. Repairs, therefore, are limited to minor cosmetic cover-ups.

Some cleaners and stain removers are worth a try on those areas that may be stained, but are still basically intact. Most RV supply stores carry a variety of plywood and wood panel care products. Many also carry colored putty and patching materials that may be helpful in some cases.

Determine the composite of the damaged panels and choose an appropriate cleaner, patch or polish. Carefully read the directions on the container to verify it will apply. Chances are, however, replacement will be the only care.

Unfortunately, because of the construction of the RV, interior wall and ceiling panel replacement is extensive and better left to the professional, unless there is a covered work area available, plenty of time, and some expertise in the construction trade. Most panels are assembled and attached during the building of the coach. For instance, the completed ceiling and roof, as one piece, is set on top of the sidewalls and secured. In other words, the ceiling panels extend over the top of the sidewalls and cannot simply be removed and replaced without first removing the roof section. Many times the rubber trim molding, or gimp, located in the corner at the intersection of the upper sidewall and ceiling, is stapled to the top of the sidewalls before the entire roof section is even lowered in place.

Additionally, interior cabinets are usually attached to the walls from the outside before the exterior siding is in place. Therefore, in order to completely remove the interior paneling, the exterior "skin" needs to be removed along with the wall insulation. Then the cabinets can be removed so the damaged panels can be taken down and replaced. It is quite extensive and usually requires pneumatic tools and heavy equipment.

Matching paneling can be cut and installed over an existing damaged panel. This can be accomplished by making a cardboard template of the cutouts around cabinets, windows, etc., then transferring the template design to a new piece of matching paneling. The new panel can then be cemented or stapled to the old panel. This may prove to be successful in repairing a small area. For larger areas with extensive damage, call a reputable body repair shop for an estimate.

Water damage detected early can be rectified easily. Left unchecked, it may become a major repair. Assertive, competent inspections may avoid these issues altogether. The key is to find the leak and repair it immediately. Do not wait for that spring shakedown.

Remember, water will seek its own level; therefore, just because water stains appear in the galley, do not assume that is where the entry point is. The rear 14-inch vent may have deteriorated sealant allowing the water to gain entry into the void between the ceiling and the roof. Water, powered by gravity, will travel until it is absorbed by the ceiling and/or the insulation, or it may continue until it finds a low spot to pool and then begin its negative action. Investigate carefully.

The key, therefore, is early detection and immediate action. Inspect regularly.

CHAPTER ELEVEN

Rubber Roofing

Few innovations in the RV industry can boast of continued interest over an extended period of time. Along with other leading-edge design concepts such as the basement model motorhome and slide-out rooms, the advent of EPDM rubber roofing has generated a lot of interest. Equipped on RVs since the 1980s, EPDM rubber (ethylene propylene diene monomer), has now enjoyed industry-wide acceptance on many RVs and many decades of successful use in other industries. So popular now, most RV manufacturers offer at least some of their product line, if not most, equipped with an EPDM rubber membrane as the finished roof surface.

So just what is all the excitement about? Why is rubber roofing on RVs so popular? According to a published polymer selection guide spec sheet, EPDM membrane is ideal for outdoor applications, such as the roofs of RVs, because it has an excellent resistance to ultraviolet light (UV), ozone, oxidants and can withstand severe weather conditions. Such characteristics allow many EPDM manufacturers to guarantee their membrane for long periods—10 to 12 years. Realistically, EPDM membrane could last closer to 20! Additionally, it has excellent resistance to heat which makes it extremely well-suited for RVs in any climate. It is capable of enduring

Typical Rubber Roof

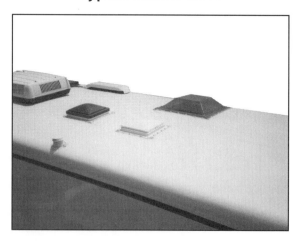

temperature variations from −50 degrees Farenheit, to 240 degrees Farenheit, without cracking or deteriorating. Its sunlight aging rating is excellent. Compression set, abrasion resistance and its resilience factors have all been rated good. On the downside though, tear resistance only came in at fair, and the solvent and oil resistance rating is poor. Other inherent negative characteristics include a susceptibility to absorb oils, fats and waxes from solvents having a low polarity. An example would be the resultant bubbling or wrinkling that would occur if an oil-based roof coating, commonly used on aluminum RV roofs, is mistakenly applied to EPDM membrane.

EPDM rubber requires no protection from UV rays or ozone bombardment, though it is prone to oxidize. Normal oxidation is a condition caused by the disintegration of surface binders or elastomers by weathering. Other destructive environmental conditions can also add to the degree of chalking. The result is that surface chalking actually removes a portion of the rubber. This is a normal occurrence, and the RVer should not be concerned about the direct effect on the rubber. Oxidation will, however, usually manifest itself as long, unsightly streaks running down the sides of the RV. We have all seen it. The streaks are usually caused by dirt, road grime and air-borne pollutants that settle and adhere to the roof and are washed over the side along with the loosened powdery surface elastomer. Some white streaking may also contain remnants of titanium dioxide, which is used as a whitening agent along with calcium carbonate, used as a filler compound.

The simple solution is to keep the roof clean. The degree of chalking associated with EPDM may vary from coach to coach, but tighter controls during the copolymerizing procedure leads to a slower rate of oxidation though most will surrender up to 10 percent of the overall thickness during the life of the roof. Since EPDM is itself an elastomer used generally in conjunction with other elastomers, copolymerizing the EPDM with other modifiers can substantially improve the quality. But that is for the manufacturers to worry about.

INSTALLATION TECHNIQUES

All rubber roof installations require a solid decking under the EPDM rubber membrane. Called the substrate, it typically consists of one-quarter-inch or three-eighths-inch plywood. Thinner substrates can be utilized, but the thickness is usually dependent upon the amount of load and the number of accessories that will be installed on the roof.

Rubber roofing material is cemented to the prepared substrate. If a bonding-type cement is used, such as a contact cement, it must be applied to the bottom ply of the EPDM as well as the plywood substrate. When a water-based adhesive or a pressure sensitive cement is used, it is applied only to the plywood.

Usually EPDM rubber is rolled out to the entire length of the RV resulting in a simple, one-piece layer of rubber as the finished roof material. During installation, the rubber extends the length of the coach, with excess rubber also extending over the sides of the RV, enough to fold down behind the drip molding or awning rail.

The membrane is folded back, front to rear, about halfway, and cement is applied by brush, roller or spray gun. Solvent-based contact cement is applied to the substrate, and the EPDM rubber and allowed to dry. Once dry, the rubber is laid out and adhered to the substrate decking. If a water-based, pressure sensitive adhesive is used, the membrane is laid in place while the cement is still wet.

Air pockets are rolled out from the centerline of the coach to the sides with a lightweight roller or a push broom. At the front and rear of the RV where the EPDM terminates, an insert molding bar is installed across the entire width of the RV. This termination bar should overlap the exposed edge of EPDM rubber. Be sure to use a compatible butyl caulk underneath the molding bar before it is secured to the roof. This same technique is used on those RVs with front and rear fiberglass caps as well, although the caps may overlap the edge of the EPDM rubber.

At the RV sides, the EPDM material is folded over the edge of the roof and stapled to the sidewall on top of the siding material. Butyl tape or caulk is applied to the back of a drip channel or awning rail which is then secured to the sides of the RV. Excess material hanging below the molding or rail is simply trimmed off with a razor knife or scissors.

After the roof is completely cemented in place, all the openings for the sewer vents, the refrigerator vent, the 14-inch vents, the roof air conditioner opening etc., must be cut into the EPDM. This is accomplished by carefully cutting the membrane with a sharp pair of scissors. When cutting the openings, avoid square-cut corners. Always radius the corners to eliminate the possibility of the EPDM tearing. When possible, have excess rubber fold into the opening which can then be stapled to the sides of the opening. This is not practical with circular roof vent openings, yet sage advice for rectangular openings in the roof. Once all the openings have been cut, apply butyl tape and install the vents as usual and seal all screws, flanges and edges with an appropriate lap sealant. When working with EPDM rubber and lap sealant, do not smooth out the bead of sealant after application.

The relative ease in which EPDM membrane can be installed has resulted in many older coaches going through an upgrade process by removing the old, soft aluminum roof, for example, and adding new insulation, a substrate decking and the EPDM rubber material. When RVs have experienced water leaks that simply cannot be resolved, oftentimes the best cure is a new roof topped with EPDM rubber.

EPDM REPAIR

As hard as we try to avoid them, sometimes accidents just happen. As stated earlier, one of the pitfalls of EPDM rubber membrane is its propensity to easily tear. Such tears can occur while backing into a campsite with low, overhanging tree limbs or by a careless repair person or RV owner walking on the roof. Flying projectiles launched during a severe rain or wind storm can also result in damaged EPDM rubber membrane. So what is to be done if such damage is incurred?

Repairs can easily be accomplished by adding a layer of EPDM membrane over the damaged area. This is how it is done.

1. Cut a piece of rubber roofing material three inches larger than the damaged area (RV paint and body shops are a good source for small pieces of EPDM). Be sure to cut the patch using rounded corners.
2. Center the patch over the tear or hole and draw a line around the entire patch.
3. Lift the patch and clean the damaged area under the patch with an aftermarket splice cleaner or a clean cloth lightly dampened with mineral spirits or hexane. The section to be repaired must be clean. Also clean the entire bottom area of the patch itself.
4. Apply adhesive to the patch and the damaged section of the roof. Spread the sealant evenly to extend beyond the perimeter of the mark by about one-quarter inch. When the adhesive has dried, align the patch and press it into place. After the patch is secured, apply a bead of lap sealant around the entire patch.

A recent addition to the aftermarket is a ready-made patch kit produced by Carlisle Syn Tec Incorporated, one of the leading EPDM producers, and distributed by Dicor. Called Patchit, this handy repair kit comes complete with a peel-and-stick EPDM patch coated with an appropriate butyl adhesive sealant and a standard tube of industrial lap sealant. Simply following the detailed instructions on the kit will easily result in a successful repair.

Another effectual method of repairing EPDM membrane damage is by using a product called Liquid Roof, produced by Pro Guard Coatings. Liquid Roof is simply a liquefied version of EPDM rubber. It is self-adhering and self-leveling. According to the manufacturer, Liquid Roof does not chalk and can actually be employed to eliminate chalking of existing membranes. It has proven to be extremely effective at sealing around roof appurtenances. Simply brushed on, it creates a thin, single layer of EPDM rubber that acts like a shield to protect existing caulks and sealants around vents, etc.

MAINTENANCE

As mentioned earlier in the chapter, the best preventive maintenance is a clean roof since EPDM requires no special treatments or protectants, although many exist today. Cleaning the rubber roof should be a regularly scheduled maintenance task performed often enough to keep the EPDM surface white. Usually four to six times per year will suffice depending on the local climate and its propensity to gather and distribute dirt, and how pure the copolymerizing process was performed during manufacture.

Cleaning can be accomplished by washing the roof with a mild laundry detergent, household bleach or one of the many aftermarket cleaners available. Other contributory factors that determine how easy it is to clean EPDM membrane include the time of year, the type of stains incurred and how well the roof had been previously maintained. In short, the best prevention is frequent inspections, immediate repair procedures and regular cleaning. For extremely tough stains or grease, some manufacturers recommend a product called hexaprene, a hexane-based solvent for rubber cements and adhesives. Hexane and all of its derivatives should be treated with extreme care as it is highly flammable.

During periodic roof inspections, pay particular attention to the sealant around the various components attached to the roof. Be sure to only use lap sealants and caulking that are compatible with EPDM rubber membrane. Also, be extremely cautious when washing or cleaning the membrane. EPDM rubber becomes dangerously slippery when wet, especially if a soap solution is utilized.

One confusing aspect of EPDM care involves the use of products that contain petroleum distillates. It appears the very words "petroleum distillates" invoke confusion and controversy. EPDM, as designed and formulated by the chemists and engineers, has a poor resistance to oils and solvents—all derivatives of petroleum, but many, if not most, of the aftermarket cleaners and protectants are forever branded with the words "Contains: Petroleum Distillates" right on the container. According to the makers, they are mandated to put the words "petroleum distillates" on the label as a notification for physicians and emergency medical specialists in the unlikely event of ingestion of the product. Prominence in labeling is a requirement of the Consumer Product Safety Commission and the Code of Federal Regulations, Commercial Practices, Section Sixteen.

According to the suppliers, the term "petroleum distillates" is a very broad category that usually refers to all aliphatic hydrocarbons. Aliphatic hydrocarbons can be divided into two distinct groups: petroleum distillates and synthetic paraffinic hydrocarbons (such as the aforementioned hexane). All petroleum distillates and paraffinic hydrocarbons are good cleaners and spot removers, although the paraffinic hydrocarbons have a lower flammability level, a narrower boiling range and a higher solvency rate. Both groups are very good at removing light grease and grime common to the roofs of RVs. In fact, a recent study has revealed that most RV rubber roof products do work, even though some do contain petroleum distillates.

Proponents say trying to define the term petroleum distillates is akin to explaining the term "liquids." Liquids come in many varieties; water, milk, battery electrolyte, gasoline, cough medicine and nail polish can all be described as liquids, and each has a beneficial use when used correctly. However, nail polish used as battery electrolyte or milk poured into the RVs fuel tank will indeed have disastrous results. The fact is that all petroleum distillates begin their refined life as a petroleum distillate, but their end use can be radically different. Another EPDM fact of life is that it has been proven to be incompatible with petroleum distillates.

Immersion tests, in fact, have revealed that saturation by petroleum distillates will cause EPDM to swell, wrinkle and bubble. When used, such products must be removed quickly and not allowed to soak into the membrane. In other words, successful cleaning can be accomplished as long as the directions are followed completely and care is taken not to saturate any area of the rubber roof.

So a dichotomy still exists. Fact: warranties can be voided by using products that contain petroleum distillates if damage is incurred by its use. Fact: when used as directed, EPDM products containing petroleum distillates do work. So just where does that leave the RV owner? It beckons the RVer to try an assortment of care products and make a personal observation and decision based on his or her climate and type of grime. In other words, use what works best in your situation taking care to follow the directions explicitly. Be also advised that your warranty may be affected by using products that contain petroleum distillates. It just may come down to how well you want the roof to look, how easy it is to clean and if the risk of voiding the warranty means less to you than keeping your EPDM rubber roof membrane spotless.

CHAPTER TWELVE

Damaged Flooring

Undetected plumbing leaks, a leaky air conditioner gasket, cracks around roof vents, faulty window sealants and a few other moisture producing ills can all lead to damaged floors within any RV. Left unchecked, moisture damage can eventually ruin an otherwise usable coach. Unfortunately, most damage may be hard to detect unless conscientious yearly inspections are performed. Occasionally, damaged areas may be inadvertently exposed while performing other tasks, such as re-carpeting the RV or replacing the toilet.

If moisture happens to seep into the floor from any source, over time it will be necessary to replace the damaged sections. There is no quick fix for water induced damage—replacement is the only true solution.

The good news is that in most cases, replacing damaged flooring can be performed by anyone with access to some power tools, some common sense, a little construction aptitude, a block of time and a generous amount of patience. Many RV owners can easily handle this chore. If, however, the affected area extends beneath wall partitions or cabinets, it is best to have a professional do the job. In severe cases, all cabinets and partition walls must be removed. The repair process can then become quite complex. More often than not, though, damage is contained to a small area and repairs can be accomplished with relative ease.

In most instances, floor damage will be quite evident by pulling back the carpeting or by removing the toilet, or by simply investigating a suspicious spot or stain. If the carpeting is still usable, carefully remove the entire section and safely store it until the flooring has been replaced. The appearance of wood rot is so unmistakable, it is not easily confused with any other malady. Dark stains, softer wood, flakes of particles, mildew and the presence of moisture are all signs of an affected area.

FLOOR CONSTRUCTION

RV floor construction details vary from manufacturer to manufacturer, but the typical floor is usually bolted to a steel chassis after assembly. The floor framework may consist of a sandwich design with a pressed wood composite or metal underbelly with wood or metal floor joists, topped with a covering of plywood or pressed wood. Inside the framework, insulation fills the voids between the joists. The top floor is usually applied in four-foot by eight-foot sheets. The joists are typically 24 inches or 16 inches on center, but this dimension may vary between floorplans and categories of coaches. The size and positioning of the supports, cross beams and joists also vary depending on the weight and overall length of the RV. The floor section of the RV is usually one of the first components constructed. The rest of the RV is then built on top of this foundation.

Main support members are spaced about four feet apart from front to rear. Other braces run crosswise to form a grid configuration. Quite often, the top flooring is attached to the beams with screws, nails or staples, so a visible line of fasteners will indicate where most supports are located. When replacing damaged flooring, the replacement piece should extend a minimum of four inches into the existing "good wood"—the wood immediately around the damaged section.

DETERMINING THE THICKNESS: To replace the flooring without damaging the infra-structure (or the saw if the floor joists are made of steel), determine the exact floor thickness of the flooring material. The easiest way to determine this is to drill a hole in the damaged area, away from cross supports or floor joists. Use any size hole saw attached to an electric drill motor to accomplish this. The larger the hole saw the better. Not only will a sample plug of the floor thickness be obtained, but a large hole saw will allow for an easy inspection of the inner floor area by using a flashlight and mirror. The drilled out sample plug can be retrieved from the hole saw to determine the top flooring thickness.

REPLACING DAMAGED FLOORING:

Marking the Cut-Out Area – After determining the location of cross supports, joists or other blocking that may be in the sub-floor, lay out and mark the damaged piece to be removed. It is always best to replace enough of the flooring to extend from one joist or support to another. If the damaged area extends further, go to the next one.

The cut lines should be directly over the center of a floor joist so that when the new piece is inserted, it will be supported by an existing joist or beam on at least two sides. Additional supports running the opposite direction may have to be added in order to accomplish this. Use a framing square to be sure the cut-out area will be straight and true.

Making the Cuts – Use an electric circular saw to make the cuts. Set the depth of the cut to a little less than the measured floor thickness if the joists and supports are made of steel. If they are all wood, the saw blade depth should be set a little deeper than the thickness of the flooring. In most cases, you should be able to make at least two of the cuts with the circular saw.

If the damaged area extends to the base of a cabinet or dinette, it may be necessary to obtain an electric reciprocating saw that will enable a cut to be made closer to the obstructing cabinet. A worst case scenario may find one using a hammer and a chisel to make those cuts that adjoin cabinets or other obstacles. (Remember the patience factor.)

Once all the perimeter cuts have been made, remove any and all screws, staples or nails that may have been used to secure the original flooring to the supports. After all fasteners have been removed, lift or pry the damaged section out.

Installing the New Section – After removing the damaged piece, examine the beams and sub-floor supports for rot or damage. If unaffected, proceed with the replacement. If there has been extended damage to wooden joists or supports, those rotted pieces must, likewise, be removed and replaced.

Measure the lengths needed and cut new supports out of two-foot by two-foot or two-foot by four-foot lumber. Secure these to the available "good wood" inside the floor. (NOTE: In some cases it may be necessary to remove a larger section of plywood than was originally intended in order to secure sub-floor components to the existing, structurally sound framework. The goal is to have a solid support below the entire perimeter of the replacement piece prior to inserting it in place.)

After the sub-floor components are in place, measure the entire cut out area and transfer the dimensions to the new piece of plywood of the same thickness as the existing flooring.

Be sure to replace all wet, rotted or deteriorated insulation found inside the floor. This step is doubly important in the colder climates.

Test the new piece for a proper fit, then glue the new section to the supports and secure it with the appropriate type of flathead screws. Be sure the screw heads are countersunk into the plywood so as not to interfere with the finished floor covering. An electric drill can be outfitted with a screwdriver tip to make the installation process a snap.

Use a readily available, pre-mixed floor patch to fill in any voids or gaps around the perimeter of the replacement section. Then sand smooth any rough areas or joints. Commercial grade floor patch is available at most hardware stores or home centers.

Sealing the Leak – Water damage does not occur from one night of rainfall seeping through a leaky window seal. It happens gradually over a period of time and continued saturation. It is imperative that the source of the invading moisture be located and repaired accordingly. It would do little good to invest the time and materials needed to do a large floor repair and then not to repair the source of the water leak. When considering RV floor damage, key places that moisture may come from include:

- Directly under sink "P" traps
- Behind or around the toilet
- At or near the shower stall or tub enclosure
- Below a 14-inch roof vent or air conditioner
- Anywhere near the water pump, fresh water tank or city water inlet
- Behind the water heater

According to industry-mandated construction codes for RVs, all water connections must be accessible. It may be necessary to remove a panel or gain access by removing an appliance, but it should be possible to observe every connection in the coach. Periodic inspection of these areas can minimize major damage to the floor caused by water. A good time to inspect these areas is during the spring shakedown each year.

Do not let moisture induced damage take you by surprise. Repair all water leaks as soon as they are detected.

REPLACING CARPETING

Simply through normal use over the passage of time or from blatant abuse, the carpeting in the RV can become an embarrassing eyesore. Stains and wear patterns are a natural result of any of these occurrences. Since RVs are meant to be used and enjoyed, carpet wear may reach a point where replacement is a valid and warranted expense. Cleaners and stain removers can only go so far. Throw rugs can only mask the problem for a while. Carpets do take a beating in the RV since the foot traffic is in such a concentrated area.

For the typical RV handyman, the re-carpeting task can be handled with relative ease using common hand tools. Allow plenty of time. The key to re-carpeting the RV involves proper planning and careful execution of a few simple tasks. Obviously, if the flooring underneath the existing carpet is in need of repairs, those items must be completed before the re-carpeting can begin.

Choosing the Carpet – Personal tastes will obviously reflect the choice of colors and style, but consider this: it is best to avoid the deep pile varieties. Most crush easily under heavy foot traffic and will not recover completely. Better choices are commercial grade, close-loop piles which can be luxurious, easy to clean and reasonably simple to install. Always invest in a quality carpet pad. Padding saves wear and tear and is well worth the added expense and labor.

Removing the Old Carpet – During manufacture, some RV floors are fully carpeted before the partition walls, cabinets and furnishings are installed. This method creates a handsome appearance and makes sense at the time of manufacture, but it presents a time consuming job for anyone wanting to replace the entire carpet.

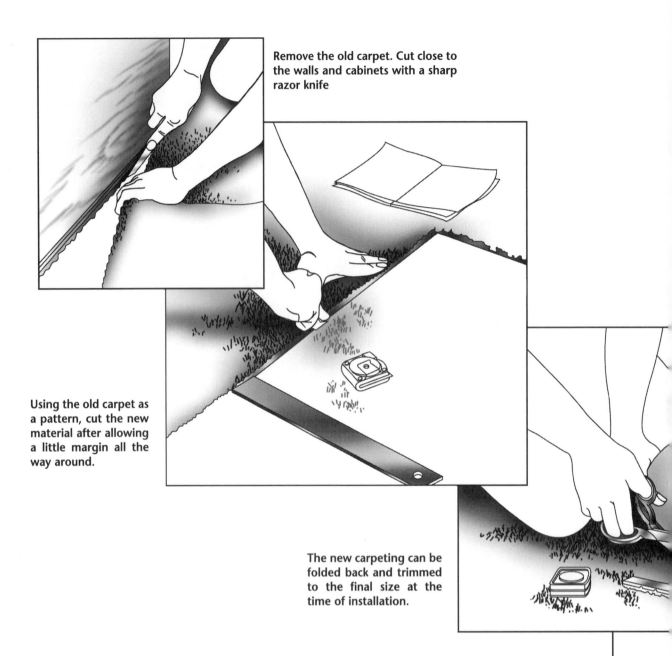

Remove the old carpet. Cut close to the walls and cabinets with a sharp razor knife

Using the old carpet as a pattern, cut the new material after allowing a little margin all the way around.

The new carpeting can be folded back and trimmed to the final size at the time of installation.

Complete removal is sometimes unnecessary since the old carpet can serve as padding or be selectively retained in closets and under storage areas. Of course, if water stains have damaged the carpet, it is crucial to remove the entire carpet, repair the source of the leak, and if necessary, repair the wood flooring prior to installing the replacement carpet. Additionally, if the original carpet contains odors as well as stains, it might be a good idea to remove the complete carpet anyway.

If the existing carpet was installed before the cabinets and partition walls, carefully cut along the walls and cabinets with a sharp razor knife to cut out the old carpet. Save these pieces. They may be used as a pattern for the new carpet. Try not to destroy or rip the old carpet.

Be sure to check the floor area carefully after removing the old carpet. Staples or tacks may still be present. Use a pair of diagonal wire cutters or pliers to remove any remaining staples. If there are any rough joints or splinters in the wood flooring, now is the time to sand and smooth them. Completely sweep the wood flooring clean.

CARPET INSTALLATION

Laying the Carpet As a preliminary step, remove any item secured at or near the floor. Cabinet doors that are low to the floor should also be removed for easier handling of the new carpet. It may be necessary to remove the LP leak detector since it, too, is mounted close to the floor. Be sure to mark the wires before cutting or removing the detector.

If a thicker carpet and pad are going to be installed, some cabinet doors may have to be repositioned to accommodate the added thickness of the carpeting. In most cases, this is not a major concern. There is usually enough room for such an adjustment without having to modify the doors.

If it is decided to use a carpet pad, install it first. It can usually be cut with sharp scissors or a razor knife. The pad can be attached by stapling or by using a spray adhesive. Be sure to vent the coach well while using a spray adhesive. Some adhesive fumes may be harmful or at least irritating, when used in close quarters.

Cutting – As mentioned, any removed portions of the old carpet can be used as a pattern for cutting the new one but it is wise to leave a little extra material all the way around the perimeter and trim the pieces to fit exactly at the time of placement. A razor knife with a new

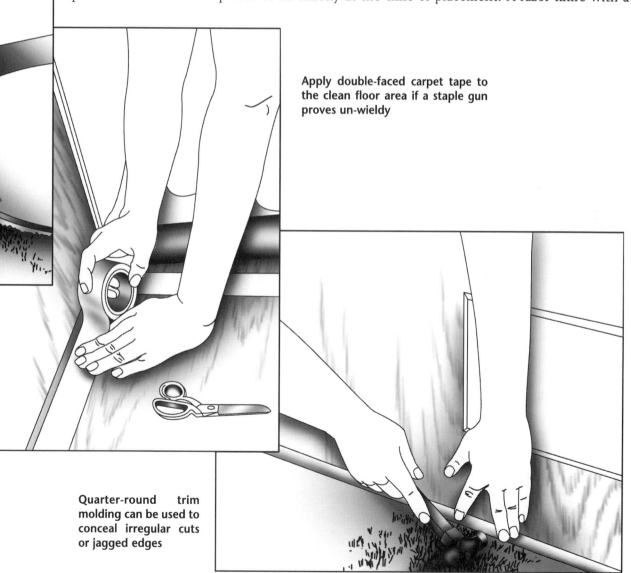

Apply double-faced carpet tape to the clean floor area if a staple gun proves un-wieldy

Quarter-round trim molding can be used to conceal irregular cuts or jagged edges blade works best for cutting virtually all carpet materials. Stock up on razor blades and change them often during the installation process. Carpet cutting will quickly dull the blades. Use a metal straight edge with the razor whenever possible to produce a nice, crisp edge.

After cutting the carpet to fit, lay it out flat inside the coach and work from one end of the RV to the other. Force the new carpet into the edges at the cabinets and carefully trim the remainder of the excess with a sharp razor knife. Remember to change blades often. Since the area in the RV is relatively small, a carpet knee-kicker is usually not needed.

Attaching – Today, the carpet tack has given way to the staple as the best method for securing the carpeting. There are other means, but the stapler reigns supreme because it is fast and easy to use and the staples are easily concealed within the pile of the carpet. It is recommended that an electric or air-powered stapler be rented or otherwise obtained for the task of securing the carpeting. Manual staplers are impractical for this size of job, and staple choice is somewhat limited.

The staple design is dependent upon the choice of pile and style of carpeting. Overall thickness of the pad and carpet also needs to be factored in to determine the length of the staple needed. Ask the carpet salesman what he recommends when choosing the carpet and pad.

Double-faced carpet tape is also quite handy for attaching the carpet in close quarters and under cabinets where a stapler may not fit. Such carpet tape is also used when joining two separate pieces of carpet. This, too, can be obtained at the time the replacement carpet is purchased.

Abutting Two Pieces – In larger RVs, it is not probable that the carpeting can be installed in one complete piece. Generally, the carpet has to be pieced together. If possible, choose a convenient location to make the butt joint, such as in a doorway leading to another section of the coach, for instance.

To make the butt joint, overlap the two pieces and using the straight edge, make one straight cut at the exact point of the joint. Cut deeply and firmly since two layers of carpet are being cut. Use the carpet tape to affix both sections of carpet to the floor at the joint. Avoid using too many staples in the area of the joint; it may accentuate it. The goal is to have the joint simply blend in with the rest of the carpet. Also, avoid making a joint in the carpet pad at the same point as the joint in the carpet itself. A few feet on either side of the finished joint is recommended.

Where Tile Meets Carpet – In most RVs, there is a point where the carpet meets linoleum, tile or a wooden section in the galley or lavatory, for instance. Usually a metal or wood threshold is used to mate the carpet to other floor coverings. Another method is to simply fold the carpet under and staple it to the floor. If there is an existing threshold, remove it. If not, purchase one of sufficient length and cut it to fit.

When folding the carpet under, try to remove any backing from the carpeting first, then cut the padding back the width of the fold (about two inches or so), so that the folded carpet lays as flat as possible. This method works well when staples cannot be used, such as when meeting ceramic tile. Check, also, with the carpet sales department. There may be another preferred method for that style of carpeting.

After the carpet has been secured to the floor, remount any pedestal bases, furnace ducts, LP leak detectors or cabinet doors that may have been removed prior to the installation. Keep in mind, it may be necessary to raise some cabinet doors to provide enough clearance above the carpet for the door to swing freely.

Miscellaneous Tips – If it was difficult to cut a straight edge under the cabinets, or along a partition wall, pre-finished molding can be added to conceal any rough edges or mis-cuts that may have been made. Always use real wood molding; synthetic or plastic molding is not recommended. Quarter-round molding works best and is relatively easy to install.

When carpeting in the bathroom, it is best to remove the toilet completely and to allow the carpeting to cover the floor all the way up to the perimeter of the floor flange. It can be difficult to accurately trim around the base of the toilet. Also, if the toilet were to need replacing at some point in time, the carpet cuts may not match the new one. After installing the carpet, reinstall the toilet. Always use a new flange wisely and be sure to test the water connection for leaks after reinstallation.

If it is necessary to drill a hole or attach a screw through the carpeting, always cut an "X" in the new carpet before doing so. This will eliminate the probability of snagging the weave and permanently damaging the carpet. Keep this in mind when reinstalling pedestal bases or furnace ducts mounted in the floor.

Should re-carpeting the cab area of a Class C motorhome be desired, the same steps can be followed, except rarely is a carpet pad used. Also, since most floor assemblies in Class Cs are made of steel, a spray adhesive or contact cement in lieu of staples to secure the carpet will have to be used. Always try to use the old carpet as a pattern.

Taking your time, double checking measurements and using a sharp razor knife will make the job of carpet replacement a fairly easy task. Additionally, a new carpet will reflect a personal touch that can be enjoyed for many, many miles.

CHAPTER THIRTEEN

Adjusting and Repairing Doors

Interior RV doors such as cupboards, wardrobes and storage cabinets, most often attract attention in transit when they bounce open. Many latches installed on RV doors simply give way to the constant jiggling of relentless vibration while in motion. The unhappy RVer usually solves this nuisance by installing positive or magnetic latches. Other complaints about RV doors include warping, poor alignment and sagging entry doors. Since these problems are more difficult to repair than loose latches, it is fortunate that they occur less frequently.

Realigning and replacing doors can be tackled by the RV owner provided the hurdle of obtaining the correct materials and parts is cleared. Specific entry doors and panels with particular finishes are readily available for RVs of fairly recent vintage, but materials are difficult to locate for older models or RVs built by manufacturers who are no longer in business. Here, the owner can take the coach to a local RV cabinet shop or body shop or improvise the repair. Professional body shop work can be somewhat costly, but the job is usually correct and professional. The drawback of doing it yourself, however, is that what started out to be a simple cupboard door replacement may blossom into the need to replace all cabinet doors.

Hardware Headaches – The most common annoyances with cabinet and interior storage compartment doors are usually caused by hardware problems. Poorly designed latches and improperly mounted hinges make a door open and close in jerky movements, or even bounce open while driving. Both can be easily corrected by the owner.

Loose Latches – The long-term solution for latches that pop open in transit is complete replacement with ones better suited for road vibration. Select replacements carefully. Examine some of the many designs stocked by RV accessory stores to find ones that require forceful turning or pulling to disengage the latching mechanism. These are the most secure.

Temporary repairs are possible with certain types of latches. For instance, one of the common designs is a barrel catch made up of plastic rollers that mount to the cabinet and a metal clip that is affixed to the door which grasps the rollers when the door is closed. If

Cabinet jamb

Back of cabinet door

Periodically the metal clip portion of this type of latch will spread and allow the door to spring open. Squeezing the clip will tighten it.

Barrel catch

Metal clip

If the mounting screws on the plastic barrel latch are tightened too tight, the plastic, the plastic will split necessitating replacement

the clip becomes distorted and no longer gaps, simply bend it back to its original shape.

Improperly Mounted Hinges – Smooth the movement of crooked doors by repositioning the hinges. Here is how. Remove the entire door leaving the hinges attached to the door. Position the door and hinges on the cabinet and mark the new mounting location. Seal the old screw holes in the cabinet with wood dough, pressing the soft dough into the holes and waiting for it to dry into a hard filler before drilling the new holes. Stuffing toothpicks or wooden match sticks in the abandoned holes is another method of filling the holes. This method, however, is not as satisfactory as using wood dough which can be sanded and drilled and produces a more attractive repair.

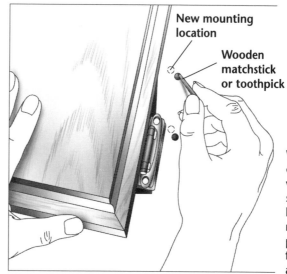

New mounting location

Wooden matchstick or toothpick

Wooden matchsticks or toothpicks work well for repairing stripped-out screw-holes. Inserting the matchstick will provide new wood for the screw to attach to.

If cabinet door will not stay closed during transit, it may be necessary to reposition the entire door. Old holes can be plugged with wood filler that matches the color of the cabinets then lightly sanded. Another option would be to insert a wooden matchstick in the old hole and dab a little matching stain, then wipe it off.

Straightening Warped Doors – Doors most prone to warping are those taller ones used for the bathroom and wardrobe closets. These can absorb moisture from repeated exposure to the humidity of cooking and hot showers. Many are reinforced with a steel brace that can be removed, bent in the direction opposite the warp and reinstalled to correct the problem. Some doors can be so distorted, however, replacement is the only cure.

Replacing a Warped Cabinet Door – Often a badly warped cabinet door cannot be repaired, only replaced. Ready made doors are available for some RVs, but if a replacement is not obtainable from a dealer, it is possible to fabricate them.

Although most high-line RVs have solid wood doors, many are equipped with doors that have a hollow-core construction made up of a frame to which thin, pre-finished plywood panels are glued and stapled. The best procedure to obtain a good match is to remove the door and take it with you to a dealer so that both the frame molding and the panels can be replaced with identical stock.

If you decide to make a replacement door yourself, start by measuring the defective door carefully. If warping prevents accurate measurements, use one of the unaffected doors as a pattern, first making sure that it is identical in size to the damaged one.

Mitering the Framing – Readily available molding can be used for the framing material. Mark the molding to correspond with the measurement, and place one piece in a miter box. Saw a 45 degree corner, sawing on the waste side of the measured line and allowing some extra so that the segments can be sanded flat for an accurate and tight fit. Prepare each piece and sand the corners to fit, then glue the frame together, securing each end in a corner clamp to make sure the 90 degree angles are retained. After the frame has dried, reinforce the corners with staples.

Preparing the Panels – To prepare the back panel, lay the frame on the paneling and trace its perimeter. Plan the front panel by tracing the inside of the frame, then measuring a lip to match the flat portion of the molding where the paneling will be glued and adding that margin to all sides. Cut these pieces, taking care to make square cuts.

Glue the front side first. Apply carpenter's glue to the lip and the mating surface on the frame and position the face panel. Use clamps to hold the pieces until the glue cures. The pressure of the clamp can dent the panel surface, so place small blocks of wood beneath the clamps as a precautionary measure.

Attach the back panel by applying glue along the frame and the corresponding part to be bonded. Again, use a clamp and let it dry. Reinforce this bond with staples or small finish nails. Sand any rough edges and check the door for a proper fit. Smooth out any irregularities with fine sandpaper. Determine the hinge positions and attach them first to the door, then to the cabinet. Test the door for free movement prior to installing the latching mechanism.

Repairing Scratches – Tiny chips or scratches can mar pre-finished surfaces. Repair these with a color putty stick sold in hardware stores. Obviously, select a color as close to the grain of the cabinet as possible. Natural stain cabinetry will require a correct color match at the local hardware store. Carefully follow the directions of the stain manufacturer.

Difficulties with Entry Doors – As with interior doors, road vibration is the major cause of problems with sagging entry doors. Over time, aluminum hinges yield under the stress of bouncing down the highway. This occurs more in coaches with the entry door located to the rear of the rear axle. Here, gravity compounds the problem and accentuates the sag.

Another problem is difficulty opening and closing the entry door. Usually, the striker plate is often at fault. This plate is mounted on the doorjamb and must align with the lock bolt. Periodic adjustment may be necessary.

Fixing a Sagging Entry Door – With some RV doors, the hinges alone can be replaced, but the more common design is one in which the hinges are integral to the door assembly and the entire assembly must be replaced. If the RV is only a few years old, order a new door from the RV manufacturer or from a well stocked supplier.

Professional technicians have the tools and expertise to install a new door quickly so that labor costs are small. The do-it-yourselfer can install a new door, but the job may be complicated by a floor that slopes or a doorway that has one or more sides out of plumb.

If the choice has been made to install the door yourself, a door assembly, putty tape, possibly new inside trim and a power screwdriver will be needed. This is where an investment in a quality cordless, reversible drill is truly appreciated. A door installation may entail screwing down as many as 70 screws.

Before installing the door, test for a proper fit by holding the door assembly in place in the opening. If the floor sags, examine it carefully. It may be necessary to shim the entire assembly to compensate for frame sag or for an irregular rough opening. Liberally apply putty tape around the edge of the door frame before inserting the assembly into the opening. Be generous with the putty tape and carefully check the installation for complete sealing. Plumb and screw the hinge side of the door first. Shim the opposite side until the door frame opening is square. A large framing square is ideal for this task. Carefully trim away the squeezed out putty tape with a razor knife after securing all the mounting screws.

Repositioning the Striker Plate The striker plate is usually mounted in slotted holes and does not have to be completely removed for repositioning. Some have aligning screws that protrude out from the edge of the door. It may be necessary to reposition these aligning screws to fit the plate on the door frame. Study the installation to determine in what direction the plate or screws should be moved. Experiment until the door closes easily, then secure the striker plate.

Additionally, it may be necessary to paint stripes or apply striping decals to finish the exterior of the door to match the original. Perhaps a local RV body shop can perform this task for a reasonable price.

Once mastered, taking care of the RV door repairs will indeed save countless dollars over the life of the RV.

CHAPTER FOURTEEN

Exterior Body Repairs

Exterior body repair techniques on RVs are almost as varied as the different types of RVs available. Construction methods are many, therefore, repair procedures will also vary depending on how the RV was originally constructed. It is imperative that prior to undertaking any exterior repair on the RV, fully explore the manner in which the coach was put together. If in doubt, or if there is a question concerning construction, be sure to contact the dealer or the manufacturer for the details before beginning.

Always allow plenty of time for exterior repairs. This is especially true if working on the roof area. Also, the larger the repair, the more it may be exposed if major portions of the RV are uncovered. If possible, perform exterior repairs inside a garage or under a covering of some type. Weather, especially moisture-laden air, makes some repair procedures more difficult. As with any repair, proper preparation is crucial to a successful job, so begin right by keeping the area clean and dry.

CONSTRUCTION METHODS

Before delving into actual repair practices, consider the different types of coach construction. Though variations of each exist, there are basically three major types of sidewall and roof construction techniques used today.
- Laminated construction
- Soft or hollow wall construction
- Aircraft design

Laminated or "sandwiched" sidewalls and roofs are multi-layered, rigid and extremely strong. It is probably the most popular method used today. The process entails gluing and sandwiching the interior finished paneling, the framework, the insulation and the exterior "skin" in one operation. One typical method allows each wall to be laid out on a large assembly table one layer at a time. The laminations are glued, pressed and clamped together and subjected to a vacuum that literally sucks the moisture and air out of the "sandwich." The result is a strong, dry, bonded, one-piece section that can now be affixed to the chassis portion and assembled with other RV sections that have also gone through this process. All cut-outs and openings for the windows, doors, vents and storage compartments are also made while the section is on the assembly table.

This type of sidewall and roof construction is the favored method by many of today's RV builders. The advantage of having a laminated roof is mainly the strength factor. Solid roofs are durable enough on which to walk, to attach storage pods, or to stow other related camping gear. Most Class A motorhomes are equipped with a roof rack and a ladder for just this reason.

Another method of construction, popular especially with the travel trailer and slide-in camper makers, is the soft or hollow wall construction. This method is most similar to house-type wood construction where a finished interior panel is affixed to a stud wall, then insulation is installed and finally the exterior siding or "skin" is applied in a separate procedure. The interior paneling is usually applied to the framework before the sidewalls are placed onto the chassis.

The advantage to this type of construction is reduced cost. It is much less expensive to build an RV with soft sidewalls and roof. The obvious disadvantage is lack of support or strength, especially on the roof.

When climbing onto or working on a soft roof, first place lengths of walking boards or supports that will span a minimum of two or three roof rafters. If anyone accidentally steps in between two rafters, damage or leaks may result. Soft roofs are not designed to be walked on. This is one reason they are popular with travel trailers and fifth wheels. Rarely do you see roof racks, ladders or stowed gear on top of such vehicles.

The third major type of construction is the aircraft type. Those sleek coaches with the non-painted, buffed aluminum exteriors have a construction technique all their own. These RVs characteristically have individually preformed sectional pieces of aluminum riveted onto a framework of aluminum or steel. Sprayed in foam-type insulation is then filled into the cavities from inside the coach, and finally, the interior sectional pieces, also preformed, are then riveted or screwed in place.

CONSTRUCTION MATERIALS

Since lamination is today's preferred construction method, it is probably only fair that this method also has the largest variety of building materials available. The interior wall paneling and ceiling panels are pre-finished, four-foot by eight-foot sheets of plywood or veneer approximately one eighth-inch to three-sixteenth-inch thick is used. Some top of the line makers may use real wood paneling instead of a veneered plywood.

The framework of the laminated wall can be constructed from wood, aluminum tubing, or steel tubing. Each has its advantages and disadvantages ranging from cost to weight. Also, many coach builders run electrical conductors inside these laminated sections. Most sidewalls will have wiring run inside, and some roof sections will also have 120 volts AC or 12 volts DC wires, or both, encased inside the bonded section.

Insulation is usually sheet or block polystyrene foam, or the equivalent, approximately three-quarters-inch to one-inch thick which is cut and inserted into the voids between the framework studs and supports. Routing channels are sometimes cut into the insulation when positioning the wires into the laminate prior to pressing and final assembly.

Next, a thin piece of plywood, usually one-eighth-inch thick, is placed just to the outside of the framework. This paneling, commonly called luan plywood, proves a smooth gluing surface for the final exterior finish. It also adds to the profound strength of the total laminated section.

The final layer in the laminated construction wall is the outside skin. This siding is made from a number of materials. Fiberglass, ABS plastic, Filon (fiberglass-reinforced plastic) and aluminum siding are the most popular materials for the exterior skin on the laminated wall. These materials are also used to form the large front and rear caps and radius molding or corners on most coaches.

Laminated roofs are constructed much the same as the sidewalls with the exception of the final outside layer of skin. Roof materials may be one-piece aluminum sheeting, rolled aluminum roofing containing seems, or the popular one-piece EPDM rubber roof covering. All bonded roof assemblies are also built on a special laminating table, and the whole assembly is set upon the upright vertical sidewalls during the construction phase of the RV.

The soft or hollow wall construction consists of an interior panel stapled, riveted or screwed to a framework consisting of wood, steel or aluminum studs or supports. Either woven fiberglass insulation or the blown-in foam insulation is applied to the back of the interior paneling, and an outer skin of aluminum is stapled or riveted to the framework.

The aircraft-type of construction is much the same as the soft or hollow wall construction except usually no wood is used at all. The framework is usually aluminum or steel square tube welded together. The exterior preformed pieces are riveted into place. Then the insulation is installed. Lastly, the interior panels, also preformed and made form aluminum, are riveted into place.

Wherever electrical wiring passes through a wooden frame member, a protective plate should be situated to protect the conductor from screws or staples that may be accidentally driven through it. One of the most difficult electrical repairs is finding and repairing a short or an "open" in a wire hidden somewhere in the sidewall or ceiling of the coach. If the RV framework is metal framed instead of having wooden studs, be sure a grommet is used to protect the wiring where it passes through. Some manufacturers protect the wiring with silicone.

Aside from the easily recognized design of the aircraft-type construction, RV aluminum siding is available in a variety of designs, corrugations and patterns with strange names and with various dimensions. Names like mesa, mesa 1, mesa with reverse, yoder, miniyoder, old and new aristocrat and greyhound are just a sampling of the various patterns that have been used over the years.

Additionally, acrylic panels of fiberglass-reinforced plastic may adorn some sidewalls as well. This material is usually available in a flat, smooth finish or a pebble-like, rough finish. Typically, all are cemented to the thin sheet of luan paneling as part of the bonded, laminated wall sections.

To find out which design is used on your RV, take the coach to a reputable and knowledgeable RV body shop and have the estimator examine and measure the siding to determine the exact size and pattern.

TYPES OF DAMAGE

In order to choose the correct repair procedure, first determine the type of damage that has occurred to the RV. Here are six different types and a definition of each.

Dent—A depression (ding) or indentation in the exterior of the RV that has not punctured the skin.

Crack—There are two distinct types of cracks. One, which resembles a spider web and is usually located near the corners of doors or windows, is called a "stress crack." It is considered a surface crack in the outermost layer or gelcoat of the fiberglass siding. The other type of crack is a little more severe. A "through-crack" is deeper than a surface crack. It will be cracked all the way through the thickness of the panel. It is common to find this type of crack on RVs with an extended overhang behind the rear axle, or at an entry door situated behind the rear axle as well.

Hole—Penetrates all the way through the siding. It could be a cut, a slice or a puncture. The damage, however, is usually confined to a very small location.

Impact—Usually causes major sidewall damage, typical the result of a collision. Frame members may be bent or broken and interior walls may show evidence of damage. Some pieces may even be missing.

Delamination—The exterior siding has separated from the cemented and bonded "sandwich." The glue simply did not hold, or was applied incorrectly and the siding appears to be bellowing out away from the sides of the RV.

Water Damage—That which is caused by a water leak that was ignored. Usually confined to the interior paneling, the insulation and/or wooden structural members inside the wall cavity. It usually does not affect the exterior skin or siding except in cases where the luan paneling has deteriorated as a result.

REPAIR TECHNIQUES

The type of damage, sidewall construction and the siding used should all be considered to determine the correct repair procedure. In many cases, the scope of the repair may be beyond the means of the RV owner. In those cases, the repair is better left to the professional body shop.

Damage so extensive the entire side sections need to be rebuilt should probably not be attempted by the owner—likewise with massive sidewall delamination damage. This usually requires complete stripping off of the siding and special prepping and gluing (remember, improper gluing was probably the original cause of the delamination in the first place).

Additionally, it is recommended that any damage so severe that an insurance carrier will be notified, should likewise be directed to the professional body shop. Body shops are familiar with insurance claims and estimating forms and paperwork. This will also expedite the repair.

Once the entire scope of the damage has been assessed and the decision is made to address the repair yourself, choose the repair option. They are:
- Band-Aid
- Patch
- Replacement

The *Band-Aid* approach is nothing more than a cosmetic cover-up of a small, diminutive dent or puncture or tear. This is where it is common (and very inexpensive) to simply install a louvered vent over the opening to hide the blemish. If the skin is punctured, fill the hole with silicone sealant prior to installing the vent. Choose the smallest, least obtrusive vent available, and simply screw it or pop-rivet it to the side of the coach over the hole. Be sure to seal the edges with putty tape. Decorative decals or other trim items can also be used to conceal small dents or holes. Literally hundreds of dollars of sidewall damage repair can be avoided with the simple purchase of a vent.

The *patch* method is a common cure for both types of sidewall cracks discussed earlier. Minor cracks are easily repaired with a patch kit. The best product for patching stress cracks is INSTA-GLAS. Distributed by Bri-Rus, Inc. INSTA-GLAS is a ready-to-use kit that can be applied to fiberglass, plastics, metal and even wood, if necessary. It is very effective and easy to carry, unlike a two-part epoxy resin and catalyst that must be carefully mixed and hurriedly applied. INSTA-GLAS is premixed and contains a photo-curing acrylic resin and strands of fiberglass. The curing process is effectuated by an ultraviolet lamp or sunlight. Once the compound has been applied, simply position the coach in direct sunlight for faster curing. This is the repair procedure:

1) Remove any moldings or trim that might conceal any portion of the crack.
2) Remove the door or window if the crack is in that area.
3) Rough sand the area at the crack and about one inch of the surrounding area.
4) Apply the INSTA-GLAS to the entire cracked area.
5) Smooth out the compound and place a piece of clear plastic over the repair area.
6) Starting at the center, slowly work any air bubbles to the sides of the plastic with a flexible putty knife or other flat object. Try to obtain a smoothness as close to the finished form as possible to avoid a lot of sanding after it cures.
7) Allow the patch to naturally cure in the sunlight or direct a UV lamp onto the repaired area.
8) After curing, remove the plastic and sand the patched area.
9) For fine surface blemishes that may exist after sanding, apply a thin layer of finishing resin and allow that to cure.
10) Finish sand the area, then mask, prime and paint.
11) Reinstall all windows or doors, trim and moldings, etc. Be sure to use the proper sealants such as putty tape and silicone.

To patch the deeper gouges, punctures, holes or through-cracks, it may be necessary to administer two applications of INSTA-GLAS. Or, if the damage is in an area with immediate access behind the hole or crack, such as in a wheel well, front or rear cap, or lower skirt area, repeated layering of fiberglass resin and glass mats can be applied to build up a reinforced segment to help strengthen the repair. The thickness of the damaged material will ultimately determine how many fiberglass layers will be needed.

After reinforcing the area behind the damage, simply apply the outer INSTA-GLAS repair patch as outlined above. Take your time. Most people have a tendency to rush body repairs. Careful sanding, inspection, filling and more sanding are the keys to a quality body repair.

The best method is *replacement*, especially regarding hollow wall construction damage .

Aluminum siding is originally installed from the roof line down. It may be in many sections top to bottom. The lowermost section slips into a locking seam on the piece immediately above it to ensure a leak-proof seam. The next piece fits into the one directly above it, and so on. RV manufacturers may choose different colors and widths of siding for an aesthetically pleasing appearance. First determine which piece of the siding is damaged. It is possible that more than one piece is damaged. Inspect the area closely.

Replacement panels are ordered through various suppliers, but keep in mind a local RV dealer may have to place the order. Many suppliers sell only to a dealer network. If you have any questions concerning ordering any aluminum siding, a source of information is All-Rite Exteriors. The company can be reached at 800-262-6541, and they can provide the name and location of the closest dealer.

REPLACEMENT PROCEDURES

Be sure to carefully evaluate any other materials that may be needed; check for damaged moldings, vent, lights, drip rails, awning rail, etc. It is recommended that all replacement materials be on hand prior to beginning the replacement procedures. Here are the procedures:

1) Prepare a clean, dry work area, preferably under a protective cover.
2) Remove all compartment doors, appliance vents, windows, wheel skirts, entry doors, moldings, trim, city water inlet, etc., virtually any item that is at or below the damaged area. If the water heater will have to be removed, be sure to turn off the source of LP at the container prior to continuing. To be safe, plug the LP line at the water heater to keep contaminants out.
3) Starting at the bottom, remove all pieces of aluminum siding up to and including the damaged area. Each piece, including the uppermost damaged piece, will have to be removed from the bottom up. If some lower pieces are unaffected by the damage, they must carefully be removed anyway and set aside for reinstallation later. Remove each piece by carefully pulling the staples located at the sides and along the bottom of the locking "Pittsburgh" or "S" seam. It is advisable to wear protective gloves when handling aluminum siding. Some edges are extremely sharp. Long, thin pieces of siding have a tendency to kink, therefore, additional help may be needed when handling these long, cumbersome sections.
4) If the damaged area does not include the uppermost piece, and there is no frame or stud damage, begin installing the new panels by sliding the top edge of the new piece into the

locking seam of the upper piece on the coach. Have someone hold the panel firmly then check to make sure it is inserted fully into the seam.

5) Staple along the lower edge below the locking seam into the wooden framework. It is recommended that an electric or pneumatic stapler be used for any siding replacement jobs. They are available at most equipment rental facilities. Use a wide crown staple horizontally along the bottom of the locking seam and a narrow crown staple when stapling vertically up the sides of the siding and around openings. Do not cut the siding for openings or for length at this point. Just allow the piece to extend beyond the edge of the sidewall.

6) Install the next lowest piece in this same manner taking care not to kink or dimple the new siding. Some thin sheets are very delicate to handle.

7) After all new pieces and any undamaged original pieces have been installed, carefully trim the edges using aviation snips or aluminum shears. Now, cut out the openings for all the peripheral components removed earlier. Take your time and trim carefully being sure to stay at the edge of the cut-out and not to wander into the middle of the newly installed panels.

8) After trimming all cut-outs, staple the siding along the ends and around the edges of the larger openings such as doors, windows, etc. It is not crucial to staple around the smaller openings such as the city water inlet. The mounting screws for the inlet itself will suffice to secure the siding.

9) Be sure to seal along the exposed vertical edges at the corners of the RV with a thin bead of silicone sealant. Apply putty tape to the backside of the molding, "J" rail and/or awning rail before securing with screws. Use a liberal amount of putty tape and trim the excess that squeezes out with a sharp razor knife.

10) Reinstall all doors, windows, etc., taking care to properly seal against leaks. As always, apply putty tape behind the mounting flange. If necessary, a thin layer of clear silicone sealant can be applied after trimming the putty tape. NOTE: Some siding patterns, like yoder, for instance, may require more than one layer of putty tape to adequately fill in the voids behind the mounting flange of doors and windows. It is vital that every portion of the void be filled with putty tape to ensure no water leaks will develop.

INSIDE THE WALL: With the siding removed, inspect the insulation and framework. If water damage has rotted a stud or frame support, now is the time to replace it. Cut a new piece to fit and secure it to existing "good wood" with nails, screws or staples.

Likewise, replace any insulation that has deteriorated. Seldom are the inside of the walls exposed like this, so carefully evaluate all that you can see at this time. Is the wiring secure? Are there any visible openings leading to inside the coach? Are mounting bolts secure? Check everything while it is exposed.

ROOF REPAIRS: Bonded, laminated roofs with seams should be sealed with a roof sealant such as Plas-T-Cote roof coating, or a like substance, once a year if necessary. Seal around every item attached to the roof, 14-inch roof vents, plumbing vents, the refrigerator vent, roof racks, antennas, pods, etc.—any place a screw penetrates the roof should be checked. Liquid Roof can be purchased and is very effective at sealing all types of roof seams or patching EPDM rubber roofing material.

If damage from low hanging branches has punctured a laminated roof, the repair is identical to that for sidewalls as explained earlier in the chapter. If, however, a soft roof has a hole, the roof can be patched by installing a flat aluminum panel that spans two rafters (if the hole is large) or simply a small piece for small holes. First fill the hole with putty tape or silicone sealant, then cover with the patch. Screw or pop-rivet the patch in place and carefully seal the entire area with Liquid Roof.

If major damage to the roof area has occurred to a soft, hollow roof, it will be necessary to replace the entire roof section. All roofing aluminum, with or without seams, comes rolled and in one piece. Roof replacement is not a quick job. It is best left to the professional body shop. It is further recommended that a soft roof be replaced with one that is covered with a thin layer of plywood and EPDM rubber roofing material. This will add strength and stability to the roof area, and the rubber roof needs no maintenance other than a few washings each year. It will also add to the value of the RV.

Patch kits are available for rubber roof repairs. Simply follow the directions on the kit for an effective repair should the rubber roof develop a tear.

Rubber Roof Comparisons

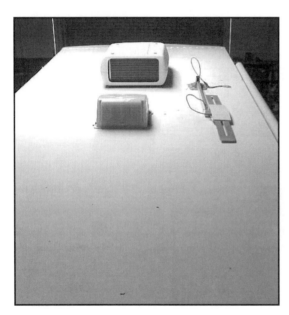

A comparison of a clean rubber roof (top), a dirty rubber roof (top right) and stained, moldy EPDM rubber on a neglected roof (bottom right).

FINISHING TOUCHES

After any exterior repair, the most important follow-up is to make sure there is no chance for water to enter. Leaks are the biggest concern.

Final touches include painting and adding decals, decorative striping or logos that were ruined by the damage and subsequent repair. It is probably best that a body shop prime and paint the damaged area, unless of course, it was a fairly small area that was patched.

Decals, striping and other manufacturer produced logos can probably be ordered through the manufacturer or an RV dealer. If the manufacturer no longer exists, perhaps a brand-specific owner's club or association can be of assistance.

Remember, only tackle those repairs with which you feel comfortable. If you think it is beyond your capabilities, call an RV body shop. Never compromise the safety factor. With proper study though, RVers should be able to easily handle almost any small exterior repair.

CHAPTER FIFTEEN

Repairing Running Lights

When one ponders just how far technology has progressed with RVs, it is hard to imagine any item more aggravating than having intermittent running lights. They sometimes burn out, flicker off and on, or can just be plain temperamental. However, it seems we must all go through this dilemma from time to time; label it an RV fact of life. The two predominant causes of problems with running lights can be categorized simply as corrosion and road vibration.

Running lights, turn signals, backup lamps and brake lamps are all subject to dirt, dust and corrosion that erode electrical contacts, along with vibration, which loosens connections. Most exterior lighting problems can be remedied easily and quickly by keeping spare bulbs and fuses on hand and by using a systematic, detective-style approach when making repairs.

If all or most of the lamps do not work, for example, one cause could be a blown fuse. This is especially true if the lights are all on the same circuit. If only the turn signals do not work, the first step is to locate the fuse block that contains that circuit. Take the suspect fuse out of its holder and inspect it visually. If the filament broken? To be doubly sure, try substituting a new fuse of the same rating, or check to see if there is continuity through that fuse by using a VOM on the ohm scale. Sometimes a fuse that appears to be good really is not. Always keep spare fuses on hand. If a short exists and the next fuse blows also, substitute a resettable circuit breaker with test leads for the fuse while searching for the short. Never substitute a fuse with one of a higher amperage rating.

One common reason why an entire circuit fails in a travel trailer, for example, can be attributed to a poor electrical contact in the wiring connector between the tow vehicle and trailer. Water can invade the tow vehicle socket or the trailer plug and corrode the contacts. A spray can of electrical

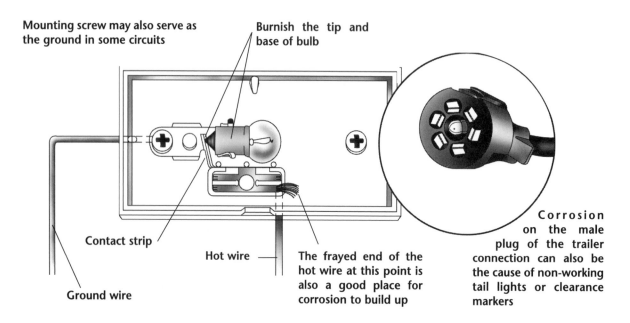

Mounting screw may also serve as the ground in some circuits

Burnish the tip and base of bulb

Contact strip

Hot wire

The frayed end of the hot wire at this point is also a good place for corrosion to build up

Ground wire

Corrosion on the male plug of the trailer connection can also be the cause of non-working tail lights or clearance markers

contact cleaner, available in hardware or electronic stores, can restore good contacts. To prevent the connector from corroding in the first place, keep both the plug and socket covered when they are disconnected.

If only one lamp is not working, remove the lens and inspect the bulb to see if the filament is broken. Although a burned out bulb is not the most frequent cause of light malfunction, it is about the easiest to spot.

If the bulb is good, the lamp may be suffering from corrosion inside the fixture. Check the wiring connections inside. They should be clean and firmly attached. Take the bulb out and brighten the base with fine sandpaper or emery cloth. Also burnish the inside of the clip and the contact strip that touches the bulb tip. Examine the strip to make sure it indeed contacts the bulb. If it does not, bend the strip to make sure it pushes against the bulb tip. If the corrosion is rampant, replace the entire fixture.

Corrosion inside the fixture can be caused by moisture seeping in around the lens. To prevent this from recurring, put a small amount of silicone sealant on the edge of the lens before it is reinstalled. If the light still does not work, very likely a bad ground exists. Another indication of a bad ground is a lamp that flickers on and off or works only when tapped or bumped.

To check for a bad ground, take the lens off and activate that circuit. Take a length of wire, or an alligator test lead, and attach one end to the side of the bulb's base. Touch the other end of the wire to one of the lamp's mounting screws or to another bare metal part on the RV (such as an aluminum window flange). If the bulb lights, invariably the problem is a bad ground.

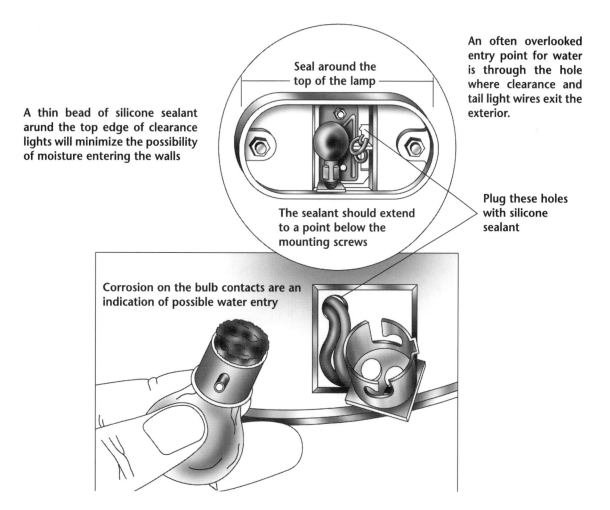

Seal around the top of the lamp

An often overlooked entry point for water is through the hole where clearance and tail light wires exit the exterior.

A thin bead of silicone sealant arund the top edge of clearance lights will minimize the possibility of moisture entering the walls

The sealant should extend to a point below the mounting screws

Plug these holes with silicone sealant

Corrosion on the bulb contacts are an indication of possible water entry

Most RV lamps have a ground wire running from the light fixture to somewhere on the chassis, or the ground path may simply be the aluminum skin on the RV. If when removing the lens cover and only one wire exists, then the ground path is to the skin through one of the mounting screws. If, however, there are two separate wires, then the ground path is usually through the second wire to a point somewhere on the chassis. This two wire setup is mandatory with coaches with non-metallic mounting surfaces such as fiberglass. Trace the ground wire to make sure that it is unbroken and firmly attached to either the chassis or the connector.

Other RVs, as mentioned, are grounded through one of the screws that hold the light fixture to the RV's aluminum skin. To cure a poor ground with this type of fixture, tighten the screw. If that does not work, take the screw out and replace it with one a size larger.

If the lights on a particular circuit are dim, it may be because the positive or hot lead to the lights is leaking or shorting current into the chassis. Follow this hot wire from the light and check for worn insulation. Damaged insulation can be repaired with electrical tape or solderless connectors. While tracing the hot wire, check any wire connector the manufacturer may have used to splice wires together. Sometimes water can get into these connectors and corrode the contacts. When replacing butt splices, it is always wise to use heat shrink tubing around the wire and the connector to protect and weatherproof the connection.

Many motorhomes have harnesses that run along the frame rails to one of the two rear tail lamp assemblies. Sometimes, in-line fuses are installed somewhere in this harness, usually close to the rear of the motorhome. These in-line fuses may be in addition to the fuse at the chassis fuse block. Look carefully, some may be wrapped completely in electrical tape or hidden behind frame members. Use a 12-volt test light to quickly locate running light circuits in a harness.

Many clearance lamp circuits for RVs begin at one of the rear tail lamp assemblies. If none of the clearance markers are working, remove one or both of the tail lamp assemblies and check the wire nuts or attaching points behind it. Chances are vibration has caused one or more of the wires to become disconnected.

Some electrical harnesses on travel trailers and fifth-wheels terminate in a void or cavity inside the sub-floor just under the front of the trailer behind the "A" frame. Here, the harness links up with the wiring inside the trailer. This connection point is also made typically with wire nuts that may be prone to separation caused by vibration. If one or more outside lamp circuits do not operate at all, it may be necessary to remove the cover to this space and check the wires and connections within. If the turn signals flash rapidly and not very brightly, install a heavy duty flasher in the tow vehicle.

Another key to troubleshooting running lamp problems is to isolate the problem area, using the process of elimination. Check individual lamps and connectors with a 12-volt test light. Try to obtain a set of electrical prints for that particular model. Many manufacturers can supply the construction prints that were used for that RV. One good habit is to always wrap electrical tape around wire nuts to make sure simple vibration will not loosen them. This one step alone could save considerable frustration while traveling.

CHAPTER SIXTEEN

Winterizing and Storing Your RV

Although many individuals and families enjoy the RVing lifestyle on a full-time basis, there are many others who appreciate the benefits on a more limited basis, such as during vacations, holidays, weekend getaways, or maybe a combination trip of business mixed with pleasure. Unfortunately, not everyone is in a position to be a full-timer. For those who utilize the RV of their choice part-time, there comes a time when the RV must be stored for a period of non-use. If located in one of the colder sections of the country, it will also be necessary to protect the RV against the cold by winterizing the coach. In either case, whether it is cold or temperate climates, certain precautions need to be taken.

Specific tasks and procedures for each of the major systems and components of the RV must be performed in order to store or winterize the coach effectively. One of the most damaging effects that can happen to an RV, short of abuse, is ill-prepared non-use. To get the most from the RV, following the procedures in this chapter will ensure the RVer of extended coach life and many more joyful RVing miles. For optimum efficiency, the following strategic and sequential steps are designed to be implemented in the order written.

As a preliminary step to winterizing the coach, completely wash the exterior. Doing so will get the storing preparation off to a good start. Washing also may reveal items that need to be addressed prior to the spring shakedown.

Fresh Water System

Probably the most demanding reason why winterizing techniques became a reality in the first place is the fresh water system. If left unaddressed, water in the lines and appliances will freeze, expand and damage virtually every type of water line found in the RV. Contamination can occur. Here is what to do.

Drain Water Completely—Most coaches come equipped today with low point drain valves for both the hot and the cold lines. Usually located at the lowest point in the RV, these valves aid in gravity draining as much water as possible from the lines. Valve positioning may be located at or below the floor level. Some are found underneath the chassis.

Accessories are available, such as a "blow out plug," which attaches to the city water inlet to aid in removing all the water from the lines. Open all the faucets and drain valves and screw the blow out plug into the city inlet and apply compressed air. Do not use gas station-supplied air. Most gas station air tanks are contaminated.

Drain Water Heater—Remember to drain the water heater. It is easy to forget that this appliance is an extension of the fresh water system. All water heaters have a drain plug or drain valve accessible from the outside of the coach, located near the bottom of the front panel. Open all the hot faucets inside the RV to aid in the draining process.

Fresh Water Storage Tank—Drain the water from the storage tank in the usual manner. Drain valves may be located on the outside of the coach, inside a compartment or underneath the chassis. If it cannot be located, contact the local dealer. All storage tanks will have a drain valve somewhere.

Empty Toilet—Regardless of which type of toilet is found in the RV, it will be necessary to remove any water from it. Usually, it is just a simple matter of operating the flushing mechanism.

Shower—Another area that seems to get overlooked many times is the shower hose. Even though it is equipped with an anti-siphon backflow preventer, many times water stays trapped in the shower hose. Simply unscrew the handheld showerhead and lower the hose to a point below the faucet attachment point.

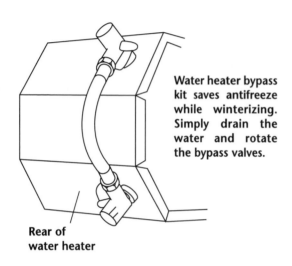

Water heater bypass kit saves antifreeze while winterizing. Simply drain the water and rotate the bypass valves.

Rear of water heater

Another recommended accessory to utilize is the water heater bypass kit. This device permanently installs to the rear of the water heater and consists of diverter valves which, when turned one direction, will completely bypass the water heater. Thereby, minimizing the amount of RV antifreeze that will be necessary.

Depending on the climate in which the RV is located, this may be all that is necessary to prepare the fresh water system for storage. However, if the RV will be stored in freezing climates, the use of RV antifreeze may also prove beneficial.

RV Antifreeze—After the lines have been blown dry or totally drained, add an appropriate amount of RV antifreeze solution. *CAUTION: Be sure it is RV antifreeze!* Standard automotive antifreeze contains poisons that will contaminate the fresh water system.

There are two basic methods of adding the antifreeze to the system:

- Water pump method
- Back fill method

The *water pump method* involves filling the fresh water storage tank with the appropriate amount of antifreeze (approximately two gallons or more depending on the size of the system), and then simply pumping it through the entire system. After pouring the antifreeze into the tank, turn on the water pump and open all the hot and cold faucets. Make sure the water heater bypass kit is in the bypass mode. (The water heater should be totally drained of water by now.) When the antifreeze appears at each faucet, the showerhead and at the toilet, close the faucets and turn off the pump.

The demand pump can also be used to pump antifreeze throughout the system.

The *back fill method* invokes the use of a hand-operated pump that attaches to each individual faucet. antifreeze is hand pumped directly from the container into the system.

Other, more sophisticated anti-freezing systems are available for permanent installation, however, the majority of RVs will be well serviced by utilizing either of the two methods above.

Back-filling the system with antifreeze is a simple, inexpensive method to protect your fresh water plumbing.

WASTE SYSTEM

During the course of pumping the antifreeze throughout the fresh water system, chances are antifreeze was also introduced through the "P" traps and into the waste system. The black and gray water holding tanks and all drains must also be prepared for storage and winterizing.

"P" Traps—As mentioned, the "P" traps probably have antifreeze in them already, but to be sure, pour another cup down the drain at the kitchen and lavatory sink and also in the shower/tub drain.

Holding Tank—Flush and clean all holding tanks. There are many aftermarket products that make this undesirable task a little easier. One, a holding tank rinser, attaches to a water hose and allows a high pressure stream of water to be directed at the sides of the black water holding tank through the toilet. If it is known on which side of the tank the monitor panel probes are installed, try to aim a stream of water directly at them to help clean any residue of waste that may be affixed to the probes. Others can be permanently installed into the sides of the holding tanks.

After cleaning, drain each tank and close the termination valves completely. If the valves are sticking or are hard to slide, lube them at this time.

Prior to storage, flush and treat all holding tanks. Here's an easy way to clean inside the black water tank. Directing the spray at the level probes will wash away clinging waste

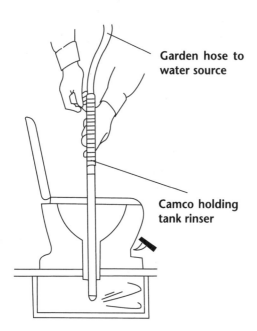

Garden hose to water source

Camco holding tank rinser

LIQUID PROPANE SYSTEM

Most of the emphasis will be placed on the four LP burning appliances, but there are a few tasks that relate to the LP system in a general sense.

LP Storage Container—The coach may have a permanently mounted LP tank located under the coach, or it may have twin upright cylinders, such that are found on the tongue of most travel trailers. In either case, make sure the service valve is turned off completely.

Remove the POL or Acme Type I fitting(s) and cover them with tape to prevent dust, dirt or critters from inhabiting the lines. If the RV is equipped with removable DOT cylinders, it is best to completely remove them and store them in a clean and dry location—never inside the RV.

Next, clean and cover the LP regulator. This prevents moisture from freezing inside the body of the regulator and keeps dirt out. Finally, if an electronic LP leak detector is in the system, be sure to disconnect it at this time. Now, focus on the individual appliances.

Water Heater—Aside from adding the bypass kit, make sure that the water heater is turned off completely. In some harsh climates it may be advisable to cut out a cardboard insert to fit inside the fold-down door of the water heater. It can simply be taped in place and the cover latched.

Furnace—Turn the thermostat completely off, and if the furnace is equipped with a manual LP valve, turn it off also. Use tape or aluminum foil to cover the intake and exhaust vents to prevent wasps or other critters from entering.

Refrigerator—Clean and dry the inside of the refrigerator after turning it off completely. Block open the doors slightly. Some units have latches that allow for this position already. Outside, at the rear of the refrigerator, cut a cardboard insert for the access door, as was done at the water heater. Tape this inside the access panel to keep dust and debris out.

Up on the roof, if not already present, it is a good idea to install wire mesh under the roof vent cover of the refrigerator. Birds and wasps love to build their nests on top of the coils located at the back of the refrigerator. This presents a fire hazard. Most newer RVs already employ mesh or other prohibiting devices here.

Range—Not much effort needed here. Just make sure the stove top and oven are turned off completely and that they are clean and dry. The range is the only appliance that is not vented directly to the exterior, therefore, there are no vents to cover or tape.

ELECTRICAL SYSTEMS

The focus here will be at the power source since most electrical devices seldom require preparation for storing or winterizing.

12-Volt Battery System—Disconnect all batteries in the system. If possible, remove each battery and store them in a cool, clean and dry place for the winter. Take the time to fully charge each battery. This is especially true if the batteries will be left in the RV. If the batteries are flooded batteries, check the level of the electrolyte and fill accordingly. It is imperative that they be fully charged after adding water. Charging the batteries will mix the electrolyte solution, thereby decreasing the chance of freezing. If the coach is stored for an extended length of time, it will be necessary to periodically recharge the batteries. All lead acid batteries will self-discharge over time.

Do not overlook the dry cell batteries in the RV. It is best to remove them also. Dry cell batteries are commonly found in:
- Digital clocks
- Smoke alarms
- Carbon monoxide alarms
- Flashlights
- Refrigerator interior lamps
- Fans

120-Volt AC System—Minimal effort here will ensure a safe, clean storage period. First, turn off the main breaker at the panelboard distribution box. Some are located in overhead compartments, while others may be combined with the DC power converter and located at the floor level or under a bed.

As a safeguard against rogue lightning strikes, unplug any 120-volt device that is plugged into a receptacle such as a microwave, refrigerator or the power converter. In this manner, a lightning strike cannot damage the components via the neutral wire in the circuit. The neutral wire is not interrupted by a circuit breaker.

Finally, wrap the shoreline plug in a plastic baggy to keep the contacts from corroding. Remember, with any electrical item, keep them clean and dry.

If the coach is equipped with a generator, it is wise to remove each spark plug and add a rust inhibitor. Reinstall the plugs just finger tight. Thoroughly clean the generator prior to storage. As done with the vents to the appliances, cover the exhaust pipe of the generator with foil or tape to keep wasps from building nests in there.

MISCELLANEOUS ITEMS

Roof Area—Prior to winterizing make sure the roof is clean and free from debris. Now is the perfect time to check the sealant around each roof vent, air conditioner, roof seam, etc. Pay special attention along the edges and across the front and rear caps. Reseal if necessary before winter sets in.

A cover for the roof air conditioner is also recommended. This is the best way to keep dirt and critters from entering, as well as to protect the condenser fines from flying debris.

Windows—Check the sealant around each and reseal with silicone if necessary. From the inside, cover the glass with foil or a protective layering of thin plastic. Even in the winter, it is possible that the sun's rays may fade upholstery and fabrics.

Tires—inspect each and thoroughly clean them with an approved product. Take the weight off the tires by placing the RV on jack stands. If a motorhome is equipped with HWH hydraulic levelers, it is permissible to extend the levelers to relieve the weight from the tires.

If it is not possible to remove the weight from the tires, periodically move the coach during its storage time to eliminate any flat spots that may develop from being in the same position for an extended period. Cover the tires to protect them from the damaging ultraviolet (UV) rays of the sun.

Undercarriage—Inspect under the RV for any openings around drain pipes, LP lines or electrical wiring harnesses. Rodent-proof the underside of the RV by plugging even the smallest of cracks or space. Rats and mice can squeeze through an unbelievably small hole. Use putty or aluminum plates to eliminate such openings.

MOTORHOME CONSIDERATIONS: Although most of the aforementioned procedures apply to virtually all types of RVs, the motorhome has a few additional steps that need to be addressed.

First and foremost, check the strength of the coolant in the radiator. It may be necessary to flush the radiator and add a stronger solution of antifreeze for the expected climate. Do not take any chances in this area. It is much better being protected for a far lower temperature than to short change the solution strength. Do not overlook the windshield washer reservoir. Either drain it or add some RV antifreeze as done to the fresh water system.

Top off the fuel tanks. The more liquid fuel in the tank, the less room for moisture. Replace any fuel filters in the system. Filters trap moisture, which subsequently may freeze if old filters are left in place over a harsh winter.

Remove each spark plug and add a few drops of a rust inhibitor. Reinstall the plugs just finger tight.

One final thought for any RV is to possibly invest in a total coach tarp. Custom designed covers are available that will completely cover the RV from top to bottom, front to rear. Special measurements are taken to allow for mirrors, air conditioners, TV antennas, storage pods, etc. This method is very effective for protecting the exterior finish from even the harshest of winters or the ravages of the hottest desert climates during temporary periods of non-use.

For a detailed video outlining each of the steps, be sure to order the video "Storing and Using Your RV." Contact the technical editor for ordering information.

Notes: _____

_____

_____

_____

_____

_____

_____

_____

_____

_____

_____

_____

_____

_____

_____

_____

_____

_____

_____

_____

_____

_____

_____

_____

_____

_____

_____

_____

_____

Winterizing and Storing Checklist

(Duplicate this checklist and place a ✓ beside each item as it is completed)

Fresh Water System	WasteWater System	Liquid Propane System
___Drain all water lines	___antifreeze in "P" traps	___Appliances completely off
___Drain water heater	___Flush/clean holding tanks	___Service valve off
___Drain fresh water tank	___Inspect termination valves	___Plug service outlet
___Empty toilet	___Lube valves	___Store D.O.T. cylinders
___Drain shower hose		___Cover regulator
___Pump RV antifreeze	**Water Heater**	
	___Completely off	**Furnace**
Refrigerator	___Cover opening	___Completely off
___Completely off	___bypass kit installed	___Cover vents
___Clean/dry inside		
___Block doors open	**Range**	**Batteries**
___Cover vent opening	___Completely off	___Disconnect all
___Screen on roof vent	___Clean and dry	___Electrolyte level
		___Fully charge
Generator	**120-Volt System**	___Remove dry cell batteries
___Clean	___Main breaker off	
___Add rust inhibitor	___Unplug appliances	**Roof Area & Windows**
___Drain fuel filter	___Cover shoreline plug	___Check sealants, seams, etc.
___Cover exhaust pipe		___Reseal as needed
	Motorhome Specifics	
Roof Air Conditioner	___Engine Coolant Strength	**Tires**
___Completely off	___Protect w/shield washer fluid	___Remove weight
___Inspect for damage	___Top off fuel tanks	___Apply protectant
___Cover	___Add rust inhibitor	___Cover

Date   **Performed by:**

CHAPTER SEVENTEEN

Spring Shakedown

After each period of non-use, regardless if the RV was winterized, stored in the backyard or kept in a closed garage for three months, each coach must go through a thorough once-over to get it ready for that next trip or for the upcoming camping season. Differing circumstances abound for different RVers, but by and large, every owner must at some point in time, go through the yearly ritual of what is termed the spring shakedown.

Keep in mind it can happen at any time of the year. It is not necessarily tied to spring. Simply stated, it is that time of year we clear out the cobwebs, dust off the road maps, pack some groceries, fill up with fuel and hit the road. If the spring shakedown is viewed from a systematic approach, checking each major component and area, system by system, there is assurance that nothing will "fall through the cracks" concerning the RV. The goal is to be back on the road safely enjoying the finer points of RVing.

SPRING SHAKEDOWN PROCEDURES

Just as it was done prior to storage, the first step of each new camping season is to thoroughly wash the RV. Starting with a clean coach puts everything in a fresh light.

ROOF, EXTERIOR AND WINDOWS: Everything should be in fairly good order on the roof if the advice was followed for winterizing the coach. However, now is the time to double-check all the roof seams, around each vent, etc. Look for damaged sealants, flaking roof coating or damage to any component such as the roof rack and ladder, if equipped.

Remove any window covering that may have been installed and open all the windows. This will help air out the coach as you go through the process of checking everything out, plus it will indicate those windows that may need some lubrication.

12-VOLT DC SYSTEM: Reinstall the 12-volt auxiliary battery(ies). Make sure all the contacts and terminals are tight, clean and dry. After the batteries are in place, check the electrolyte level. It is quite possible some of the fluid has evaporated during the storage period. Add water if necessary and fully charge the batteries.

Go through the coach and turn on the various 12-volt components to ensure the batteries are indeed powering the RV and that everything works so far. Don't forget to reinstall the dry cell batteries in the smoke alarm, carbon monoxide alarm, etc.

120-VOLT AC SYSTEM: Remove the shoreline cord from the plastic baggy and inspect the prongs for corrosion. Burnish the prongs with fine sandpaper or emery cloth to brighten the contacts. Plug in to an acceptable receptacle, then go through the RV and plug in all the components and appliances that were unplugged last fall: the refrigerator, the microwave, the converter, etc. Turn on the main breaker. An audible click should be heard as the relay in the converter closes and 12-volt power is now being produced by the converter.

Retrieve the polarity checker from the tool kit and test the polarity of the 120-volt receptacles located throughout the RV. If the polarity is anything other than okay, immediately unplug the shoreline cord and review the chapter on the electrical systems.

Test the GFCI located at or near the lavatory sink or at the panelboard distribution box. Make sure it trips and fully resets. Even though it may click, snap or make some other type of audible noise, that in itself is no guarantee the GFCI is making and breaking the electrical contact. Leave the polarity tester plugged in or any 120-VAC appliance plugged into the bathroom receptacle or the exterior receptacle to perform the GFCI tests. The exterior and bathroom receptacles are two that must be protected by the GFCI. If the circuit is not broken when the GFCI is tripped, there is no GFCI protection and a replacement or at least further troubleshooting is necessary.

FRESH WATER SYSTEM: Regarding the fresh water tank, depending on the method chosen to winterize, there will either be no water in the tank or it will have antifreeze in the tank. The goal of this step is to drain any antifreeze that may be present and to refill the tank with fresh water. It may be necessary to drain and refill it a second time.

There are aftermarket items such as water tank fresheners and baking soda products that are designed for RV use that will help in this area. Visit the local RV service center or accessory store for these and other helpful items.

Now is the time to clean or replace any filter or strainer that may be in the fresh water system. Some may be connected to the water pump or installed in-line to the pump. It is wise to replace the entire filter or the strainer element each year.

Open the valves on the water heater bypass kit if it was installed prior to storage. Include the water heater during the remaining tests of the water system.

Once the fresh water tank has been filled, turn on the water pump and begin pumping fresh water throughout the system. Open all the hot and cold faucets in the RV. When water is flowing swiftly from each faucet, close them all.

While the pump is still activated, open the pressure and temperature relief valve on the water heater. The obvious result of doing so will find water gushing out of the relief valve and down the side of the coach. This is okay. The goal here is to flush out the water heater. It has sat empty all winter (or throughout the storage time) and is in need of flushing. You can also open the drain valve or remove the drain plug to aid in this step. Let the pump continually try to fill the water heater as it is draining. Do this for 10 to 15 minutes. This helps rid the tank of unwanted calcium chips or deposits that gather on the bottom of the inner tank of the water heater. Be sure to turn off the water pump first, then close the pressure and temperature relief valve and water heater drain.

There are many handy devices available that make flushing the water heater easier. Check them out at the dealer's retail store.

Next, chlorinate the fresh water tank. This can be done by using one of many aftermarket products found in the RV accessory store or try this homemade recipe: Add one-quarter cup of bleach to the tank for every 15 gallons capacity of the tank. This bleach solution, diluted by the entire water supply, will effectively chlorinate the water, keeping it fresh and ready for use.

Now, connect the fresh water hose to the city water connection. With city pressure applied, inspect in, under and around all water piping in the RV. Look for any leaks that may have developed during the off-season. If none are found, proceed to the waste water system.

WASTE WATER SYSTEM: Drain the fresh water from each holding tank that has accumulated during the preliminary check of the fresh system. Now is the time to check the operation of the termination or dump valves. Most can be removed, disassembled and lubed if necessary. Make sure none are leaking before continuing.

Next, treat the holding tanks for odor control and waste degradation. In the past, formaldehyde-based chemicals used as a deodorant seemed to work best. However, as technology has progressed and the dangers of formaldehyde poisoning came to be understood, other options became a reality. In fact, formaldehyde and other alcohol-based chemicals are no longer recommended for use in either holding tank. Even some RV campgrounds and state parks now prohibit the dumping of formaldehyde-laced holding tanks into their waste systems.

**Holding Tank
Treatment**

The safest way to treat the holding tanks and to eliminate odors is to use a non-chemical, enzyme-based product that contains live bacteria. The live bacteria actually digest the odor causing molecules, which helps to eliminate the odor and to break down the solid waste. Add four or five ounces of a product called RM Tank Care, produced by Tri Synergy, Inc., to the tanks, along with enough fresh water to cover just the bottom of each tank. After subsequent evacuations of each tank during the RVing season, add another four or five ounces. This will ensure the tanks will remain fresh and free of odors and that you are doing your part to protect the environment.

Inspect the sewer hose and check for pinhole leaks. Also, check all the seals on the hose adapters and sewer cap. Start the season right by not having messy sewer leaks.

LIQUID PROPANE SYSTEM: Retrieve and carefully inspect the DOT cylinders or the permanently mounted horizontal LP container, depending on how the RV is equipped. If any scratches or nicks are noticed that have developed into rust, use a wire brush and some touch-up paint now to eliminate potential problems. Remove the plug or cap from the service valve(s), if one was previously installed. If one was not used, quickly open and close the service valve allowing the high burst of LP pressure to blow away any contaminates that may have accumulated in the throat of the unprotected service valve.

Now connect the regulator to the system, open the service valve and leak test the POL or Acme fitting. Many RV accessory stores carry a leak detector solution that can be brushed onto the LP fittings throughout the RV. However, a solution can be mixed using common liquid soap detergent and water and stored in a spray bottle that is handy for those hard to get to fittings in and under the coach. (Avoid using detergents containing ammonia or chlorine products.)

Before moving on to the individual appliances, remove the tape or foil previously applied to the furnace intake and exhaust vents.

Appliances—Inspect and clean each of the four LP burning appliances as is needed. Please refer to the Liquid Propane chapter for specific instructions on the water heater, refrigerator, range and furnace. Those sections detail the step by step procedures for performing the yearly cleaning and maintenance tasks necessary for safe, trouble free operation. (In addition to the written procedures, consider ordering the companion videos for these steps by contacting the technical editor.)

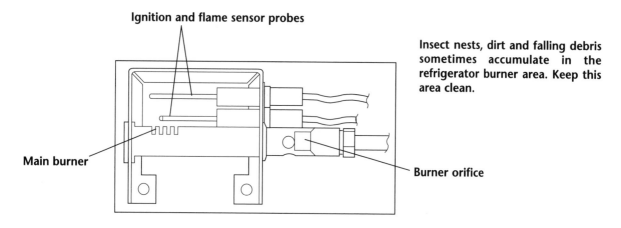

Ignition and flame sensor probes

Main burner

Burner orifice

Insect nests, dirt and falling debris sometimes accumulate in the refrigerator burner area. Keep this area clean.

Water Heater Burner

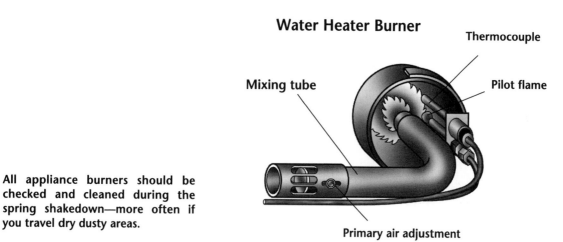

Thermocouple

Pilot flame

Mixing tube

Primary air adjustment

All appliance burners should be checked and cleaned during the spring shakedown—more often if you travel dry dusty areas.

The first step concerning the appliances is to rid the system of air. Light a stove burner and simply let it burn while the other appliances are lit. Prior to lighting the other three appliances, however, here are three things to verify:

- Foil or tape is removed from the furnace vents.
- Cardboard is removed from refrigerator and it is level.
- Cardboard is removed from water heater and it is filled with water.

Now, light the remaining three appliances. After cycling each appliance through its sequence of operation, turn them all off and verify that the LP pressure is set correctly. This can only be ascertained by using a manometer. Refer to the details for properly setting the LP regulator operating line pressure in Chapter 6. The RV must be taken to a service facility at least once a camping system to have this step performed if a manometer is not available. Finally, activate the LP leak detector.

Roof Air Conditioner—Remove the cover and inspect for any damage that may have incurred during storage. Clean or replace the air filters. Refer to the owner's manual for the particular brand and model air conditioner. Most filters are accessible from inside the RV. Cycle the air conditioner through a cooling cycle. Listen for unusual noises or vibrations.

Generator—If the RV is equipped with a generator, change the oil according to the manufacturer's recommendation. Replace all appropriate filters such as:

- Oil filter
- Air filter element
- Fuel filter

Clean and lube the throttle linkage at all the pivot points. Manually move the governor arm to ensure there is no binding. Log the hours on the hour meter. Check it against the maintenance chart for other periodic maintenance that may be due.

Clean and reinstall the spark plugs. Remove the tape from the exhaust pipe. Wipe the entire unit down with a damp rag. Make sure the generator compartment is clean.

Test fire the unit. Remember, it may be a little rusty from sitting so long. Never try to "prime" the carburetor by pouring gasoline into it. The fuel pump on the generator itself will suffice for drawing the correct amount of fuel. However, this is a good reason why it is important to fully charge the batteries.

The generator will blow a lot of blue smoke at first because of the rust inhibitor put into the cylinders prior to winterizing. This is normal and should burn off fairly rapidly. If the generator continues to rev up and down uncontrollably over a period of time, further troubleshooting may be in order.

Once the generator has started and is running smoothly, allow it to power the coach. This happens normally in one of three ways:
- Manually plug the shoreline into a 30-amp receptacle inside the RV
- Manually throw a switch or manipulate a breaker
- An automatic switching device makes the connection

Consult the RVs manual to determine the particular method. Once connected, turn on a roof air conditioner to put a larger load on the generator. Let it run for a minimum of thirty minutes. If it fails to power the air conditioner and simply sputters and dies, further troubleshooting is needed.

MOTORHOME CONSIDERATIONS: Aside from following the manufacturer's recommendations, check all the fluid levels for the motorhome chassis. Those that are typical to most gasoline powered chassis include:
- Engine oil
- Transmission fluid
- Rear axle differential oil
- Power steering fluid
- Brake cylinder fluid
- Radiator coolant
- Battery electrolyte
- Windshield washer fluid

(For diesel chassis', follow the recommendations in the owner's manual for that chassis.)

Reinstall the spark plugs, check the air cleaner element and test-fire the engine. As with the generator, it is common for blue smoke to be prevalent due to the rust inhibitor induced into the cylinders prior to storage. Check the mileage to see if it is time for a tune-up. Remember, non-use can, at times, be harder on an RV than abuse.

TRAVEL TRAILER CONSIDERATIONS: Inspect the electric brakes. It is recommended that one side of an axle and the opposite side of the other axle be inspected at least annually. If the trailer only has one axle, inspect both brake assemblies. The spring shakedown is just as good a time as any for this inspection. Look for abnormal wear patterns on the brake shoes and an uneven pattern of wear on the brake magnets. Also, the drum, armature and all mechanical components should be checked.

Replace like components on each end of the same axle regardless of the condition of the opposite side. If the left side magnet of the forward axle is in need of replacement, replace both magnets on that axle. Keep like parts the same age on the same axle.

Check the outer bearing during disassembly for the brake inspection and re-pack if necessary. Check the shoes and around the backing plate for evidence of a seal that might need replacing. Consult the axle manufacturer's recommendation for mileage intervals for packing and replacing the bearings and races. They vary considerably.

After reassembly of the brake assemblies, and while the trailer is still on jackstands, spin each tire and activate the trailer brakes. (The trailer must be plugged into the tow vehicle or it is possible to jumper across the electrical connector from the battery terminal to the electric brake terminal.) Each tire should immediately come to a stop.

Spin each tire again and this time pull the pin on the break-away switch located on or near the "A" frame of the trailer. Again, each tire should come to an immediate stop. Be sure to reset the pin fully into the switch so as not to drain the battery. Now also is the time to adjust each brake assembly if necessary.

UNDERCARRIAGE CONSIDERATIONS: Hopefully the vehicle is in a location that is suitable for crawling underneath and inspecting the undercarriage. If the coach was stored in a grassy or wooded area, be on the lookout for insects or other choice critters that love to hide and maybe hibernate under the cool confines of a dormant RV.

While under the coach, look for any obvious signs of damage or discrepancy. Loose wires, twigs, rocks, etc., are items that may need to be addressed prior to moving the RV. Take a close look.

MISCELLANEOUS CONSIDERATIONS: A good habit to get into at the start of each camping season is to lube all the compartment door and entry door locks and latching mechanisms. Many irritating nuisances can be avoided by this one, simple, small step. A silicone spray or Teflon lubricant with a long tubular nozzle works best for most door locks.

Check all running lights, trim lights, turn signals, backup lamps, headlamps, tail lamps, spot lamps and the horn for proper operation. If a small car is towed behind the motorhome, be sure to check out the electrical wiring between those two units as well.

Check the air pressure in all the tires. Do not overlook the spare if there is one. Pull the RV forward a few feet listening for strange sounds not heard before. If all sounds fairly normal, take a short spin around the block or so. As you feel more comfortable with the way it handles and sounds, take a longer excursion—maybe a one-day trip. Once totally comfortable, load up and go on that much needed vacation or weekend getaway. The spring shakedown has been a success!

For a complete visual guide to the spring shakedown be sure to order the video tape, "Storing and Using Your RV." Contact the technical editor for ordering information.

Spring Shakedown Checklist

(Duplicate this checklist and place a ✓ beside each item as it is completed)

Roof Area	Windows	Batteries
___Inspect all seams, vents, etc.	___Uncover, open to air out	___Reinstall or connect
___Reseal as necessary	___Lube as necessary	___Clean/tighten terminals
		___Electrolyte level
120 Volt System	**Fresh Water System**	___Fully charge
___Clean shoreline plug contacts	___Drain antifreeze/flush tank	___Verify voltage
___Plug in appliances	___Fill tank, pump water	___Reinstall dry cell batteries
___Main breaker on	___Add chlorination	___Test alarms
___Verify polarity	___Apply city water/leak test	
___Test GFCI	___Drain, refill tank	**Waste Water System**
	___Add freshener	___Inspect termination valves
Liquid Propane System		___Drain/flush holding tanks
___Inspect LP container for rust	**Water Heater**	___Add enzyme treatment
___Connect regulator assembly	___Remove covering	___Inspect sewer hose & seals
___Leak test	___Blow out burner area	
___LP pressure test	___Fill with water	**Refrigerator**
___Service valve on	___Test fire	___Remove vent covering
		___Blow out burner area
Furnace	**Range**	___Level refrigerator
___Remove vent covering	___Clean, test fire	___Test fire
___Clean near combustion area		
___Clean thermostat, test fire	**Roof Air Conditioner**	**Generator**
	___Remove cover, inspect	___Change oil, replace filters
Motorhome Specifics	___Clean filters	___Lube throttle pivot points
___Check owner's manual	___Test run	___Clean plugs, reinstall
___Check all fluid levels		___Uncover tail pipe
___Test drive		___Clean unit & test fire

Spring Shakedown Checklist (cont'd)

(Duplicate this checklist and place a ✓ beside each item as it is completed)

Under Coach Inspection	Travel Trailer Specifics	Miscellaneous
___Check all, clear debris	___Inspect/adjust brakes	___Check all running lights
___Tie up loose wires	___Check break-away switch	___Check fire extinguisher
	___Test brake circuit	
	___Road test	

Discrepancies

Plumbing Systems	Electrical Systems	LP System/Appliances

Date: **Performed by:**

Notes: _____

_____

_____

_____

_____

_____

_____

_____

_____

CHAPTER EIGHTEEN

The Spare Parts Kit

Throughout this handbook, there have been mentions of various spare parts recommended to carry aboard the RV during travel. Obviously, space limitations and common sense should prevail when considering the extent of the spare parts kit. The optimum, of course, would be to have one of everything on hand, just in case it breaks, but that is far from the intended purpose of a spare parts kit. The purpose for carrying a few spare components is two-fold. First, it is intended to minimize, or totally eliminate any downtime encountered while traveling. Second, repair dollars can be decreased simply by having some key parts on hand, regardless if the owner installs them, or a service technician installs them. By performing the preventive maintenance tasks described in the *RV Owner's Handbook*, it is hoped the spare parts kit will never even need to be unpacked. But just knowing the required part is on hand is reassuring, especially when traveling off the beaten path around the backwoods of the countryside. Who knows, it may even be possible to help out a stranded fellow RVer with a crucial part from the kit. It is just simply a cost-effective investment, an insurance policy, if you will.

There will be no attempt to list spare components for the chassis portion of motorhomes or the automotive portion of any tow vehicle. Obviously, items like spare belts or a lower radiator hose would be beneficial, but it would transcend the scope of this chapter to consider the automotive side of RVing. This chapter will list, system by system, those components that will be helpful in compiling a spare parts kit. Some may or may not apply to all exact situations. The utility of such a spare parts kit is that it can be customized for any RV. Here then, are some recommendations.

ELECTRICAL SYSTEM

Generator tune-up kit—If the RV is equipped with an on-board generator, it is advisable to carry a generator tune-up kit. This kit should contain spark plugs, points, condenser, fuel filter, air filter, oil filter, ignition circuit fuses and a schematic wiring diagram of the generator. Obviously omit those items that are not applicable.

12-volt fuses—Inspect the 12-volt DC fuse box and determine which sizes of fuses will be needed. Be sure to check all in-line fuses common to either system. Be aware that the automotive fuse block may have a different type of fuse altogether. Check the owner's manual when a doubt exists.

12-volt circuit breaker—Some applications call for a 12-volt automatic resettable circuit breaker instead of a fuse. The electric brake controller circuit is an example. Carry spare 12-volt breakers for the sizes needed.

In-line fuse holders—In case of the necessity for an emergency wiring repair, an in-line fuse holder can be spliced in at any point in the circuit. Carry two spares in the kit.

12-volt light bulbs—These are clearance lamp bulbs, stop lamp bulbs, single fixture incandescent bulbs, etc. Go through the rig and list each bulb number that is used. Typically, bulb numbers 57,

1157, 1156, 1141 and 1003 are the most common. The bulb number is located on the brass colored base portion of each bulb. This addition to the kit could prevent a moving violation in some states!

Dry cell batteries—Clocks, smoke alarms, carbon monoxide monitors and refrigerator fans all use dry cell batteries. Keep a couple of spares of the needed sizes in the refrigerator.

Battery terminals—Carry at least two spare battery terminals. Terminals may become corroded beyond cleaning and will need to be replaced.

PLUMBING SYSTEMS

Sewer drain cap—This is not a life-threatening component to be without. It certainly will not leave an RVer stranded somewhere should it be lost, but the fact is, some campgrounds are sticklers and rightly so. Some may not allow check-in without a leak-free drain cap in place.

Toilet water valve—This could be the second most important spare part to carry. Also called ball valves, this component could truly save a vacation, especially when dry-camped in the boondocks. Most toilet manufacturers package their spare parts on convenient and protected cards. This keeps the part clean and ready to go when needed.

Toilet to flange gasket—This may be a wax ring, but the rubber gasket-type is preferred. The rubber one is easier to store and will not melt during hot summer days. Always replace the seal whenever the toilet is removed for repairs or maintenance.

Spare toilet parts—Consider other toilet parts to carry as spares, such as a vacuum breaker or spare nuts for the closet bolts. Flush mechanism seals and gaskets are also recommended as an addition to the spare parts kit. Check the parts listing in the owner's manual for specific parts for the toilet.

Termination valve "T" handles—These are recommended especially if the RV has a habit of bottoming out at driveways or low dips in the road. When in the closed position, the dump valve is not usually the lowest component, but if left in the open position, such as immediately following a tank evacuation, they are prone to damage. These "T" handles and lock nuts generally just thread on to the shaft of the dump valve.

Shower vacuum breaker:—Some are made of plastic and therefore, are prone to being broken. Having a spare vacuum breaker fitting will guarantee no loss of shower facilities if one is damaged or broken.

Holding tank patch kit—If the holding tank is ABS plastic, it is recommended to carry at least one of these patch kits. They are also useful for patching a leak in any ABS fitting or pipe joint as well. A must when traveling off the beaten path. They are only truly effective on ABS tanks. They will work only as a temporary fix on polyethylene or polypropylene tanks.

Spare fresh water line fittings (asssorted)—This broad category is determined by the type and size of the fresh water line in the RV. Spare unions, couplings, as well as plugs and caps. should be in the kit. If the toilet needs to be removed, for instance, by plugging the incoming line, other portions of the fresh water system can still be utilized without interruption. Look through the RV and choose those fittings which will be needed the most.

Water pressure regulator—Why bother to carry a spare? Sad to say, some have been known to disappear overnight or when the campsite is vacated for a day trip. Plus, it is always nice to have a loaner on hand to help out a novice RVer who forgot his or hers.

Fresh Water Hose Repair Kit—Male and female ends can be easily repaired without tools with this kit. Every RVer at some time has flattened an end on the fresh water hose. Having one each of these on hand will insure the city water will be ready to supply the RV.

LIQUID PROPANE SYSTEM

LP pressure regulator—This is by far the most important spare item to carry during travel. A defective LP regulator can render the RVer "dead in the water" without an alternative plan. Having a spare dual-stage regulator has saved many vacations from becoming disasters and has kept many full-timers from becoming temporary motel dwellers. All regulators are pre-set at the factory, so they can be installed safely without having to pinpoint the exact pressure. However, always test the system for leaks whenever any device or component has been replaced.

LP container sending unit—If the monitor panel is depended upon to determine how much LP is left in the tank, consider carrying a spare sending unit. Since it is commonly exposed to the elements, they sometimes become damaged, frozen, or otherwise rendered useless. They are easily replaced by removing just two mounting screws at the LP container.

Thermocouple—This can be a very inexpensive insurance policy. Universal thermocouples are available that will work on the water heater and the furnace. The thermocouple used on some refrigerators is a different size thread on the button end. Still, it is recommended to include a spare thermocouple for each of those three appliances. There is no thermocouple on the range.

Electrode assemblies—The most common operational component associated with water heater and furnace troubles is the electrode assembly. Some become carboned, pitted and corroded beyond the resolve of a simple cleaning. Others become damaged if the ceramic insulators are cracked or broken. By carrying an electrode assembly for both the water heater and the furnace, downtimes can be minimized or eliminated in the DSI models of those appliances.

Three-eighths-inch flare plugs—Easily installed since they require no sealant on the threads, these flare plugs are needed whenever an appliance is removed for maintenance or repair for two main reasons. First, a flare plug keeps dirt and dust from entering the LP system while the appliance is being worked on, and second, it is a safeguard in case someone inadvertently turns the LP gas back on. Sometimes an appliance may have to be transported to a service facility for repairs. The flare plug will enable the remaining appliances to be operated while the other one is out being repaired.

There are many other items to consider for inclusion in the spare parts kit such as cabinet latches, a spare sewer hose, etc. Consider those items that you would not enjoy living without should they become broken or otherwise useless.

Aside from specific components, many supplies should be carried by the RVer. In order to accommodate the replacement or installation of many items, some supplies are also mandatory. The following list may be considered a recommended list of RV supplies:
- Electrical tape
- Duct tape
- Masking tape
- Putty tape
- Silicone sealant (caulking)
- Silicone or Teflon lubricating spray
- Bri-Rus Insta-glas—quickly repairs fiberglass damage.

- Pipe thread sealant—able to be used with LP gas, hot and cold fresh water systems and plastic threads; read the label to make sure it will work with all the above
- RM Tank Care—Holding tank treatment
- Loc-Tite thread sealant
- Nylon wire ties
- Solderless wire terminals and wire nuts
- ABS patch kit
- Small can of ABS cement
- Liquid Roof—Repair sealant for roof seams, etc.
- Rubber Roof Patch Kit

By having these supplies on hand, you will be equipped to handle almost any chore around the RV.

CHAPTER NINETEEN

Master Maintenance Schedule

Throughout this book, there has been generous detail given to specific maintenance procedures for every system and major components found on today's RVs. An attempt has been made to relate to all types of RVs as generically as possible when listing and explaining the various procedures.

As a general guide to help remember the many aspects of owning and operating an RV, this chapter will, in chart form, list many maintenance tasks along with the time intervals at which to perform them. They are presented system by system or by broad category. These charts are designed as a reminder only. Use these reminders and then refer to the specific chapter if more details are needed. Also, refer to the owner's manual that came with the RV for other information.

Keep in mind not every element may be listed here. Your coach may contain additional aftermarket products that also need maintenance but are not featured in this handbook. An example would be a satellite TV system or hydraulic levelers, for instance. This master schedule is tailored to the typical RV containing the "usual" accouterments.

Please notice that there may be more than one check mark for each individual item on the chart. Here is why. Some components may need attention at varying times throughout the year. If more than one check mark appears, the longest interval mark should be considered the minimum, while the shorter duration interval marks may be the recommended time frames. Here is an example.

On the LP System chart, for the item "Leak Test Entire RV," it is recommended that this maintenance procedure be performed as part of a pre-trip check-out, or as necessary (in case of an LP gas smell for instance). But at the very least, check for leaks twice a year.

As mentioned, use these charts as a guide only, then refer to the main text for the specific details. For instance, on the Fresh Water System chart, for the item, "Flush & Sanitize Tank," turn to the Fresh Water System section in Chapter 5 for the details on how to flush and clean the fresh water tank. These charts are to be considered simply time interval reminders.

Factors such as extremely dusty conditions, RVing full-time or when traveling in extreme heat or cold may demonstrate a need for a certain amount of flexibility within these guidelines. Be prepared to modify the maintenance schedule based on the particular set of circumstances and traveling habits as they relate to your RV.

It is hoped that by following the procedures within this book, many miles of trouble-free operation will be attained and you will glean an abundance of leisure memories and traveling enjoyment from your RVing experiences. And remember, RVing is more than a hobby, it is a lifestyle!

Master Maintenance Schedule

— Chassis and Running Gear —

Task	Pre-Trip	As Necessary	Weekly	Monthly	Quarterly	Semi-Annually	Annually
Inspect Brakes		✓					✓
Inspect exhaust system						✓	
Tighten lug nuts	✓			✓			
Check tires	✓			✓			
Check running lights	✓			✓			
Check fluid levels	✓	✓		✓			
Check fan belts	✓				✓		
Check/test battery	✓		✓				
Check shocks						✓	
Engine tune-up		✓					
Check A/C operation	✓	✓					
Inspect suspension							✓
Pack wheel bearings							✓
Test alternator output	✓					✓	
Test drive vehicle	✓						

Notes: _____

_____

_____

_____

_____

_____

_____

_____

_____

_____

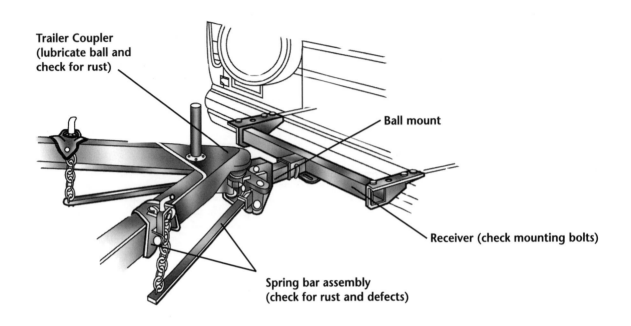

Trailer Coupler
(lubricate ball and
check for rust)

Ball mount

Receiver (check mounting bolts)

Spring bar assembly
(check for rust and defects)

— Towing —

Task	Pre-Trip	As Necessary	Weekly	Monthly	Quarterly	Semi-Annually	Annually
Lube hitch ball	✓		✓				
Inspect ball mount	✓				✓		
Inspect receiver	✓				✓		
Inspect spring bars	✓						✓
Lube sway control	✓						✓
Check trailer coupler	✓					✓	
Check tongue jack	✓						✓
Test break away switch	✓			✓			
Test electric brakes	✓						✓
Adjust brakes	✓	✓					✓
Check electrical cord	✓				✓		

— Electrical Systems —

12-volt DC System

Task	Pre-Trip	As Necessary	Weekly	Monthly	Quarterly	Semi-Annually	Annually
Battery electrolyte level	✓		✓				
Clean terminals	✓	✓					✓
Tighten connections		✓					
Test converter output	✓						✓
Check system drains		✓					

120-volt DC System

Task	Pre-Trip	As Necessary	Weekly	Monthly	Quarterly	Semi-Annually	Annually
Test GFCI	✓			✓			
Check breakers							✓
Check shoreline cord	✓						✓
Test polarity	✓	✓					
Generator	Maintenance schedule based on hours of operation (See Volume 2, Chapter 6)						
Test ground wire							✓
Test inverter output						✓	
Test AC appliance	✓	✓					
Test CO monitor	✓						✓

Notes: _____

_____

_____

_____

_____

_____

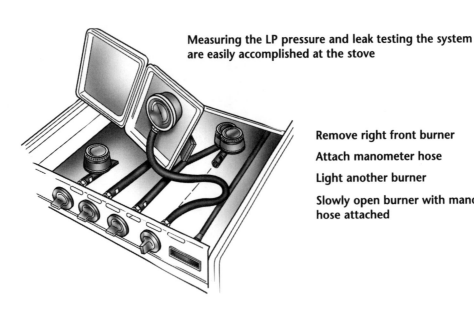

Measuring the LP pressure and leak testing the system are easily accomplished at the stove

Remove right front burner

Attach manometer hose

Light another burner

Slowly open burner with manometer hose attached

— LP System —

Task	Pre-Trip	As Necessary	Weekly	Monthly	Quarterly	Semi-Annually	Annually
Test fire appliances	✓	✓					✓
Clean appliances		✓					✓
Inspect LP container	✓					✓	
Leak test entire RV	✓	✓				✓	
Test LP leak detector	✓		✓				
Set pressure regulator	✓					✓	
Tighten fittings		✓					
Inspect LP hoses	✓						✓

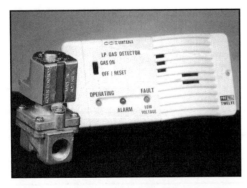

Be sure to test the LP leak detector at least weekly during your travels. Likewise be sure to turn it completely off when not in use to avoid a drain on the battery.

All new RVs that have an internal combustion, engine driven generator must be equipped with a carbon monoxide detector. It's a wise choice to add one if your coach is not so equipped. Periodically test the detector to be sure it is in working order.

— Fresh Water System —

Task	Pre-Trip	As Necessary	Weekly	Monthly	Quarterly	Bi-annually	Annually
Visual Inspection	✓						✓
Flush & sanitize tank	✓	✓			✓		
Leak test system	✓					✓	
Clean/replace filters							✓
Check hose clamps							✓
Tighten fittings		✓					
Flush water heaters	✓						✓
Clean faucet aerators							✓
Chlorinate system	✓	✓					

— Waste Water System —

Task	Pre-Trip	As Necessary	Weekly	Monthly	Quarterly	Bi-annually	Annually
Visual Inspection	✓						✓
Rinse/flush tanks	✓	✓					✓
Check for leaks	✓	✓					
Lube dump valves	✓	✓				✓	
Treat tanks	✓	✓					
Lube toilet flush mechanism		✓					✓

Notes: _____

_____

_____

_____

_____

_____

_____

— RV Exterior —

Task	Pre-Trip	As Necessary	Weekly	Monthly	Quarterly	Bi-annually	Annually
Clean & Wash	✓	✓					
Lube door locks		✓					✓
Inspect roof areas	✓				✓		
Seal roof seams		✓					✓
Inspect doors/windows	✓					✓	
Reseal doors/windows		✓					

— RV Interior —

Task	Pre-Trip	As Necessary	Weekly	Monthly	Quarterly	Bi-annually	Annually
Clean	✓	✓					
Check for leaks						✓	
Check/lube hardware							✓
Check escape hatch	✓					✓	

Notes: _____

_____

_____

_____

_____

_____

_____

_____

_____

_____

_____

_____

_____

Contributing Suppliers

We would like to thank the following suppliers for providing information and/or product samples used in compiling this RV Owner's Handbook. We encourage all RVers to contact these suppliers for more information regarding their products.

303 Products, Inc.
PO Box 966
Palo Cedro, CA 96073-0966
www.303-products.com

All-Rite Exteriors
1500 Shelton Drive
Hollister, CA 95023

Atwood Mobile Products
4750 Hiawatha Drive
Rockford, IL 61103-1298
www.atwoodmobile.com

Bri-Rus, Inc.
1186 Broadway, Suite B
El Cajon, CA 92021

CAMCO Mfg., Inc.
121 Landmark Drive
Greensboro, NC 27409
www.camco.com

Carefree of Colorado
2145 West 6th Avenue
Broomfield, CO 80020
www.carefreeofcolorado.com

CCI Controls
5052 Cecelia Street
South Gate, CA 90280
www.ccicontrols.com

Demco-Dethmers Mfg. Co.
PO Box 189
Bowden, IA 51234-0189
www.demco-products.com

Dicor Corp.
PO Box 1806
Elkhart, IN 46515-1806
www.dicor.com

Eaz-Lift Spring Corp.
PO Box 489
Sun Valley, CA 91353-0489

FLOJET Corp.
12 Morgan
Irvine, CA 92618-2092

Gear Vendors, Inc.
1717 North Magnolia
El Cajon, CA 92020
www.gearvendors.com

Hayes Lemmerz International, Inc.
38481 Huron River Drive
Romulus, MI 48174

Heart Interface Corp.
21440 68th Avenue South
Kent, WA 98032
www.heartinterface.com

continued on next page

Hehr Power Systems
4616 Fairlane Avenue
Fort Worth, TX 76119
www.hehrpowersystems.com

Heliotrope General
3733 Kenora Drive
Spring Valley, CA 91977
www.hg1.com

HWH Corporation
2096 Moscow Road
Moscow, IA 52760-9612
www.hwhcorp.com

Jordan Research Corp.
6244 Clark Center Avenue, Unit 4
Sarasota, FL 34238

Kwikee Products Co., Inc.
230 Davidson Avenue
Cottage Grove, OR 97424

Magellan
960 Overland Court
San Dimas, CA 91773
www.magellangps.com

Manchester Tank & Equipment Co.
1749 Mallory Lane
Brentwood, TN 37027
www.mantank.com

Marshall Gas Controls
1000 Civic Center Loop
San Marcos, TX 78666
www.mgc-mbc.com

Michelin North America, Inc.
PO Box 19001
Greenville, SC 29602
www.michelin.com

Microphor, Inc.
452 East Hill Road
Willits, CA 95490
www.microphor.com

Norcold Inc.
PO Box 180
Sidney, OH 45365
www.norcold.com

Onan Corporation
1400 – 73rd Avenue NE
Minneapolis, MN 55432
www.cummins.com

Optima Batteries
17500 East 22nd Avenue
Aurora, CO 80011
www.optimabatteries.com

Patrick Industries
PO Box 638
Elkhart, IN 46515
www.patrickind.com

Powerwatch Technologies
PO 22988
Denver, CO 80222

Pro Guard Coatings
172 Shillington Road
Sinking Spring, PA 19608
www.proguardcoatings.com

Protect All Inc.
1910 East Via Burton
Anaheim, CA 92806
www.protectall.com

PullRite/Pulliam Enterprises, Inc.
13790 East Jefferson Boulevard
Mishawaka, IN 46545
www.pullrite.com

Reese Products, Inc.
PO Box 1706
Elkhart, IN 46515
www.rvamerica.com/reese

Remco Products
4138 South 89th Street
Omaha, NE 68127
www.remcotowing.com

RV Power Products
1058 Monterey Vista Way
Encinitas, CA 92024
www.rvpowerproducts.com

SeaLand Technology, Inc.
PO Box 38, Fourth Street
Big Prairie, OH 44611
www.sealandtechnology.com

SHURflo Pump Manufacturing Co.
12650 Westminster Avenue
Santa Ana, CA 92706-2100
www.shurflo.com

Siemens Solar Industries
4650 Adohr Lane
Camarillo, CA 93011
www.siemenssolar.com

Statpower Technologies Corp.
7725 Lougheed Highway
Burnaby, BC, Canada V5A 4V8
www.statpower.com

Suburban Manufacturing Co.
676 Broadway Street
Dayton, TN 37321
www.suburbanmanufacturing.com

Sure Power Industries, Inc.
10189 SW Avery
Tualatin, OR 97062-9517
www.surepower.com

Tekonsha Engineering Co.
537 North Church Street
Tekonsha, MI 49092
www.tekonsha.com

Thetford Corporation
PO Box 1285
Ann Arbor, MI 48103
www.norcold.com

TR Industries, Inc.
11022 Vulcan Street
South Gate, CA 90280

Tri-Synergy, Inc.
PO Box 27015
San Diego, CA 92198-1015
www.trisyn.com

Uponor TuffPex
401 West Bristol Street
Elkhart, IN 46514
www.uponor.com

U.S. Catalytic Corp.
871 Latour Court
Napa, CA 94558
www.uscatalytic.com

Western Reserve Camper
Specialties, Inc.
7898 Mayfield Road
Chesterland, OH 44026
www.rvresource.com

Winegard Company
3000 Kirkwood Street
Burlington, IA 52601-2000
www.winegard.com